695 AE
ms

INSTANT COLLEGE

THE TAMPA TRIBUNE

J. C. Council, Chairman of the Editorial Board
James A. Clendinen, Editor   *Robert L. Hudson, Managing Editor*

Instant Junior College

Dr. R. William Graham comes to Tampa with impressive credentials for a challenging task — getting the new Hillsborough Junior College off the ground within five months.

As president of the new institution, Dr. Graham will work part-time until June while he completes his work as vice president of the Junior College District of St. Louis and administrative head of · its Forest Park Community College.

But by the scheduled opening date in September he must find a place to hold classes, hire a staff, and establish some sort of curriculum. Both his education and experience should stand him in good stead.

For he joined the St. Louis Junior College system in 1964 only two years after its founding, and while it operated in temporary quarters before its permanent buildings were completed. His master's degree major was in curriculum, his doctorate in higher education administration.

There is no legal requirement that the new junior college open its doors in such haste. School officials say, however, that because of unavoidable delays in so many phases of the establishment of the institution, they feel that it will benefit now from momentum and be in better position to bid for funds in the 1969 Legislature if it is actually in operation.

The plan, to open with 500 students in temporary quarters, is the same as that which successfully started the Orange·County Junior College in Orlando. It does not envision an all-day schedule of classes at first, but rather evening and night classes, perhaps in one or more of the county's high schools.

In his first interview after arrival here, Dr. Graham indicated he was looking for a challenge, not a place where he could "retire immediately." That he already has 150 applications for jobs indicates others share his enthusiasm, and that of the County School Board, to get the college going.

So doubtless, do the college's potential 4,000 enrollees from Hillsborough County. They are meeting increasing difficulty in gaining admittance to neighboring counties' institutions, sorely taxed to handle their own residents. So although Dr. Graham is virtually whipping up an instant first term for Hillsborough Junior College, there's certain to be no lack of applicants for those first 500 enrollments.

INSTANT COLLEGE

By

R. WILLIAM GRAHAM

Boston
BRANDEN PRESS
Publishers

Standard Book Number 8283-1291-5
© Copyright, 1971, by Branden Press
Printed in the United States of America
Library of Congress Catalog Card Number 70-127368

TO MOM

TOPIC INDEX

PREFACE

Even though its roots are firmly implanted in England and Western Europe, the American system of education has produced two unique institutions, the four-year liberal arts college and the two-year college, or community college. While the liberal arts college, which is less professionally oriented than the university, has contributed greatly to American education, the junior college is the fastest growing segment of higher education and stands to make an even greater impact on society in the coming decades.

In 1921 there were 207 junior colleges, of which two-thirds were privately supported (even though one-half of the total enrollment of 16,000 students were in tax-supported junior colleges). Over the past decade the opening of at least one to two new community colleges per week has brought the total to over 1,000. If the present growth continues, it is likely that the number of two-year colleges will exceed 1,200 by 1972.

According to the American Association of Junior Colleges, "Establishment of the new junior colleges in most of the states represents long-range planning aimed at putting opportunity for higher education within commuting range of all citizens. Moreover, the public institutions operate at a low cost to students and provide educational programs that will appeal to a wide range of interests and abilities . . . . This expansion will bring total enrollment in the country's junior and community colleges close to the 2,000,000 mark."

The fantastic growth of the comprehensive community college provides the background for this narrative, which describes the problems, traumas, and successes which accompanied the formation of Hillsborough Junior College in Tampa, Florida, from its conception through its opening in the fall of 1968. During this period almost all of the facets of this exciting new institution, the community college, were scrutinized by the citizens of the community, the board of trustees, the president and the professional staff. By preparing this documentary report, it is hoped that the reader will gain an understanding of the purpose and function of America's truly new concept in higher education.

The author is indebted to the many friends and colleagues who have assisted with the preparation of this book. Special commendation should be accorded to Mr. Clark Everett of Hillsborough Junior College English department for literary criticism and extensive proofreading. An expression of appreciation is due the author's wife and family for their willingness to live a life shaped mainly by his professional ambitions. And finally, without the foresightedness of the citizens of Hillsborough County, the statesmanship of the political and educational leaders of the state of Florida, and the enthusiastic support of the college trustees, Hillsborough Junior College might not exist today. The author is grateful to have been extended the opportunity to help mold the future of this institution of higher learning.

In several instances in this volume the author has recounted the details of interviews with certain unsuccessful applicants for various positions at the college. In order to protect the professional reputations of these candidates geographic locations of employment and details of experience and academic preparation have been altered.

R. W. G.

FOREWORD

No segment of our society is so completely uninformed about America's fastest growing institution of higher education as the communities whose needs the public two-year college is designed to serve. Yet, in the seven states in which forty percent of our country's total population is concentrated, ninety percent of the people are already within commuting distance of a community college. It has been stated on defensible grounds that during the next decade up to seventy-five percent of our society will feel the impact of the "people's college." This change makes a fuller understanding of the role and purpose of the community college a necessity.

In its attempt to tell simply and candidly the community college story, *Instant College* combines the general features of an autobiography, history, and case study of one of America's new community colleges.

At its simplest level *Instant College* may be read merely as a documentary history—an account of the birth of one of America's newest comprehensive community colleges: how it came to be; how it reacted to skeptics, including a sometimes unfriendly press; how it was organized and financed; and how it plans to meet present and future needs of the community of which it is a part.

At another level the work may be read as an autobiography in two phases. The first phase, "Chapter I," describes the author's background, his interests, and important people in his life. The reader comes to know the man and thus understands the motives and rationale for many of the decisions which shape the character of the new community college he heads. Moreover, because of the author's experiences as a student, teacher, and administrator in institutions of higher learning, the reader becomes aware of the need for and role of the public community college in our culture today and how it differs from other public as well as private institutions.

The second phase is the story of a president who started a

college with meager tools: how, in a few short weeks, he employed a faculty and staff; developed a curriculum; secured temporary facilities; purchased furniture and equipment; organized counseling services, registration procedures, and a student records system; prepared salary schedules and a budget; and worked with a new board of trustees in long-range planning and site selection for permanent facilities.

Both for the college trustee, whose knowledge of community college operations must be thorough if he is to play a proper role in developing policies, and for the layman, *Instant College* provides general answers, as viewed by the author, to such questions as: "What is the community college?" "What are its purposes?" "Who plans it?" "What is the role of the community college president?" "How is he selected?" "What is the relationship of the community college to the four-year college?" "Who can enroll in the community college?" and "Who does enroll?"

For the community college administrator, counselor or teacher, the document provides some insights into the author's attitudes, judgments, consideration, and the operation of a new comprehensive community college.

Few people have the opportunity to know a college president. Even fewer get to know what goes on behind the scenes when this person is thrust into the public eye and is subject to the political pressures brought ot bear on his office. Included in the book are newspaper accounts which allow the reader to compare the public image created by the media with the situation as seen by the president.

Instant College is a personal version of the community college story. Its informal style makes an interesting story with which the lay reader can identify. While the book reads easily with a minimal use of pedagogical terms, the content is comprehensive and articulates the philosophy of the writer. *Instant College* offers the reader a glimpse into the future as the president and his associates at Hillsborough Junior College dream of education as it will develop in the years ahead.

CHARLES E. CHAPMAN

President of the American Association of Junior Colleges (1970-1971)

INTRODUCTION

The community college has sometimes seemed to defy accurate classification because it is both higher education and less than that, both community oriented and more than that, both highly structured and totally unplanned. Now that the development of the public community college extends over almost three quarters of a century, many more people are still trying to describe this product of American inventiveness.

The early establishment of these colleges in California and in Illinois has been repeated in many other states. Local impetus has been a major factor in almost every locality, although since the early 1960's state legislatures and state level boards have played increasingly more important roles.

EARLY DEVELOPMENTS IN FLORIDA

In Florida the historical development of the community college began in the late 1920's when a group of civic-minded leaders approached Captain Lynch, Superintendent of Public Instruction in Pinellas County, with the request that he help them start a college. Although the St. Petersburg Junior College was established at that time as a private institution, the cooperation of public officials including Superintendent Lynch was very much in evidence. This cooperation included the use of the new high school facilities as well as providing professional leadership from local school officials and teachers. A primary factor, however, was the local orientation of the planning associated with due consideration of the state level university. This latter concern was in some measure alleviated through encouraging words from the representatives of the University of Florida assuring the St. Petersburg leaders that transferred hours of credit would be accepted by the University as contributing toward a four year degree.

On the opposite coast of Florida the members of civic clubs in West Palm Beach in 1932 made a request to their Board of Public

11

instruction that a junior college be established. They proposed that this new junior college be a part of the public school system. Their major rationale was centered around the fact that the depression had made it impossible for numbers of youth to leave their homes to continue their education in a distant university. Not only were these young people preventd by finances from continuing their education, they also found it nigh to impossible to obtain jibs. Ennui and hopelessness seemed their lot.

Palm Beach County School Tax District Number One became the parent of Palm Beach Junior College which opened its doors in 1933. Here, as in St. Petersburg, the high school provided facilities and faculty as well. Here, as in St. Petersburg, the enthusiasm of local civic leaders was the major force in establishing the institution. Also, here, as in St. Petersburg, a statement of encouragement from the University of Florida in Gainesville provided an assurance of continued opportunity and confirmed a tacit state level approval.

Elements of rugged, historic American individualism were present in these early days of Florida's junior college development. The cooperation which helped pioneering settlers raise the roofs on their new barns and established civilized law and order was much in evidence here. The desire for things to be better for one's children was also influential as well as the unreasoned awe for higher education which has been typical of American society since colonial days. And fmally, an appeal to state level authorities to assure quality developed as an essential ingredient.

These factors have been an essential part of the subsequent development of junior colleges as well. The emphasis upon local initiative, the respect for a diversity of educational opportunity, and the recognition that state leadership is needed in assuring quality have all become essentials in a community college system in Florida which is second to none other in the nation.

The 1933 establishment of Palm Beach Junior College and the 1927 founding of St. Petersburg Junior College mark the beginning of the Florida system. The legislative authorization in 1967 completing the Master Plan culminated in the establishment of a total system of twenty-eight colleges geographically placed in such a way as to locate a college within commuting distance of ninety-nine percent of the state's population.

The time in between these two dates may be considered as the developmental period. Population pressures after the ending of hostilities in World War II sharply pointed up to the Florida Legislature some hard facts about potential problems in higher education in the state. At that time a Board of Control operated three universities, one for boys at Gainesville, one for girls at Tallahassee, and one for blacks at Tallahassee. A citizens study of education in the state reported to the 1947 Session of the State Legislature that troubles were in the offing. As a result of their recommendations, the two larger institutions (about 4,000 students in the University of Florida and less than that at Florida State College for Women) became coeducational institutions and moved toward the multiversity category. Florida Agricultural and Mechanical College also became a University and began to develop programs similar to those offered at the other two universities.

These steps were only the beginning, however, of very rapid increases. By 1951 it was clear that further study would be required. Accordingly a Council for the Study of Higher Education was established to develop plans for higher education in Florida. This Council, under the directorship of A. J. Brumbaugh with Myron Blee as his Associate Director, began to develop longitudinal studies to consider Florida's needs in Higher Education. Their work was so intensive and so thorough that it required several years before even preliminary reports were ready for public reaction.

The Council did, however, recommend to the 1955 Session of the Florida Legislature in an interim report that a special Community College Council be created to develop long-range plans for the establishment of a system of community colleges which would provide the first two years of a baccalaureate degree, vocational-technical programs, and courses for adults. This recommendation was received with enthusiastic approval by the president of the four junior colleges then in existence;

13

by the State Superintendent, Thomas D. Bailey; and by the professional leadership of the public education system. The Council was created and was charged to report to the next Session (1957) of the Legislature.

During the years between 1933 and 1955 there had been very limited growth in Florida's junior colleges. In terms of enrollment the existing colleges had developed very slowly. Only one college was on a permanent campus and programs were very much limited. However, the postwar pressures of enrollment once again brought pressures upon these institutions as well as the elementary schools, high schools, and universities. The 1947 Citizens Committee report had also provided encouragement for their continued growth by providing for state support for the first time for junior colleges and by including legal encouragement for their establishment. Palm Beach Junior College had received legal sanction through a special law passed in 1939, six years after its establishment. The 1947 omnibus school bill provided that groups of counties which met the population criterion of 50,000 persons could establish a junior college as well as single counties with this total population.

After this law was put into effect, St. Petersburg Junior College requested public status. Financial problems were becoming too great for continued operation of a private institution with little or no endowment and a great need for funds. Thus in 1947 there were two public junior colleges in Florida.

Shortly thereafter Escambia County requested authority from the State Board of Education to establish Pensacola Junior College—a request which was granted under the new law. This was followed by a request from Jackson County in cooperation with two other counties for authority to operate Chipola Junior College. This institution had been established by a church group during the previous year at an air base near the town of Marianna. The following year Negro leadership in Pensacola requested that the Escambia Board of Public Instruction provide a junior college for blacks. Pursuant to operating customs in 1948 this request was duly approved by the State Board of Education for implementation. Washington Junior College was the result.

14

Therefore, when the Community College Council was established in 1955, Florida had five junior colleges located in four widely scattered geographical areas serving less than 4,000 students in total enrollment. These five institutions, however, were supported very poorly both in reference to operating expenses and capital outlay. The same session of the Florida legislature provided more than four million dollars for junior college capital outlay—the first state funds appropriated for construction of junior college facilities. This constituted a beginning for state support for community college facilities.

A MASTER PLAN FOR JUNIOR COLLEGES

The Master Plan for Community Colleges had its origin at that point in time. Not only did the law itself require that long range planning be carried out, but the law also required that the three historic functions of junior college education be a major concern in this long-range planning. These functions were described as the freshman-sophomore courses parallel to those offered in the university, vocational-technical courses, and courses for adults. No further instructions were given.

The Community College Council provided the state level concern which was pointed out in the early development. However, the function of local initiative was not assured in the basic law. When the Council (made up of ten men, seven who were already serving on the State Advisory Council on Education and three who were actively engaged in college or university administration) faced its tasks, it found that several basic considerations had to be developed.

The early principles adopted by the Community College Council included the following basic assumptions:
1. Education is necessary for democratic government.
2. Education is valuable for the improvement of society.
3. Education is valuable because it helps to equalize opportunity for all people.
4. Education to be truly democratic and to achieve greatest success must be locally controlled and locally oriented.

With these as guiding forces the Council worked with the ex-

15

isting community junior colleges and with citizen groups, school boards, and professional leadership to evolve a plan which would be considered workable and appropriate for Florida. The best consultants from outside the state were called in. These included such persons as L.V. Koos, professor emeritus of the University of Chicago, and long-time student of the junior colleges; S. V. Martorana, at that time a staff member of the U. S. Office of Education; R. L. Johns, professor at the University of Florida and generally recognized as an expert in public finance in education; D. Grant Morrison, the director of junior colleges in the State of Washington; Roy B. Minnis, who held a similar post in Colorado; Norman Harris, an expert in the field of vocational-technical education; Thomas A. Van Sant, a similarly regarded expert in adult education; Arthur Hitchcock, with special competence in guidance and counseling; John Carr Duff, a professor of adult education from New York; and C.C. Colvert, a highly regarded junior college expert from Texas. These men, working with groups in the state and with the Community College Council, evolved basic recommendations which served as the foundation for the Master Plan.

An essential part of this plan, however, was the local survey. This survey became the basic study upon which all decisions at the state level were made. This survey preserved the essential *local* character and *local* emphasis of the entire Florida Community Junior College System. Guidelines were developed to aid local people in conducting such surveys and consultants were provided to help.

After collecting and analyzing demographic data about the state as a whole, as well as about each county in the state, after collecting and analyzing similar socio-economic information, and after examining the post high school opportunities available at that time, the Community College Council concluded:

1. There is indicated a great increase in numbers of young people who will need facilities for continued education beyond high school.

2. An increasing percentage of Florida's high school seniors have indicated interest in many kinds of post high school education.

3. The public community junior colleges would help to eliminate many of the barriers to continued education which now influence the decisions of high school seniors.

4. Local surveys reveal a great amount of local support for and interest in the development of community junior colleges with broad programs.

5. The long range plan in Florida would require the eventual establishment of twenty-seven new junior college areas if the barriers to continued education are to be eliminated.

These findings were supported by data drawn from each of Florida's sixty-seven counties and were followed by twelve specific recommendations from the Council:

1. That the State of Florida adopt a long-range program for expanding community junior college facilities in the state in order that the expected increase in numbers of young people may receive appropriate education near their homes for two years beyond high school.

2. That community junior colleges be charged with continued responsibility to develop broad and diversified programs to serve the needs and abilities of all post high school youth in their respective communities.

3. That these institutions be also charged with the responsibility for providing programs of adult education needed by the people in Florida.

4. That guidance and counseling services be provided to enable each person to be encouraged to study those areas most appropriate for his own abilities and interests.

5. That in keeping with sound planning and feasible financing a priority system be adopted to promote establishment of new community junior colleges in an orderly fashion.

6. That the well established pattern of local control and local orientation of these community junior colleges be continued and strengthened.

17

7. That joint state and local participation in the financial support of these institutions be preserved.

8. That the State Board of Education which has Constitutional responsibility for all levels of education in Florida give special attention to its responsibilities for the community junior colleges.

9. That the State Advisory Council on Education be specifically charged with responsibility to advise the State Board of Education on matters relating to community junior college development.

10. That a Liason Committee of professional people be appointed by the State Board of Education to advise the State Advisory Council on Education and the State Board of Education on matters having to do with the development of sound programs of post high school education and with policies of transfer from the community junior colleges to the universities.

   a. That this committee have members recommended by the Board of Control, the Florida Association of Public Junior Colleges, and the State Superintendent of Public Instruction.

11. That the State Board of Education be aided in its supervisory responsibilities through a Division of Community Junior Colleges established as a part of the staff of the State Superintendent of Public Instruction.

   a. That the research and study carried on by the Community College Council be continued as a responsibility of the Division of Community Junior Colleges in the office of the State Superintendent of Public Instruction.

12. That buildings, equipment, and other facilities be provided for the community junior colleges according to potential enrollment and demonstrated need.

Following recommendation number 5, the Council divided Florida's sixty-seven counties into four priorities:

Priority 1: Those areas which are characterized by larger concentration of population, high indications of need for educational services, a demonstrated positive attitude toward such expansion, and definite indication of ability to contribute to the support of a community junior college.

18

Priority 2: Those areas which met the requirements of population and need for educational services but do not reach a comparable level in the expression of a favorable attitude toward a community college and the ability to support such a program.

Priority 3: Those areas which should continue to be studied and which should be considered for later development.

Priority 4: Those areas which should be developed in the future when additional evidence of need and support becomes available.

Several of the counties were too small to be considered alone as a potential community college area and were therefore combined into larger areas. In the final designation 31 areas were identified as potential community junior college areas. Four of these were at that time supporting community colleges leaving 27 new areas to be established.

Obviously the Council could not recommend the establishment at one time 27 new community colleges. Two essentials were not completed—the determination of the level of local interest and support and the sequence of priority movement. Both of these essentials could be obtained through the local survey.

Therefore the next step followed by the Community College Council was to offer each area in Priority Two the opportunity to request officially when that area should procede in establishing a community college. At this point a Priority One list would be developed.

Hillsborough County, which included Tampa with a population of about 150,000, was obviously in a Priority Two category until it had determined that the local commitments for support of the community college existed. However, the Board of Public Instruction of Hillsborough County after proper consideration decided that that county was not ready to conduct the required local survey at that time.

Several factors were influential in aiding the Board in reaching this conclusion:

1. There was consideration being given at this same time to the establishment of a fourth state university in the Tampa-St.

Petersburg area (Hillsborough and Pinellas counties). Some persons in Hillsborough County expressed the opinion that the establishment of a community college in Hillsborough County at this time might deter the approval of a university there. The continued confusion in the minds of many people between the functions of the community college and that of a university was not entirely surprising. The fact that Pinellas County was the location of St. Petersburg Junior College was considered a plus factor by some individuals in the claims of Hillsborough County as the proper site for the new university. In any case, this factor was a consideration in the decision of the Board.

2. The vocational program in Hillsborough County was much further developed than was the case in most of the other counties in Florida. In addition to other vocational opportunities a well developed Vocational High School was in operation which conducted a sizeable program for adults as well as for high school students. Many of the individuals responsible for this program viewed the community junior college as a rival to the vocational program and were active in their opposition to the establishment of a community college. Their influence upon the Board which was in charge of their activities was naturally strong and this opposition became a second factor in the decision of the Board to delay its survey.

3. Perhaps the most important factor, however, was the financial situation. Local taxes on the real property constituted the major source of local revenue for support of education. The establishment of a community college would require that a portion of these local tax revenues be diverted from support of grades 1-12 to support of the new community college. While this was not a great sum of money, it was large enough to cause the Board to hesitate in making a commitment. The financial situation was the third factor which influenced the Board's decision.

Nine other potential community college areas did conduct their local surveys, however. Six of these returned with strong commitments and enthusiastic support from local people. The Boards of Public Instruction of these six areas requested Priority One status and these requests were approved. The other three remained in Priority Two.

The Community College Council presented to the 1957 Legislature in accordance with the law which created the Council a long plan for the development of community colleges, a list of six Priority One areas, and a list placing all other areas of the state in Priorities Two, or Three, or Four.

The laws necessary to effect these recommendations were passed with one negative vote in the House and one negative vote in the Senate. Governor Collins signed the bill and Florida's Community Junior College Program was officially launched.

The six new institutions were authorized and actual planning was begun. A plan which incorporated the important aspects of local initiative and control with state level coordination and leadership was put into operation.

During the next ten years, 1957-1967, eighteen new community college areas were studied through local surveys. Local Boards of Public Instruction formally requested Priority One status with commitments for support in each instance. The 1967 Legislature approved the last of the 28 community college areas completing a plan which placed a college within commuting distance of almost everyone in the state.

NUMBER TWENTY-SEVEN—HILLSBOROUGH COUNTY

During 1964 Hillsborough County requested approval from the State Junior College Board (a coordinating board which replaced the Community College Council) to conduct their local survey. This survey indicated that the need for a community college in Hillsborough County was great. The President of the University of South Florida, Dr. John S. Allen, was a leader in helping people understand that the university could not meet the need for education for everyone. Many students who could not attend the University needed the opportunities provided by the community colleges. The Board of Public Instruction after due study reached this conclusion and requested a Priority One status.

21

There were still problems at the local tax levels, however. While the Legislature had taken some action which allieviated the local stresses, the effect in 1965, of this legislation was not entirely adequate. For this reason in the authorizing law the approval to begin operation was delayed until fall, 1967. The law also stipulated that certain requirements for grades 1-12 support must be met prior to State Board of Education approval to operate a community college.

These requirements were met in the opinion of the State Board of Education and the Community College for Hillsborough County was authorized early in 1967. The local Advisory Committee which is a legally constituted body charged with responsibility to advise the Board of Public Instruction on all matters related to the college was appointed by the State Board of Education and actual planning began in October of that year.

One of the activities of the Advisory Committee was to begin the search for a president. To aid in this search the Board employed Associated Consultants in Education as a search agency. This consultant group examined the credentials of more than 100 candidates living in all parts of the country before presenting to the Committee a selected list of three individuals. From this list the Committee selected persons for final interview.

To aid them in this process of selection the Committee and the Board listed the following qualifications for the president:
A. Professional Preparation:

A person having an earned doctorate is required. A major in junior college administration is desired, although appropriate successful experience in a junior college administrative position will be accepted in lieu of a major in junior college administration.

B. Professional Experience:

A person with educational experience which includes the following:
1. At least two years of actual classroom teaching experience in a junior college, a technical institute and/or a college or university.

22

2. At least three years of significant and successful administrative experience with at least one year in a junior college or post-secondary level technical institute.
3. A well defined field of personal professional competence. Preference will be given to a person with such competence in curriculum planning and development at the post-secondary level.

C. Personal Competencies and Characteristics:
1. He must possess the demonstrated technical competence to perform the duties and carry the responsibilities of the office of President.
2. He must possess the demonstrated ability to understand people, to work with them and to secure their cooperation.
3. He must possess a thorough knowledge and understanding of and a commitment to the junior college program including a special concern for both technical and academic phases of the program.
4. He must possess demonstrated ability to implement programs through the processes of democratic leadership.
5. He must possess a sensitivity to community educational needs, the research ability to guide the discovery of these needs and the leadership competence to supervise the implementation of programs required to meet them.
6. He must demonstrate ability to interpret the purpose and role of the community and to promote good public relations on behalf of the college.
7. He must demonstrate above-average organizational ability, be diplomatic, be able to delegate responsibility and authority and have the capacity to gain the confidence and respect of associates and community leaders.
8. He must have good moral character and high ethical standards.

At the same time as the presidential search was begun, other planning activities were also started:
1) the overall survey of the area was extended to examine potential sites for locating the campuses;

23

2) the potential staff needs and educational specification for facilities were projected; and

3) a program of public information about the functions of community junior colleges was started.

Consultants from existing community colleges in the state, from the universities, and from the firm conducting the presidential search were brought in to work with the local leadership. A staff member of the Hillsborough County grades 1-12 supervisory staff was appointed to serve in an executive position for the Committee until the college president was appointed.

In all of these activities the state level staff participated in accord with requests for aid from the local officials. The concommitants of local orientation and control and state level coordination and leadership were actively present in the entire prologue.

JAMES L. WATTENBARGER
Director, Institute of Higher Education
University of Florida

CHAPTER I

Right Place — Right Time

I first became aware of the junior college movement when I was an eighth grader at a small junior high school in Highland, California, a town of about 200 people located six miles east of San Bernardino. Our next-door neighbor, who was the local junior high baseball coach and algebra teacher, used to take me with him when he officiated at football games at the junior college in San Bernardino. At that time I never dreamed that I would even become a junior college student, much less a college professor and eventually president of three different junior colleges.

My maternal grandparents migrated from Georgia to Texas after the Civil War and then to California at the beginning of the citrus boom around the turn of the century. Thus, like all the boys in my class, it was assumed that I would some day become a citrus grower. However, because both my mother and father were musically inclined, I was introduced to the piano at an early age. Dad played trumpet occasionally for enjoyment and my mother was a contralto soloist in our local church and sang frequently at local functions. As soon as I became sufficiently accomplished on the piano, I was pressed into service as her accompanist, a chore I didn't especially relish. I would have much preferred singing the solos myself.

I am sure my parents never dreamed that I would become an educator. (In fact, Mother always hoped I would be either a citrus grower or a minister—in that order.) Teachers, or even college graduates for that matter, had very little prestige in our community. I recall a family discussion about one of our church members whose niece was majoring in Greek at UCLA. My grandmother couldn't imagine a greater waste of time. However, my dad did encourage me to finish my education even though he did not himself graduate from high school. He always said, "You can lose all your money, but they never can take your education away from you."

25

Admittedly, for reasons other than his insistent proddings, I was proud of my father. Even during the depression he retained his job in the freight office at the Santa Fe Railroad where he earned the title, Night Chief Clerk. Moreover, he built us a cabin in the mountains north of town, not too far from Lake Arrowhead. There we passed the long summers in complete surrender to the out-of-doors and, of course, to Mom's torturous prophecies about my future as a citrus grower. But somehow, between her proddings and Dad's insistence that I continue my education, I managed to practice for hours on the piano. During my first year at San Bernardino High School, I pursued my interest in music by joining one of the high school dance bands. This was during the Benny Goodman-Glen Miller era when pianists who could play popular music and also read notes were much in demand.

While I excelled in music, I was not pleased with my performance as a student. My training at the small junior high at Highland, where academic achievement was frequently sacrificed at the expense of accomodating the sons and daughters of itinerant fruit pickers who came to the community each year, had not prepared me to compete in a large urban high school. In fact, so inadequate was my background in mathematics (at Highland our baseball coach had taught elementary algebra) that I passed Mr. Baer's advanced algebra class only when I promised never to study mathematics again.

In any case, after two years of academic struggle, I welcomed Dad's transfer to Los Angeles in a new department of the railroad. Because I was approaching my senior year, Dad suggested that we live in Pasadena rather than in Los Angeles so that I could attend Pasadena Junior College. Its 6-4-4 organization would enable me to complete the twelfth grade and the first two years of college in the same institution.

Much to my disappointment, however, Pasadena was as unexciting as San Bernardino had been before. Furthermore, I was lonely. The junior college had more than 5,000 students, which made it virtually impossible for an "outsider" to break into the social activities. However, thanke to the inspiration and influence of Bernard Katz, a staff pianist for CBS in Hollywood with whom I studied piano, I was content to practice from eight to ten hours a day while carrying a few subjects to complete my high school diploma.

Dad's promotion and transfer to San Francisco the following year I welcomed as much as I had his transfer from San Bernardino to Los Angeles. Again, however, I was faced with the dilemma of wanting to attend college but not knowing how to go about it. My counselor helped me to evaluate several possibilities, including Stanford University, the University of California at Berkeley, San Francisco State, and San Mateo Junior College. Even had my grade average qualified me for admission to the first two, the cost, especially at Stanford, would have been more than my family could afford. While tuition at San Francisco State was low, it was a brand-new college and we knew nothing about the quality of the music department. When we examined the catalog of San Mateo Junior College, however, it appeared to have everything I needed, including an "open door" policy (which meant that any 18-year-old could enroll) and no tuition or fees (which meant that Dad had only to pay for my books). Dad's decision to rent a house for us in Burlingame, only four miles from the campus in San Mateo, meant that my first two years of college could be inexpensive because I would be able to live at home.

My acceptance at San Mateo was followed by two shocks. The first came during registration in September, 1940, when I discovered that few of the music courses listed in the catalog were actually being taught. Feeling that I had made a mistake in choosing San Mateo, I talked with Mr. Rohr, the only music instructor on the staff, who assured me that he could teach such catalog listings as counterpoint, canon and fugue and orchestration if enough students requested them. Unfortunately, there were hardly enough students to justify offering even an elementary harmony course. At any rate, it was too late to change my mind, so I completed my registration at San Mateo—and I'm certainly glad I did. Because it was a small school, I was able to sing in the chorus, play in the band and orchestra (even as a rank beginner) and try my hand at orchestration. These opportunities would not have been available to me as a freshman at the University or at San Francisco State. Moreover, because my classes were small and the instructors were willing to pay special attention to my particular needs, I began to fill the gaps in my academic background.

My second shock came at the end of my freshman year, when Dad and Mom announced their intention to file for a divorce. When they asked my reaction, I told them that they had their lives to live and I had mine. Even though I said it didn't make any difference to me, I know now that it was more traumatic than I realized.

Anyway, the divorce resulted in Mom's and my return to Pasadena, where I enrolled again at Pasadena Junior College—this time as a college sophomore. In order to help support a mother who was too emotionally upset to seek employment, I played on weekends with various dance bands in San Bernardino. With the country at war and the older musicians being drafted, the more accomplished musicians were compelled of necessity to teach me the ropes. But when I threatened to quit school and become a full-time musician so that I could more adequately support my mother, they unanimously discouraged me, insisting that music was no good as a full-time career.

At their insistence I concentrated on my studies and even qualified for membership in Alpha Gamma Sigma, the college scholarship society. In addition, I played French horn in the college orchestra while keeping an eye on a cute string bass player. Eventually I asked Director Milton Mohs if I might switch to string bass, and for several weeks I practiced night and day to become proficient enough to share the same music stand with Jeanette Joy. Although I liked her, I did not like her name because, according to my dad, Jeanette was the name of grandfather's old mule. So I called her Jeanny, and it has been that way for twenty-seven years.

Next to winning Jeanny's affection, perhaps my most rewarding experience at Pasadena came in April of that year, when I was asked to write the music for an all-student production. When I

28

stopped to consider the precedence for high-quality performances set by talented grads like Nat King Cole and Stan Freberg, I concluded that composing original music for "Operation Mickey" meant even more to me than membership in Alpha Gamma Sigma. This awareness prompted me to go a step further and orchestrate the songs for a thirty-five piece, all-student orchestra which included such fine young musicians as Ian Kerr, who later played with the Philadelphia Orchestra, Jean Ober, French hornist with the Twentieth Century-Fox Studio orchestra; and Mary Emery, who played with the Kansas City Symphony. Jeanny's younger brother, Al, a trumpeter of sorts, offered to help out and play cymbals during the overture. However, like Walter Damrosch in his debut with the New York Philharmonic, he missed his cue and the thunderous cymbal crash was never heard.

As a result of my efforts, I was nominated for membership in the Omicron Mu Delta Honor Society, a recognition I did not expect because I was in competition with students who had four straight years at the college. But I was flattered that my efforts had not gone unnoticed.

The next summer, Mom and I moved back to San Bernardino so that she could be near her sisters. She took a job as a switchboard operator in the county hospital and I enrolled in the University of Redlands in September of 1942. While the tuition was high, I knew I could work regularly with bands in the area and my living expenses would be nominal if I lived with Mother. It never occurred to me to seek financial aid from the University. While my college academic record was good and I certainly needed financial assistance, I was proud and wanted to make my way on my own resources. For most of the fall semester I worked in a nightclub called The Cave for $27.50 a week. I played piano from 8 o'clock until 2 in the morning six nights a week while carrying a full academic load at the University. I am not certain how creative and inspired my music was because, in order to get my homework finished, I had to read my textbooks while playing. I propped the books on the music rack in front of me and read Homer's *Iliad* while playing "Honeysuckle Rose." I finally got fired after I

29

had almost fallen off the piano bench three times in the same evening because I couldn't stay awake.

As a liberal arts college, Redlands exposed me to the humanities and a broad liberal arts curriculum. I was required to take a course in religion (a study of the Bible) and attend compulsory convocations weekly. At the convocation I always intended to ignore the speaker and spend the time reading my class assignments. Invariably, however, I found myself engrossed in what he had to say. Even now, I can remember little of what I learned in my classes, but many ideas gleaned from the convocation programs stay in my mind.

Jobless and draftworthy, I concluded that my chances for remaining in school were very slim. Being an aviation enthusiast, I tried desperately to get into the Air Corps as an aviation cadet. But an astigmatism and hay fever frustrated my efforts. Still, I tried every way I could to enlist in a branch of the service where I would not have to be a foot soldier. Fortunately, in February, 1943, the military fouled things up and my application papers got in the wrong stack; I was accepted as a meteorology student in an Air Force training program at Pomona College, one of the group of Claremont Colleges which now includes Pomona, Scripps, Harvey Mudd College of Engineering, and Claremont Graduate School.

Typical of the liberal arts colleges which do not emphasize vocal training, Pomona prefers instead that a student get a broad background in general education subjects covering many fields. In the meteorology program I was a fish out of water, at least at first. The detachment included 300 cadets from all over the country, most of whom had been math, physics, or engineering majors in college. Fortunately, while waiting for the last group of men to arrive, the profs decided to review math up to calculus. Of course, for me it was brand-new all the way. The concentrated math and physics curriculum was not as interesting as the humanities, but we lived in dormitories, had maid service, and ice cream for dessert every day of the week. Further, the college was located just thirty miles from Jeanny's home in Pasadena and thirty miles from Mom in San Bernardino. On the weekends I alternated visiting my two girlfriends.

30

Even though I had my academic problems, I somehow managed to survive the periodic washouts. By the end of the year, only 100 of the original 300 cadets were still in the program. To make my academic status even more precarious, Jeanny and I were married on New Year's Day in 1944. Why New Year's Day? That was the only time I could get a three-day pass. I was pleasantly surprised when the day before we were scheduled to finish the military program, the dean called me into his office and asked if I would be able to attend the graduation ceremony. It appeared that they had been counting units and found that I had enough to graduate.

After forty-eight weeks at Pomona, we suddenly awakened to the fact that the Air Force no longer needed meteorologists; they had sent the fellows who washed out of our training program directly to weather observer's school, then to O.C.S. where they had received commissions as weather officers. It was purely accidental that, as a music major, I ended up with a degree in mathematics, but I never did find out who decided that instead of being commissioned a Second Lieutenant in the Air Corps I should be shipped off to the infantry equipped with only a bachelor's degree. I can assure you that the newly acquired degree didn't make the rifle any lighter or easier to handle in the field.

I was assigned to the infantry as a buck private rifleman at Camp Adair, Oregon. Jeanny followed me and worked in the service club as a hostess. About that time my hay fever, which I had been able to keep under control while in the Air Corps, began causing trouble. Over the next six months I proceeded to sneeze my way out of the army. While training in the field, I fouled up every maneuver with my sneezing. Finally, in November, 1944, I was discharged and returned to Pasadena with slightly over $50 in my pocket.

At that time I would not consider buying anything on credit. Figuring that I had $50, and no more, to pay for an automobile, I bought a 1929 Chevrolet touring car that resembled the Amos 'n Andy fresh air taxi cab. The doors were wired shut with bailing wire. When I drove it home, it coughed once and died right in front of the house. During the six months I drove that car, however, it ran on kerosene almost as well as the gasoline we were able to buy.

Several weeks later I became a weight engineer at Douglas Aircraft in Long Beach. Although the position was shortlived, it enabled me to contribute to the war effort and to be near the airplanes which fascinated me. When it became evident that the war was about to end, I left Douglas and went to work for a hydraulics company in Pasadena as a time study analyst. While on this job I decided that I really wanted to give the music business a try on a professional basis.

So a few weeks before Clark Aero Hydraulics folded with the rest of the war factories, I organized the Airliners, a vocal group made up of four boys and a girl. One of the singers, Jimmy Joyce, eventually married the girl, Betty Perkins. Jimmy, who remained in show business as choral director on the King Family television program, later conducted the Jimmy Joyce Singers on the Smothers Brothers Comedy Hour.

Because those were the days of gas rationing, I shared my gasoline with the other members of the group. At our rehearsals I found it difficult to sing because I kept belching the gasoline fumes I had inhaled while siphoning gas from my tank.

Our first professional engagement on the Ginny Sims NBC Radio Show on VJ Day was followed by a few guest appearances and a motion picture during the fall. Our agent, Maurice Duke, was co-producer of the Sam Katzman production, *Teen Canteen,* which was distributed by Monogram Pictures. This was a low-budget film which was economically profitable but aesthetically atrocious. In the film I had such great speaking lines as, "Sure, Freddie, I'll have them for you in the morning," and "What about the decorations my dad sent us?" Some years later my young sons had fun watching the TV movie that showed Dad when he was a kid.

In the spring of 1946 the Airliners joined the Alvino Rey dance orchestra to tour the country for nine months. Alvino had just reorganized his band after the war and, while the King sisters were the featured vocal group with his original band, they were now occupied giving birth to the King Family. Other than our trip to Oregon, Jeanny and I had never been out of California and were anxious to see the other sections of the country. We played all the ballrooms and theaters which featured the last of the big name bands in the late 40's. It was fun giving seven shows a day at the Strand Theater in New York and playing nightly at the college Inn in the Sherman Hotel in Chicago. I enjoyed my role as a celebrity in the entertainment field, but I never did get used to the 300 mile bus rides between one-nighters. Jeanny was the band's librarian and chief babysitter for Louise (King) and Alvino's son, Robbie. We were on the roof of the Astor Hotel in the Starlite Room when the lights in Times Square came on again after the war-enforced "Brown Out." For a couple of young marrieds this was really living.

During the time we were with Alvino Rey we recorded for Capitol Records and always hoped that the big hit would be forthcoming. When we could not find the magic formula, the group disbanded in the winter of 1946. Jeanny and I returned to California where I replaced Mel Torme when he left the Meltones to become a soloist on his own. For a short time the group, which included Les Baxter (now with Capitol Records), furnished the vocal backgrounds for the singers on the Bob Hope Radio Show. We sang with guests Bing Crosby and Doris Day while Desi Arnaz and his orchestra furnished the accompaniment. Our main function, however, was to sing a Pepsodent Toothpaste jingle twice during each program. Hope would try his best (with some success) to make us break up while we sang the tale of Poor Miriam who finally discovered Irium. While the job paid well, it was not very gratifying to one who wanted to leave his mark on the world.

The realization that the music business was in the doldrums, that I was not going to become a star overnight, and that our first child was due in September, 1947, prompted me to enroll at the University of Southern California to pursue a master's degree in music. In those days USC had an enrollment of 12,000—enough students to cause a graduate of a small liberal arts college to feel lost and somewhat frightened. I chose to attend USC because of the stature of the music department and because, as a graduate student, I would be able to study with its name instructors rather

33

than with teaching assistants working on graduate degrees. I have always felt that I was fortunate to be able to attend a junior college where the freshman and sophomore courses are taught by experienced, full-time teachers.

I lasted only one semester as a music major, however. Even though I had been orchestrating and arranging music professionally for some time, I was told that I would have to complete undergraduate music courses in elementary orchestration, conducting, and counterpoint. Although I rebelled at the thought of more boring music theory classes, I did enjoy my music composition classes with Ernst Toch and Michlos Rosza. I'm afraid, however, I was disillusioned by my classes in musicology. (Who was it defined a musicologist as a person who knows every time Beethoven went to the bathroom but can't hum the Moonlight Sonata?) Further, I couldn't understand a word Madame Ehlers said in her course on Bach because of her thick German accent. When on a final examination I was asked to recall the number of Dominant Seventh-Tonic Chord progressions in one of Rameau's sonatas, I gave up.

I had decided that I would work toward a teaching credential strictly as an insurance policy in case I could not continue my career in professional music. However, while much of the work I studied in the music department was old hat, all the ideas and concepts in education were completely new. I enjoyed my work with Claude Crawford because he espoused a philosophy of functional education which appealed to me. He contended that students learn better if they see the practical value and relevance of what they are studying rather than being asked to amass a body of theoretical knowledge.

I found my courses in educational philosophy and psychology stimulating and my background in mathematics helpful when studying statistics. I received my master's degree in 1948 and continued work toward a doctorate. Because I did exceptionally well on my first series doctoral exams, I was allowed to complete my final examinations before my doctoral committee suddenly discovered that I had no teaching experience. Therefore, on

34

the 20th of August they informed me that, even though the college catalog did not mention it, they would not recommend the Doctorate in Education until I had at least three years' teaching experience in the classroom.

With plenty of theoretical course work behind me I thought I would have no problem finding a teaching job. I soon discovered, however, that because additional salary is paid for advanced graduate work, I was forced to compete with experienced teachers from out-of-state who could be hired for less money than I would have to be paid. Finally, I landed a job teaching English and band in South Pasadena High School. I was delighted because it was in a very desirable location and the salary was relatively good. Then I discovered why the job hadn't been filled previously. During my interview the principal had asked me if I was willing to direct a small band which had to be taught under rather awkward circumstances. I said I didn't mind teaching small music groups, but I wasn't prepared when only five students enrolled. One of them had never played any instrument except bass drum. That left me with four musicians, a drummer and two weeks to prepare for the first football game. Also, there was no class period for the band; it met at 7:00 in the morning, an hour before classes began. By aggressive recruiting I managed to put twenty-five bandsmen in uniform by the last game of the season. After football season was over and the star fullback, who was also the best trumpet player in school, decided to support the band, we were off and running. Over the next three years the band gained the support of the community and was invited to march in the Tournament of Roses Parade in 1952.

After the usual traumas that accompany the writing of a dissertation, I was awarded my doctorate. During the previous summer, when Steve was four and Ken was two, Jeanny and I hired a babysitter so that we could go to the city park every day and tabulate by hand a questionnaire which was a part of my doctoral study. On my salary we couldn't afford to use punch cards and have the data recorded by machine. I'm certainly glad that no one challenged the accuracy of my data, because by the time we were through I really didn't care what any of the answers were. But I did learn how to conduct and interpret a research study.

In the fall of 1953, when Jeanny's folks moved to a smaller house, we purchased the home in which Jeanny had spent most of her life. Our third son, Dave, had arrived in February and we needed more room. Also, that fall I joined the staff of the music department at Pasadena Junior College where I taught harmony, organ, and men's glee club, and was Assistant Director of the Official Tournament of Roses Band.

It is always difficult to be accepted as a fully professional teacher by colleagues who were your former instructors. However, to make it doubly difficult, I soon discovered that I disagreed wholeheartedly with the philosophy of the music department. I felt that the administration was more interested in using the students to publicize the college than it was in educating them. I was even called on the carpet because I had allowed one of my organ students to play for the college Christmas program. I was reminded that it would have looked much better on the printed program had Dr. Graham's name appeared. It didn't matter that the student actually played better than I did. At any rate, my contract was not renewed the next spring.

I should say, however, that the overall philosophy of the junior college and its curricula were excellent. In addition to a full assortment of courses which would parallel the offerings of almost any college or university in the country, Pasadena had extensive vocational curriculums. Courses were even taught to apprentices in programs sponsored by the various trade unions. Moreover, a fine commercial art department and an outstanding cooperative education program allowed students to spend part of their time taking courses at the college and the rest of the time working in industry under the joint supervision of the college and on-the-job supervisors. A full complement of courses in construction, for example, enabled students to build a house every semester. After the house was completed, including wiring, painting, cabinet work, etc., it was auctioned off and removed from the site. All of the courses taken in these programs were credited toward the Associate in Arts Degree, which was awarded after two years of post-high school work.

While, technically, I resigned from my position, it was quite a shock to my ego to realize that I had been fired. I now realize I should not have attempted to change my colleagues' attitudes overnight. At any rate I immediately set out to prove that I could get an even better job. I accepted a summer assignment teaching in the graduate school at the University of New Mexico. Just before I was ready to leave for Albuquerque, I told Jeanny I thought I should accept the associate professorship which had been offered at East Stroudsburg State College in Pennsylvania. With little fanfare we piled in the car our three small boys, ages two, four and six, hooked up our fifteen-foot camping trailer and took off. After spending six weeks at the University of New Mexico, we took another month sight-seeing before arriving at Stroudsburg.

During my two years in Stroudsburg I directed the chorus and taught professional courses in education. It was a typical "college on the hill" institution where all of the students lived in dormitories. Also, being a state teachers college, it was assumed that every student would become a teacher. Upon talking with the students, however, I soon discovered that less than half of the student body of 800 were interested in teaching careers. They attended the college only because their other alternatives were either an expensive private liberal arts college or the selective state university. The curriculum was quite rigid, with offerings limited to general liberal arts subjects and professional education courses. Unlike the junior colleges in California, there was no attempt to serve the adult population in the community by offering classes in the late afternoon and evening.

A professor's life in Stroudsburg, even with the hard winters, was extremely pleasant. Jeanny and I enjoyed both the Pocono Mountains and our home which overlooked the Delaware Water Gap. Because I taught only twelve hours per week, I had adequate time to pursue my professional interests. While I was able

37

to publish many professional articles, I had difficulty finding a publisher for the textbooks I wrote. Several publishers told me that they would publish my books if I were to get a professorship at a well-known university. On the other hand, university deans insisted that if I were to publish the books they would then consider me for employment.

Thanks to President Noonan's monthly faculty meetings, I wrote at least one professional article each month. These meetings, which began at seven o'clock in the evening, lasted until at least 11 p.m. and sometimes as late as midnight. And were they dull! For the most part Noonan read to us from reports which he prepared after accreditation visits to other colleges in the area. Apparently he felt we would develop a good college if we heard his criticisms of other institutions. It was amusing, however, that even though the meetings were not scheduled to begin until 7:00, by 6:30 you couldn't find a seat in the back two rows. Those of us who wanted to accomplish things got there early so that we could crouch down in the back seats and do our work.

To make ends meet financially, I played in a summer resort several nights a week during the tourist season. In fact, the main objection I had to the job at the college was that there was not enough salary for us to keep up with our circle of friends.

Finally, in 1955, I succumbed to the lure of the dollar and became a sales representative for the F. A. Owen Publishing Company in Dansville, New York. Jeanny and I then proceeded to spend the most miserable year of our married life. I covered Ohio, West Virginia and Kentucky as my territory, returning home every two weeks for a weekend with the family in eastern Pennsylvania. While the financial rewards were great, the altruistic rewards were nil. At the end of each day I could only count the dollars I had made, not my contribution to society.

The next summer we returned to California, ostensibly to visit the family. I had hoped to secure a professorship in one of the California colleges but found it difficult since I had now become an out-of-stater. Finally, late in August, I accepted a position teaching in a junior high school in Ventura. I figured I could

38

take the next year to locate a professorship. However, before the academic year was out, a position which interested me opened up at the junior college in Ventura. The college had a very extensive continuing education program with twice as many evening students as day students. (At that time it enrolled 2,000 day students.) Evening courses were offered in income tax accounting, prevention of drug addiction, interior decorating, pilot training, sailing techniques, and electronic organ, in addition to the credit courses designed to serve the area's adult population. I applied for the job and, while I was not appointed to the position, I so impressed the screening committee that I was offered a position in student personnel services.

For the next six years I served as dean of men and head counselor. Ventura College was one of the seventy-five junior colleges in California where the community college movement developed an initial thrust. The college served a diverse and well-rounded student body, even though the University of California restricted its enrollment to the top ten percent of the high school graduating classes and, theoretically, the state colleges limited their applicants to the top third. For financial, social, and many other reasons many students who were qualified to enter the university as freshmen chose to attend the junior college. While in California the tuition and fees are nominal at all of the public-supported colleges, many students find it desirable to get part-time jobs and economize by living at home with their parents. Therefore, like most junior colleges in the county, Ventura is designed as a commuter college.

I found counseling students at Ventura to be very gratifying. One of the first students I counseled was an engineering major who, before entering the junior college, had majored in coffee shop at the University of Idaho. His transcript listed a solid string of "F" grades. I remember telling him that from the looks of his record he would never be able to overcome the deficiencies and graduate from an engineering school. I believe I even quoted his odds in terms of a 60-to-1 shot in a horse race. He decided to try the curriculum anyway. For a while he had difficulty getting adjusted to a new college, but because he had

39

recently married he had a new source of motivation. He eventually transferred to the university and eight years later dropped by to let me know that he had finally received his bachelor's degree. He told me that my telling him that I didn't think he was capable of completing the degree so angered him that he vowed to become an engineer just to make me out a liar.

In addition to serving as head counselor, I was also director of Ventura's Student Financial Aids Program. In that capacity I urged community organizations to spend their scholarship funds on junior college students who were ready to transfer to the university with junior standing rather than to confine their efforts to high school seniors who felt they must go away to college instead of taking advantage of the low-cost education in their own community. Helping worthy students was indeed rewarding; however, I sometimes found it difficult to explain to a student who felt he was very much in need of financial assistance that there were those who were needier. I'll always remember the young girl who tried to convince me that her family could not afford to pay for her education because they had payments on a new $50,000 home and two Cadillacs to meet each month. I suppose it was really a case of relative values with her parents.

Over the years, because of the administration's tendency to make decisions without consulting the staff, the faculty developed a negative attitude and exhibited a complete lack of confidence in the administration. Throughout my tenure in Ventura I kept hoping that, as the college grew, the new faculty members would modify this attitude. I found to the contrary that it was only a short time before the new staff members adopted the attitudes of the veterans.

Jeanny and I found the Pacific Coast a delightful place to make our home and raise our children. My mother remarried and came often to visit us, and it was nice to spend the holidays with Jeanny's folks, Phyllis and Fisher. After all, I have always liked Jeanny's family, especially Jeanny's dad, Fisher, who is a remarkable example of a self-educated man. His mother died when he was very young and, unable to get along with his stepmother, he was sent to the West Coast to live with an aunt

40

whom he ended up supporting. Consequently, he only finished the eighth grade. However, he reads omnivorously and is extremely talented, interesting and balanced. I have always valued his counsel.

While in Ventura, our three sons, Steve, Ken, and Dave, participated in Cub Scouts and Little League baseball activities as we became more and more a typical suburban family. The boys even became reconciled to the fact that our family had been planned for three sons and that the little baby brothers and sisters for whom they campaigned were not in the game plan. Consequently, when in the fall of 1959, Jeanny announced to the family that she was pregnant, we were all stunned. Ken sat down on the couch, put his head in this hands and said "Gosh, Dad, what are we gonna do? We're splitting the allowance three ways as it is!" When Robin showed up on schedule the following spring, the whole family glowed. In fact, she has always been a family baby, with four daddies.

As time passed and my job became routine, I developed more and more interests outside the college. I even decided to pursue my interest in aviation. I knew I couldn't afford to buy an airplane of my own, and the thought of joining an aviation club did not appeal to me. Also, I have always enjoyed working with my hands on projects around the house. Therefore, I became interested in the Experimental Aircraft Association and the home-built airplanes which were being constructed in Southern California. However, Jeanny shook me up one day when she reminded me that I had never flown an airplane. So, with no further deliberation, I found my way to the local airport and proceeded to take flying lessons. After spending approximately twenty-five hours in a 1941 Interstate, I concluded that I thoroughly enjoyed flying. I immediately sent for the plans and started on what I thought was to be a two-year project.

While the family enjoyed living in Ventura and the leisurely pace at the college gave me time to pursue my hobbies, internal problems at the college convinced me, at age 40, that if I remained I could expect no further promotions.

Therefore, in the summer of 1962, when I was offered the presidency of Palo Verde College in Blythe, California, Jeanny and I decided that the excitement of the unknown and the challenge of a new situation were more intriguing than the possibility of spending another twenty-five years in Ventura. With mixed emotions we sold our new home overlooking the Pacific Ocean and moved to the middle of the desert on the Colorado River half way between Los Angeles and Phoenix.

At that time Blythe was a town of less than 6,000, situated, as we used to say, 100 miles from the nearest grocery store. While we were disappointed in the cultural void in the community, we enjoyed the mild winters, hot summers, and the water sports on the Colorado River. The entire family learned to water-ski and everyone except Jeanny learned to handle the single slalom ski with aplomb.

Palo Verde College was a small instituition (approximately 125 full-time students) which utilized a condemned elementary school for a campus. Because the college was administered by the public school system, I reported directly to Dr. Larry McGee, superintendent of schools. Being situated in a rural area, Blythe had a very low tax base which provided insufficient funds to run the schools adequately. In fact, the small population made it difficult to justify the inclusion of a junior college in the system. However, because of the extreme distance to another college, the community felt that it wanted to offer at least a token college curriculum to the students. We had ten full-time faculty members on the staff; I was the only administrator. I served as my own dean of instruction, prepared the class schedule, supervised instruction, assigned classrooms, and worked with the faculty to evaluate the curriculum. Because the college was so small, each instructor had to teach six different classes every semester. We usually offered only one section of each course at a time, which meant that each teacher had to prepare a different lesson for each class he taught. While we did have some excellent instructors, it is difficult for any person to prepare himself adquately at the college level to handle such a diversity of assignments.

42

Even though we had a part-time counselor who also assisted with the student activities, I got to know each one of the students quite well. The business office in the public schools handled most of the routine business operations, but I did receive invaluable experience in building and administering a budget, supervising a bookstore, and directing the efforts of the custodians and maintenance personnel. All in all, because the operation was so small, it resembled a laboratory experiment in college administration.

I got along very well when Dr. McGee was superintendent, but when he resigned and the principal of the high school was promoted to the superintendency, life became difficult. Because the operation of a junior college is considerably different from secondary and elementary school administration, certain problems are inevitable when a junior college is administered within a public school system. For example, most high school teachers are required to be on the school grounds from 8:00 in the morning until at least 3:30 in the afternoon. However, because junior college classes do not meet five days a week, most junior colleges do not require their faculty members to be at the college when they do not have office hours or classes to attend. Therefore, a district directive that all faculty will be in their classrooms eight hours per day does not make sense in the junior college. Further, if the junior college teachers do not have to honor this request, the high school teachers are unhappy. I tried to explain these differences to the superintendent, but invariably he would say, "I don't know anything about running a junior college, but this is the way I want it done." As the situation grew increasingly worse in the spring of 1964, I decided a change had to be made.

Fortunately, the previous spring we had been visited by an accreditation team made up of presidents of junior colleges throughout the state. They had been impressed with the work I had been doing with the limited resources available. When I asked for their support in helping me locate another position they were cooperative. Bob Swenson, president of Cabrillo College, introduced me to Leland Medsker, from the University of Cali-

43

fornia, who in turn told Ed Gleazer, executive director of the American Association of Junior Colleges, about me. In passing, several of my colleagues suggested that I should contact Joe Cosand, who had just established a new junior college in St. Louis.

Dr. Cosand had been president of Santa Barbara Junior College while I was at Ventura, but I had never met him. I attempted to contact him but was unable to get a response. Therefore, when I flew to be interviewed for a state department position in Pennsylvania, which was just in the process of starting a community college system, I took the opportunity to stop in St. Louis on the way back to speak with Dr. Cosand. After talking briefly with him I decided to take a rather brash approach. I told him that since I had spent some time in show business I thought I knew a pretty good fluff when I saw one, but I had never been fluffed quite as smoothly as I had in St. Louis. He looked a bit startled, then with a sheepish grin said, "I'll have to admit that knowing the poor resources available at Palo Verde College and being familiar with the faculty morale at Ventura, I can't imagine anything or anyone of value coming out of either of these two institutions." After a few more minutes of small talk, I caught the airplane back to California to discuss with Jeanny and the family the firm offer that I had received while in Pennsylvania.. At that point the Pennsylvania job looked very good because the salary was excellent and I thought it would be fun to be on the ground floor of the organization of a state system of community colleges.

The next day, however, Dr. Cosand called to say that his colleagues in California insisted that I was the man for the job in St. Louis. Now I was confronted with two excellent job opportunities. While the job in Pennsylvania paid considerably more, the St. Louis job would enable me to help master plan and develop one of the largest community colleges in the Midwest.

The next day I went to Los Angeles to attend a conference of junior college administrators and discuss my dilemma with some of my professional friends. Without exception they told me, "If you have the opportunity to work with Joe Cosand, take it.

44

This is a chance to work with one of the best in the business."

So in June, 1964, we put our house on the market and I left for St. Louis to become the director of Forest Park Community College, the urban campus designed to serve the city of St. Louis.

After my stint at Ventura and Blythe, working in St. Louis was like a breath of fresh air. The faculty and staff were enthusiastic and the three colleges in the district—Meramec, Florissant Vally, and Forest Park—were developing at a breakneck speed. There were no traditions to worry about and the staff members had not worked together long enough to let rivalries get in the way of progress. Further, the environment encouraged creativity.

When I was an administrator in California and had a problem, I immediately telephoned three or four of my colleagues to find out their solutions. As a consequence, few creative approaches were attempted because each of us chased the other around the mulberry bush assuming that if it would work at El Camino it would work at Pasadena and Cerritos as well. In St. Louis, however, we were in sort of an oasis in the Midwest, with no comprehensive community colleges in the immediate vicinity. We had to think through our problems and come up with logical and workable answers, even though they might not have been attempted before.

Also, in California you learn to live by the book, the California School Code, a thick volume containing all of the laws which affect the operation of school districts. When a faculty member or an administrator asked if he could try a new approach to a probfect the operation of school districts. When a faculty member or an administrator asked if he could try a new approach to a problem we first looked in the book to find out if it was authorized. If there was no authority stating that it could be done, the answer was an emphatic "No." Administering a college in Missouri imposed no such limitations. The state law is very broad and gives considerable latitude to the local junior college district. One of the strengths of the public junior college is that it puts the institution directly under the control of a local board of trustees. While the state colleges and universities are governed by Regents operating at the state level, the junior college is free to react to the needs of the local community.

The Forest Park campus served mainly the central city with its slum area in the north and the small neat homes of the German-extracted south St. Louis population, in addition to the county suburban population. For a campus site the district purchased the thirty-five acre amusement center which had been erected prior to the 1904 World's Fair, and which was located across the street from Forest Park, a several thousand acre park with a planetarium, amphitheater, art museum, zoo, golf courses, tennis courts and playing fields. The Highlands Amusement Center was located "on the Hill," the Italian community in which baseball's Yogi Berra was raised. During the initial part of the construction of the campus, the roller coaster was left standing and, for a while, I was the only college president in the country with a roller coaster on his campus.

I went to St. Louis just before ground was broken on the new campus; so for three years the college held classes in Roosevelt High School after 3:30 in the afternoon, when its 3,000 students were dismissed. In order to house the faculty and administrative offices, we leased an abandoned restaurant across the street from the school. While the surroundings weren't plush, they were adequate. We had offices in the Gun Room and held some meetings in the Hide-away Room. However, the fireplace in the faculty lounge wasn't used too often because we couldn't keep it from smoking.

The two other colleges in the county serve typical suburban areas. Florissant Valley Community College to the north is located near an industrial area which lends itself to the development of heavy technology programs in engineering and the related fields. Meramec Community College, in the southwestern part of the district, caters to a typically middle class suburban population.

In November of 1965 a bond issue was passed (by a 4 to 1 margin) to provide almost $50,000,000 to complete the three campuses. The Forest Park Campus was master planned for

46

7,000 full-time equivalent students, while the two suburban campuses were designed to accommodate 4,500 each. It was a wonderful experience for me to be able to work with the Chicago-based Harry Weese Architectural Firm from the master planning stage through the actual construction of the campus. We moved into our first core of buildings in the fall of 1967. Also, as a vice president in the district, I was in on many of the discussions concerning the two suburban campuses.

Because of a talented staff and aggressive leadership, the district was able to enlist the support of a number of private foundations. The Carnegie Foundation established a technical education center in St. Louis which is run by the Junior College District, and the Ford Foundation funded a program to train junior college teaching interns in technical education. The students take their theoretical and academic work at the University of Missouri and Southern Illinois University, then gain practical teaching experience on junior college campuses.

More recently, the Kellogg Foundation granted $168,000 to help identify the needs of the St. Louis area so that two-year training programs could be established in the allied health field. In an urban area such as St. Louis, the needs for two-year college trained personnel are so great that it would be possbile to spend the entire operating budget in these training programs. To get maximum benefit for the tax monies which could be used for this purpose, we needed a list of priorities. Therefore, we employed a hospital administrator from Amarillo, Texas, to direct a team of four researchers, first, to survey the field and then, to work with advisory committees made up of practicing technicians and professionals to develop curricula which would train competent health technicians.

We also used citizen advisory committees to help us keep our curricula up-to-date in other fields. Executives in industry tell us that the educational life of an engineering technician is four years. In computer technology it is only eight months. It is frightening to realize that it may be physically impossible to turn out two-year graduates who are not already obsolete. To

47

avert this, it is necessary to incorporate within the training programs provisions whereby employed technicians can constantly upgrade their skills and techniques.

As an open-door college serving the urban area of St. Louis, we attracted an extremely diversified student body at Forest Park. The faculty became concerned about the lack of preparation of many of the recent high school graduates who attended the campus. In the city of St. Louis many graduates did not have sufficient backgrounds to compete with students who graduated from the more college-oriented high schools in the suburban areas. Also, in many of the inner city high schools, yearly promotion was more dependent upon students' conformity to the rules and regulations than upon subject-matter achievement. When we accepted a student into the college we felt morally obligated to provide a program which would enable him to succeed and improve his skills and understanding. We felt that to put a student arbitrarily in a college-level program who had not progressed beyond the fifth or sixth grade reading ability was to court disaster. Therefore, the faculty suggested we develop a unique program for upgrading the basic skills of students who technically qualified for admission to the college but who, because of their weak backgrounds, were unable to succeed.

The Danforth Foundation became interested in our approach to the problem and funded a $250,000 program to develop our General Curriculum. General Curriculum students took part of their work in traditionally organized classes designed to stimulate their interest in learning. We encouraged the teachers to concentrate less upon topics covered, the transferability of the courses to the universities, and what their colleagues thought about their teaching methods than upon making education the most exciting experience these students had ever had.

Divided into groups of 100, the students worked with five full-time teachers, including a full-time counselor. The counselor's role was to help the student assess his ultimate potential—a task for which standardized tests are of little value because they assume that all students are from the same ethnic group and have the ability to read and interpret the tests. If a student scores poorly on an achievement test, it is difficult to tell whether the student has latent talents which do not show because of cultural and educational barriers. Our team of five instructors attempted to identify the promising individuals by devoting full time to a small number of students.

In order to upgrade basic skills in reading, writing, and arithmetic, the students spent approximately three-fifths of their time in a Learning Laboratory. Under the close tutelage of eductional diagnosticians, they used programmed instruction textbooks, teaching machines, and a varying assortment of teaching aids to work on an individualized basis at their own speed. Some of the more serious students spent as many as thirty-five hours a week in the laboratory. While we did not pretend to have solved the problem, our approach appeared to make more sense than forcing the students into classroom situations similar to those that had been unsuccessful in the public schools.

Because the district's projected enrollment for 1973 was 15,000 full-time students drawn from a 500 square mile area, the board of trustees decided to build three relatively small campuses instead of one large one. Moreover, because many students worked part-time and couldn't afford to spend long periods on the road, the board thought it advisable to place the campuses near the students' homes. Yet, even in a college of only 7,000 students, as Forest Park will be, many students will attend the college for two years and never have a class with a student they've been in class with before. The larger the school, the more impersonal it becomes.

However, three different college campuses operating under a single board of trustees posed problems of administration which are considerably different than those encountered in a single college. Under the multi-campus structure in S. Louis, a maximum of autonomy was extended to the colleges under the broad control of the board. Problems arose, however, when the faculties of each of the colleges developed curricula along slightly different lines. For example, as a system of compensatory educa-

49

tion for disadvantaged students, the Forest Park faculty developed the General Curriculum, but it was not considered to be appropriate at the two suburban campuses. Therefore, the selection procedures for the program were slightly different than those in the developmental courses on the other two campuses. To help solve this type of problem, Dr. Cosand met with the vice president (the three campus heads and the vice president for business services) twice a month to coordinate the efforts of the district. This President's Council, which also served as a sounding board for Dr. Cosand as he prepared materials to present to the board of trustees, was a key group in the administration of this multi-campus district.

As a junior college administrator in California, I attended many conferences throughout the state, but never had a chance to see what was going on in the other forty-nine. We always took the position that, because California was a leader in the movement, anything worth seeing could be seen in California. However, as an administrator in St. Louis, I was given the opportunity to participate in national conferences and study groups. I soon discovered that much of the leadership in the movement is taking place outside of California. In addition to conferences sponsored by the Sears Foundation on urban problems, I attended the national conventions held by the American Association of Junior Colleges. At these conferences educators join together to discuss critical issues in junior college education and to hear speakers espouse both old and new ideas. In this connection, it is only fair to admit that the bull sessions that occur between scheduled events are as contributory as are the formal sessions. And it certainly helps your own image in your college to know on a first-name basis the outstanding authorities in the field.

While my job in St. Louis was exciting and rewarding, the family reacted to the move in several ways. Robin, of course, made friends rapidly and was ecstatic at being old enough to go to school. On the other hand, Steve, a senior in high school, was not happy in his environment. In a large suburban high school, social groups are pretty well established, and it is difficult for a new stu-

50

dent to be accepted. Within a few months he was completely demoralized and his studies showed it. When he entered Kirkwood High School, he needed only two semesters of English to graduate, but before the year was out he had failed one of them.

The next summer we sent him 150 miles north of St. Louis to Culver Stockton College, a small liberal arts college where considerable individual attention is given to a student in a home-away-from-home setting. The dormitories are closely supervised and the classes tend to be small. Of course, the tuition was more than we had anticipated paying for Steve's entire college education, but we felt that the circumstances warranted the sacrifice. Steve finished his requirements for the high school diploma and attended the fall semester there as a college freshman. Then he decided his main problem was his own attitude. While he made passing grades, he did so without enthusiasm or interest in his studies. Therefore, he decided to enlist in the Armed Services for three years so he could study electronics.

Ken and Dave adapted to the new situation slowly, but found increasing interest in the rock 'n' roll band which they organized. Eventually both boys developed groups of friends and somewhat drifted apart. Ken participated in varsity basketball and baseball at the high school, while Dave became interested in studying piano.

It took us almost a year to sell the house in Blythe. The additional expenses incurred in moving from a warm to a cold climate, coupled with double house payments and Steve's tuition, made for rough going for a while. To help make ends meet, Jeanny sold real estate on a part-time basis. In addition, she sang with the church choir and maintained a very busy life raising a family and helping me with my college obligations.

By the fall of 1967, I was again at a crossroad in my career. I had just completed three years of pioneering—developing new buildings and curricula for one of the largest single junior college campuses in the Midwest and was finally in a position to enjoy the fruits of my labor. Yet, during that period five administrators had resigned to become presidents of their own junior college districts, and I was already older than any one of them. Many of my colleagues asked when I was going to "make" and head my own college.

Over the years when confronted with similar dilemmas, I have often used Jeanny's dad, Fisher, as a sounding board. While he is not a professional educator, he has always been a good listener and an incisive thinker. Even when we moved away from Southern California, I could always rely upon Fisher to clarify my thinking. Since January of 1968, when I discovered that a junior college district was being formed in Tampa, Florida, Fisher has been my confidant in a most literal sense. The Hillsborough Junior College story thus unfolds through our correspondence.

CHAPTER II

Search

St. Louis, Missouri
Thursday
January 18, 1968

Dear Fisher:

I just got home from work late, as usual, to find Jeanny has gone to church for choir practice. I suppose I really should go sing at least an hour with the choir, but frankly I'm tired. Anyway, I think I'd rather sit at home by the fireplace and get caught up on some of my letter writing.

I received an interesting announcement of a junior college presidency yesterday. A notice came from the University of Southern California Placement Office describing the formation of a new junior college district in Tampa, Florida. Because it covers all of Hillsborough County, it appears to have the potential to become a large multi-campus district. I'll have to confess that even though I studied geography in college, I had to dig out the atlas to find that Tampa is located about half way up the West Coast on the Gulf side. It appeals to me as a place to live because I imagine it has the foliage found in the southern states as well as the tropical features of the West Indies. As you know from our West Coast background, we have enjoyed the mixture of plant life found in California. I received the announcement the day before the deadline for submitting applications; so instead of responding to the University Placement Office, I dashed off a letter directly to a Dr. C. W. McGuffey, executive director of the Associated Consultants in Education located in Tallahassee, who is screening presidential candidates. I have never heard of the firm, but I imagine it is one of the many educational consulting firms in the country.

I talked with my boss, Joe Cosand, today about my future in St. Louis. We agreed that now is the time for me to spread my wings. Joe is right when he says I have prepared myself to be the

53

president of a junior college district rather than simply the head of one campus, even though it may be one of the largest in the United States. Frankly, I was a bit shocked when he insisted that I find myself a position immediately rather than play around with possibilities as I have done over the past two years. I suppose he is right.

If I could pick my job, I would find one that had the financial structure found in Illinois, the climate of California, the board of trustees of Cleveland, and the staff that I have here in St. Louis. I guess I would have to call the college Utopia U. Being more practical, I realize that any position I take will probably be a compromise. I know that Joe is interested in my professional development, but nobody likes to feel that he is being pushed out of his present position. Really, though, as I have told you before, he is a great guy to work with, and I'm flattered that he thinks I have the potential to head a larger operation with more responsibility.

As you know, I have interviewed for several jobs which I have not found to my liking. In this business rumors run like wildfire, and it is impossible to keep it a secret when you interview for a job. Each time I have been interviewed by a board, Dr. Cosand and other members of our staff have known what I was doing. Naturally this causes feelings of insecurity within the entire staff. I really don't blame him for wanting me either to "put up or shut up"—to take a job or remove myself from the job market. I had a long talk with Jeanny and we finally agreed to the inevitable: I will not really be happy or feel that I have made the most of my potential until I become the president of a college where I report directly to a board of trustees. So—here we go again!

Sunday
January 21

Boy, things are really moving fast. Before I even had a chance to finish this letter I got a call from McGuffey. He told me I was one of the top three candidates screened to interview for the job

54

in Tampa. He really caught me by surprise; I was honest with him, though. I told him I didn't have the slightest idea what my reaction might be to the Hillsborough County position but that it might be fun to find out. I asked him if my friend Jim Wattenbarger, who has until recently been head of the Florida Junior College System in the State Department, would know anything about the situation. Dr. McGuffey said that Wattenbarger is a member of their consulting firm and could give me all the details. He also suggested that I contact a Frank Farmer in the courthouse in Tampa to arrange the travel details.

McGuffey took it rather good-naturedly when I said that as a native Californian who spent his childhood on an orange grove, I have a biased opinion of Florida. Somewhat facetiously I told him I spent part of my boyhood praying for a wet winter for California and a hard freeze for Florida. You will recall how the citrus prices fluctuated with the climatic conditions.

I told McGuffey that Jeanny and I would be happy to come to Tampa and discuss the position except that I wanted to be under no obligation. We plan to take an objective look at the situation. Yet, I'll have to admit the thought of warm weather is rather appealing. Here in St. Louis the temperatures have been hovering in the 20's for the past several weeks. At least it should be fun to spend a few days in sunny Florida.

I plan to be in California for a couple of days next week. There is a conference at UCLA on Teaching Innovations which Dr. Cosand asked me to cover for him. We are organizing a consortium of colleges which are taking the leadership in developing new teaching techniques. I will call you as soon as I arrive.

Jeanny and the kids are well and, as usual, are up to their necks in activities. Ken's band is playing regularly and his hair is growing steadily. I really can't stand the music he plays, but he certainly brings in the money—as much in one evening as I did in a whole week when I was his age. The band with which he plays is called the . Belaeraphon Expedition (whatever that means). I'll send you a photo so that you can see the "darlings" with whom he works.

55

Dave is driving us out of our minds playing the piano. It's hard to believe, but he practices between twenty and thirty hours a week. He is engrossed with Debussy, Mozart, and Haydn. It hardly seems possible that a few years back I had to berate him constantly to practice his music lessons. The other day I ran across the picture which I took of him sitting at the keyboard with transistor radio on the piano, the ear plug in his ear, his ball glove on the piano bench, while he practiced his lessons and listened to the Dodger baseball game. Of course, he is improving by leaps and bounds and we think he has the promise of making quite a pianist.

Robin is still the cute little Brownie she has been all year. My, how she does like being a part of the Girl Scout program! She can hardly wait from week-to-week for the Brownie meetings.

Jeanny is trying to recuperate from all of her activities during Christmas. My mother came to visit us, and Steve came home from Ft. Bliss. Steve is a soldier of sorts, but doesn't appear to be accomplishing very much. He drives a truck most of the time and is assigned to KP only when they can catch him. Jeanny has spent very little time with her real estate activities this winter, and I would prefer that she call the whole thing quits. Frankly, it is not worth the time she puts in.

Love to all,
Bill

St. Louis
Tuesday
January 30, 1968

Dear Fisher:

I just got back from UCLA, where I had a pleasant weekend with my colleagues from California. Of the twelve colleges represented, nine are located in California. Of course, I knew all of the California presidents as well as Oscar Shabot, president of the Chicago Community Colleges, Joe Fordyce, president of Santa

56

Fe Community College in Gainesville, Florida, and Bill Priest from Dallas.

Dr. Fordyce filled me in on the Tampa job. It is a tough situation, but, in Joe's opinion, one with considerable potential. The newspapers have reported problems in the public schools, but a new superintendent has been on the job since the first of last year. Fordyce thought the Tampa position would be good if the new man has been able to gain the confidence of the community. Joe said he'd been asked to give a recommendation for a local man whom he had rather coolly endorsed. He said I could use his name if I felt that it was advantageous to have the endorsement of a local Floridian.

I also had a talk with Dr. Milton Jones. I don't think I told you about him; he is serving a year in St. Louis as an American Council on Education intern. He is dean of students at St. Petersburg Junior College in Clearwater, which is just across the bay from Tampa. Milton said he thought the West Coast of Florida was a delightful place to live (although he preferred Clearwater to Tampa) and that he felt that the Tampa position would have great potential. He said he was sorry the job had developed as soon as it did, because after he finished his internship he would like to have been considered for the job himself. Well, we'll just have to see what happens.

Our plans for the trip have changed slightly. Betty and Bob Benz have decided to take a vacation and fly with us to Tampa. You will recall this is the couple with whom we flew in the Beech Bonanza to Cleveland for the air races this past Labor Day. Bob is always anxious to log a little cross-country time, and we have found that the four of us can fly as cheaply as Jeanny and I can fly by commercial jet. We had to tell them why we are going to Tampa, but they have assured us that they will keep our secret.

Jeanny and the kids have mixed feelings about my taking another job. We all remember how tough it is when you move into a new town, a new school, a new church, and a whole new community. I suppose it isn't as difficult for me since I have new professional colleagues and am up to my ears in the new assignment. It's really much harder on the family, but that's the way it is with most executives who move around the country these days.

57

Ken especially seems upset with the prospect of our leaving because he still hopes to be able to land a recording contract with his band. Dave really doesn't have too many friends here and is engrossed in his piano. Of course, Robin is so young that she will adjust easily, and Steve is out of the fold at the present time. We haven't heard anything for several weeks from him, but we assume that no news is good news. At least, he must be all right or we would have heard otherwise.

Boots, the newest member of our family, is quite a character. I don't know whether Jeanny told you in her last letter that we traded in Sam, the cocker spaniel we got from the Humane Society, for a more docile animal, Boots the Beagle. Now three years old, Boots has had his problems, though. When he was a pup, he was hit by an automobile which broke his pelvis. Therefore, it is impossible for him to hoist one leg to christen the plants. Being a rather innovative animal, however, he has solved the problem by learning to stand on both forepaws. You should see him standing in the snow with both hind legs cocked at an angle doing his duty. I always did say where there's a will there's a way.

Jeanny is excited about our trip to Florida. We try to delude ourselves into thinking that this is a vacation trip, but experience has taught us it will be impossible to relax completely and enjoy ourselves. Perhaps it's partly a guilty conscience, since we're spending tax funds to consider a job while trying to mix in a few days' vacation. You're aware, of course, that your daughter is a real brick when it comes to rolling with the punches. She finds it just as difficult to move as the rest of the family, but never complains when it's time to get up and go.

Regards to Al, Betty and Phyllis.

Bill

St. Louis
Friday
February 16, 1968

Dear Fisher:

We just got back from an exciting week of combined vacationing and job-hunting in Florida. After the weather we have

58

been having in St. Louis, it was great to be able to spend a few days in a warm climate. When we left for the airport the temperature was hovering in the teens and flying conditions were miserable. Ordinarily I would have been a bit apprehensive about taking off in marginal weather, but, fortunately, Bob Benz is a real old maid when it comes to flying.

We arrived at the airport shortly before 9 a.m. but it took us three hours to get the plane ready to get in the air. First, Bob had to pack every suitcase and package in its own special nook. Then we found out we were renting a new model Bonanza which was unfamiliar to Bob. This necessitated his flying with an instructor three times around the field to get checked out. It's a nice model airplane with a three-blade propeller, lots of baggage room, and a cruising speed close to 200 miles per hour. But I really don't see what good the 200 mph cruising speed did us when we sat on the ground for three hours. Incidentally, this plane has almost the same flying characteristics of my little home-built model in the basement. However, mine is about half the size of the Bonanza and will carry two passengers rather than four. Also, it will burn seven gallons of gasoline an hour rather than twelve. There is one major difference, however. The Bonanza we flew is finished; the one in my basement, even after six years, is still not completed.

We flew most of the morning IFR (instrument flight rules), which simply means that we went up through the clouds and on top. Up there it was a beautiful day with the sun shining on the tops of the airborne white caps. Once again I got my kicks handling the controls. Ordinarily Jeanny is quite comfortable while I am flying, even though I still do not have a license. But one incident really shook her up. We had been having a little bit of difficulty with the gasoline gauges, so we decided to run the gas out of the right tank so that we could see just where the needle indicated when the tank was drained dry. However, we neglected to say anything to the girls in the back seats. You can imagine Jeanny's reaction when the engine coughed once and went completely dead while we were flying absolutely blind in the middle of a cloud. Incidentally, the Bonanza only has one control wheel.

59

When you change from the pilot to the co-pilot you have to swing the wheel over and the co-pilot flies rather than the pilot. I don't know whether Jeanny thought we were going to stop and jump out at 6,000 feet, but she changed from a state of drowsy sleepiness to a rigid upright, wide-awake condition in less than a tenth of a second. Of course, all we did was to switch to the other gas tank and the engine came to life immediately. The rest of the trip was uneventful. We landed after dark, coming in over the lighted city and swinging over darkened Tampa Bay into the Tampa International Airport.

We called for the courtesy car and made our way to the International Inn. After checking in we sat down for a minute to relax. No sooner had I taken my shoes off than the phone rang. Frank Farmer was on the phone; he was waiting for me in the lobby and asked if we wanted to chat for awhile. Quite frankly, after waiting for three hours to get airborne, then sitting above overcast for five and a half hours, I didn't feel like presenting my first impression to a person who undoubtedly would be influential in my selection or rejection. I apologized profusely and told him I would prefer to postpone our talk until the next day.

After breakfast the next morning Jeanny and I took up our vigil in the lobby of the hotel. After about ten minutes' standing around staring at everyone there and peering into every car that drove up to the front door, a rather quiet man stepped from behind a pillar to ask if by chance we were the Grahams. Of course, it was Frank Farmer who then took us to his office in the courthouse. The day was sunny and rather cool—in the low 60's—but after a winter in St. Louis the wind-blown palm trees were a pleasant sight.

At his office Farmer talked with us for about forty-five minutes, giving us general background on the junior college and the public school system. I did a bit of probing myself to find out what sort of image Dr. Raymond Shelton, the new superintendent, had made in the nine months that he had been on the job and what sort of loyalties he had developed among his staff during that period. Farmer assured me that Shelton was a good man and that things

60

were on the upswing in Tampa. Farmer said that the formation of the junior college itself, however, had generated only mild enthusiasm in the community.

At the present time there are twenty-six public junior (community) colleges in the state of Florida. The largest, Miami-Dade, has a current enrollment of 30,000 students. The formation of Hillsborough County is the next-to-the-last junior college district necessary to make a community college available to 98% of the students in the state.

It seemed rather strange to me that Florida's third largest city would be next to last in securing its junior college. I learned that while it had been a number one priority area for several years, Tampa had not been able to secure the matching funds necessary to organize a junior college because of financial problems in the school district. Apparently this is one of the things that Ray Shelton has been able to help accomplish.

Jeanny and I were able to chat with Dr. Shelton for about ten minutes before our scheduled interview with the Junior College Advisory Committee. Florida has a strange system which at the present time includes two boards. The county-wide public school systems are responsible for education from kindergarten through junior college. However, each school board must appoint a junior college advisory committee to make recommendations pertaining to the 13th and 14th grade programs. One of the delegated functions of the advisory committee is to recommend the employment of a president for the junior college. Therefore, the group interviewing me was really an advisory committee rather than a *bonafide* board of trustees. During the week we were in Florida, however, the legislature passed a new bill which, as of July 1, will make the advisory committee a legal board of trustees with rather hazily defined powers. The school board will still have all powers of taxation and must legally approve the budget, but the Junior College Board of Trustees will be the official governing body. I'll have to admit that it sounds like a rather weird arrangement, but I like it better than having to take all matters to the public school board for action, as we did in Blythe.

One by one, the advisory committee members entered the board

61

room; this stage of an interview is always rather awkward. The committee members looked me up one side and down the other as I frantically tried to keep names and faces together so I wouldn't mix identities. Mr. Thompson, the rancher, was the first one I met. He is a ruddy-faced man who seemed pleased that I knew enough about the citrus industry to be able to ask a few intelligent questions about the fruit market. By the time the fourth board member arrived I really wasn't sure just which one was which. Fortunately the interview began almost on schedule.

Committee Chairman Ken Hardcastle, whose thick Nashville drawl I found very difficult to refrain from mimicking, began by asking Jeanny to take a seat at the table. This took us both by surprise because at previous interviews the board members, upon being introduced to Jeanny, would then have her politely squired off to some other location to meet a board member's wife who showed her the city. Most boards apparently feel that the wives should be interviewed but only to see if they use good English, wear clothes which are in style, and are at ease in unfamiliar surroundings. In this case, however, Jeanny was asked specific questions concerning her role in the development of the junior college. The board members wanted to know what she thought she could do in a team effort to get the junior college accepted in the community. They wanted to know, moreover, how she felt our family would adapt themselves to the new community. Finally, they wanted to know what she thought was the main difference between the junior college and the four-year liberal arts college.

Handling the questions like a pro, she referred to the fact that she and I met in a California junior college over twenty years ago before I transferred as a junior to the University of Redlands; that she was aware of the many technical-vocational offerings then available at Pasadena City College; and that it was so obvious that many of the students attending the junior college really were not prepared to go directly into the university but were able to find more appropriate careers in fields such as auto mechanics, vocational nursing, engineering technology, and the like.

After about a half hour Jeanny was excused and the board

devoted its attention to me. Mr. Hardcastle was extremely interested in my attitude toward the treatment of controversial issues on a college campus. When asked this type of question, I have always made it a point to pull no punches and answer honestly rather than try to determine the bias of the questioner. So, I told Hardcastle quite pointedly I felt that, as an institution of higher learning, it was the responsibility of the junior college not only to foster the discussion of controversial issues but to make sure that objectivity is maintained and that a proportionate amount of time is devoted to each side of the topic. I had a little difficulty convincing him that controversy is relative. For example, during World War II there was relatively little controversy over the fact that the United States was at war, whereas now there is considerable controversy over the Viet Nam conflict.

After an hour and a half of questioning, I was finally asked, "Do *you* have questions?" Quite frankly, I had many questions but felt that there was no point in attempting to probe too deeply too soon. I did attempt to determine their understanding of what their role was to be by asking if they were willing to support a quality institution. The answers I got were quite nebulous—a good sign that they admit that they are a novice lay board which does not have preconceived ideas of what the character of the college should be. They feel that their job is to select the best qualified president and see that he furnishes the leadership necessary to make it a great institution.

Of course, as with most new boards, the various members were still attempting to establish their relative roles. Every time you get a group of five people together you usually find one who has something to say on every subject, and another who, as the philosopher, likes to generalize and point out all ramifications. This board was no exception.

Mr. Hardcastle wanted to know my political affiliations. My first reaction was to ask, "Does it really make any difference?" I refrained, however, not knowing exactly how my retort would be interpreted. Instead, I gave him an answer which wandered around the bush three or four times by saying that my Southern background tended to make me a Democrat by birth. (They even

63

thought it humorous when I told them that my mother had been expelled from school in California when she refused to admit that the South lost the Civil War. Mr. Thompson responded, "Good for her!") I suppose I straddled the fence when I told them that in St. Louis we call a California Democrat a Missouri Republican.

Before the interview was terminated, Mr. Gray, the banker, wanted to know my reaction to the suggested salary range. I couldn't even remember having heard one mentioned. The figure they then quoted did not really surprise me because I am well aware that in Florida you receive part of your take-home pay in sunshine. I replied that while my salary in St. Louis is slightly higher than the figure they were considering, money is not the most important factor in my decision. I told them that I didn't expect them to offer an initial salary that was completely non-competitive, but would hope that, if pleased with my performance, they would make the necessary adjustments to compensate me in accordance with the responsibility of the position. Further, I intimated that I considered the initial salary to be an indication of the level of confidence that the board had in my potential. (I have learned that it never works to make a power play when it comes to salary. Before I interview a candidate for a position, I always have a pretty good idea of his present salary. It goes over like a lead balloon when he looks me straight in the eye and tells me that he has to have a salary that's exactly double what he is now making.)

After the interview, Frank Farmer drove Jeanny and me back to the motel and promised to meet us after lunch to show us around the area. When he returned, he asked whether we would like to look at housing or do a little sight-seeing around Tampa. Because he had had lunch with the advisory committee, I asked him to hint to me as broadly as he could. If I were still in contention for the job, I would like to look at housing; if I had not impressed the committee, we might as well see what Tampa has to offer. He rather tersely indicated that it would be a good idea to look at houses.

64

So we drove around the area examining the tract developments and custom homes along Tampa Bay. He drove us to the Carrollwood area north of town, took us through the home which he had recently purchased, and gave us some idea of the price of housing. Because there are no basements in most of the houses, no enclosed garages, and little insulation, the cost of houses appears to be cheaper than in St. Louis. However, water-front housing costs considerably more. And I don't see much point in living in Florida unless you live on the water.

When we got back to the hotel Mr. Farmer asked us to join him for some liquid refreshment. He was very helpful in answering some of my questions concerning the college. However, when it was time to leave, over his objections, I insisted on paying the bill. While industry readily provides expense accounts for entertaining customers and visiting firemen, I had a feeling Farmer would have to handle this expense out of his pocket. He later confirmed my suspicion that Florida law prohibits this kind of expenditure. Once again I appreciate the small budget account I have in St. Louis which enables me to be gracious when we have visitors. It's not that I am not well-paid; it's just that I find it difficult to anticipate when I'll be called upon to entertain a college guest. And Jeanny would scream if I used her grocery money!

That evening Jeanny and I went to the Kapok Tree Inn in Clearwater, which had been highly recommended by a friend in St. Louis. A rather unusual restaurant, it is so large that we lost our way and entered through the kitchen. Because there are so many dining rooms and so much bric-a-brac, one of the hostesses had to escort us to the front door. To say that the decor is gaudy and overdone would be an understatement. The building itself is really a large Quonset hut, or series of steel buildings. Hanging from the girders are flower pots with live plants and all sorts of odd decorations. I hate to sound like Grandpa Joy, who wrote only about the quality of the food, but the steaks at the Kapok Tree Inn were out of this world. Furthermore, Jeanny and I shared a jug of rosé wine from a contraption which looks like a urinal on a stand. So help me, it stands upright and when you push the wine glass up from underneath, it relieves itself and you get a sparkling glass of wine. What a way to live!

On Saturday we met A.C. and Ann Wright, who are friends of the Benz's. They are a delightful couple who live in a manner to which Jeanny and I would like to become accustomed. A. C. has done very well in land investment and cattle ranching. They picked us up at the hotel and squired us in their Cadillac around the Clearwater beaches and into St. Petersburg. We had dinner at the Port-o-call, a restaurant which Guy Lombardo started a number of years back but never could make a financial success. As Grandpa Joy would say, the lobster (Maine lobster, that is) was delicious. We saw another interesting sight in St. Petersburg, The House of Parakeets. An early resident raised them, let them escape, and now they inhabit the island quite profusely. Just driving down the street near the House we must have seen a hundred of them flying around.

After the Wrights had let us off at the hotel, Jeanny and I went out looking at houses. Right now we think we would like to live somewhere on Tampa Bay. There are many fingers of land, or, perhaps I should say, sand, which have been pumped out into the bay. I think it would be great to have a boat moored in the back yard, don't you?

Sunday morning the Benz's, Jeanny, and I attended the Florida State Fair. It reminded me so much of the National Orange Show in San Bernardino, which, as a youngster, I delighted in attending. I guess I'm still a kid at heart. The next day unsettled weather conditions caused us to fly a few miles eastward to the home of the Wrights rather than attend the Gasparilla Day Parade. José Gaspar in the early days supposedly buried his treasures somewhere on Tampa Bay. Every year Tampans celebrate his notoriety by bringing in a sailing vessel similar to the one featured in *Mutiny on the Bounty* and having a pirate parade. Some day Gaspar Community College may serve part of Hillsborough County.

In the late evening we boarded the Bonanza and took off from Tampa, flew down the coast from Clearwater to St. Petersburg,

66

and then swung eastward to Ft. Mead. Because the VOR radio was not too accurate at the low altitude at which we were flying, we mistook Bowling Green for Ft. Meade. After we found our bearings, we landed blushing at the Wright ranch east of Ft. Meade.

We spent two days with the Wrights. They have a lovely home complete with riding horses, grazing cattle, a swimming pool in the back yard, and three boats. The weather was a bit cool, so we didn't get a chance to water-ski. I suppose there is no valid reason for Wright's owning three ski boats, except that his children didn't particularly like the first two that he purchased. Also, they have a new electronic organ which has all sorts of built-in percussion effects. I spent most of Sunday evening experimenting with the organ. By the time I got through, I could get a fairly decent sound out of it. It took me back to my night club days. I'm glad I no longer have to play music for a living, although, admittedly, I did enjoy the period during which Jeanny and I played for dances on weekends.

On Tuesday morning we got up bright and early to prepare for the flight back home. However, Bob was his usual tortoise self. To climax the entire ordeal, he lost his sunglasses. For an hour and ten minutes we frantically searched the house, the airplane, and the auto, only to find the glasses in the first bag in which he had looked. I really don't mind flying with someone as meticulous and thorough as he is, but I will have to admit that at times it taxes my patience.

We flew home along the East Coast and had a very enjoyable view 100 feet above water from Daytona Beach to Jacksonville. From Jacksonville to home I handled the controls most of the way—at a respectable altitude, of course.

After being gone almost a week, we were pleased to be home again. I had better close for now. I'll keep you posted as to any developments.

Bill

St. Louis, Missouri
Wednesday
February 21, 1968

Dear Fisher:

It has now been more than a week and still no word from Florida. Since the committee was anxious to make an appointment, I have to assume that I am no longer in the running. Several days ago I talked with Milton Jones, the intern from St. Petersburg. Milt thinks the Florida teacher walk-out might hold up the decision to appoint a president. You will recall that the advisory committee must act through the school board; under the circumstances, I imagine Superintendent Shelton has more pressing matters on his mind than the appointment of a president for the new junior college. Further, if the walkout results in any changes in local financing, it is possible that the college opening might be postponed for a year. At any rate, it has been my experience that when you have not heard by telephone within a week, it is only a matter of time until you receive a "Dear John" letter.

I leave next week for the annual conference of the American Association of Junior Colleges in Boston. Frankly, I looked forward more to going to Florida in January than I am to going to Boston in the middle of February. Do you blame me?

Jeanny and the kids are well, but the whole family is upset over the prospect of our making a move. It's not that they feel St. Louis is the only place to live, but the unknown makes everyone insecure. The prospect of having a house on the market for a long period of time and settling in a new town while making double house payments doesn't make me very happy either. Now that we have definitely decided to make a move, I really wish I could find something in a hurry and eliminate the suspense.

Just have time for a note now—will write more later.

Bill

68

St. Louis
Friday
March 1, 1968

Dear Fisher:

I returned late last night from the AAJC Conference in Boston. The weather was a wee bit on the nippy side when I caught a plane just before a snowstorm hit the area. It's times like this that make me wish that I could go to sunny California—even muggy Tampa.

Speaking of Tampa, I walked into the Sheraton Hotel in Boston to attend the first general session of the conference and happened to sit beside Dr. Charles Chapman, who is President of Cuyahoga Community College in Cleveland. He leaned over to me and asked if I was going to take the job in Tampa. It seems that one of his top administrators is also a candidate for the position.

There seems to be very little secrecy as to the candidates for the position. In fact, Joe Cosand arrived late to make a presentation and told me that he had heard from three different sources that I went to Florida looking for a job. He added that one of the sources of his information works on my campus, so I did a little bit of hell-raising today. It seems that every time I take a trip out of town, not at district expense, the staff in the business office assumes I have been invited to interview at the new district's expense. In this case they were absolutely right, but it doesn't do the local morale any good to have this sort of rumor floating around.

In many respects, the AAJC Conference serves as a slave market for faculty and administrative recruiting. But this year the amount of negotiating made it absolutely ridiculous. In 1966-67 it had been predicted that fifty new junior colleges would be formed. The actual number was almost twice that amount. Therefore, with all the new colleges to staff, personnel is a real problem. In fact, I used the conference as an opportunity to get my name pretty widely spread as a potential president. I talked confidentially to Ed Gleazer, AAJC Executive Director; Norm Harris of the University of Michigan; Leland Medsker of University of California; Max Smith of Michigan State; Dr. Sebastian Mortorana of New York State; and any other person I thought might be in an influential position to give me some leads. It really didn't take very long to get results, because during the three days that I was at the convention, I was interviewed by representatives from three boards of trustees.

A new college being formed in Muskegon will add to the twenty new junior colleges recently organized in Illinois. I knew a little bit about the situation because one of my students in a seminar on the community college at the University of Minnesota two years ago is now a principal in the Muskegon school system. He had interested me in their problems of formation and in the various vested interests which had played quite a part in the physical make-up of the final district organization and of its approval by the state. Therefore, I felt I had a basic understanding of the problems. When they asked if I would be available for an interview, I told them I would like very much to look the situation over.

My most interesting interview was with a member of the board from Johnson County, Kansas. There is really nothing unique about this new junior college which will be organized in the suburbs just across the river from Kansas City, Missouri. But the manner in which the board has organized the college and the advertising brochure certainly make the job appear very attractive.

When most community colleges are started, a descriptive brochure is developed, usually by an educational consultant. Most brochures look so much alike you get the impression they have all stolen from each other in preparing their materials. The Johnson County brochure, however, is unique. For example, instead of simply describing the function of academic courses in the comprehensive community college, and then in another section describing the vocational-technical courses, the two are combined in a section entitled, "An Inter-related Curriculum."

Perhaps this approach appeals to me because I personally feel that there should be no distinct line drawn between the two functions. The terms "academic" and "vocational" should not be

70

antagonistic concepts. The curricula demand a "both/and" rather than "either/or" approach.

Also, the brochure discusses the opportunity for innovation in the community college field. Innovation normally refers to teaching methodology. We in St. Louis have always said we would rather have our teachers try something new that fails than try something old which they know is not going to work because it never has. Therefore, there is a great deal of interest in the community college movement in finding new and better ways of teaching students than we have been able to do in the past. However, the brochure cautions that "this [newness] should not be interpreted to mean that all new ideas will be worked into the fabric of the college. Among the educational innovations which should be considered are: large and small group instruction, computerized learning programs, modular scheduling, flexible architecture, learning laboratories, independent study, comprehensive library that included electronic aids."

After examining the brochure it is obvious that either a very astute consultant was employed or the board of trustees has developed considerable insight into the community college movement. When I talked with board member Dr. Hugh Spear, I was told that the brochure had been developed by the board of trustees after a great deal of study. We must have talked for an hour or so before I was assured of his interest in my candidacy.

It seems that a year or so ago Joe Cosand met with their board as a consultant and, in passing, told them a great deal about the St. Louis District. So I am certain that my being on Joe's staff has not hurt my chances for the job. And one of Jeanny's acquaintances, who has just moved to St. Louis from Kansas City, keeps telling her how great a place it is to live. Perhaps we'll get a chance to find out. Dr. Spear indicated that he would contact me shortly to arrange an interview with the board some weekend in the near future. We'll keep our fingers crossed because this looks like a good one.

You would have gotten a kick out of observing the action in the slave market. There were so many boards conducting interviews the candidates virtually tripped over each other going and coming

71

from the various hotel rooms. In fact, for one interview I literally had to get in line and wait my turn. In a job placement agency this sort of thing is not unusual, but when applying for college presidencies, it did seem a little startling to me. In fact, while sitting in an anteroom awaiting my turn, I actually listened to one candidate being interviewed.

The presidency we were considering is in an academic junior college which has operated for years as a part of the public schools, offering almost entirely highlevel academic courses which transfer directly to the university. Several years ago, under a new community college law, it became a comprehensive community college with programs in remedial education, continuing education, and vocational-technology. I have been following the development through the newspapers, and the situation has not been particularly healthy. For one thing, a rather antagonistic press has delayed site selection and construction for a least another year, when a nationally-known consulting firm will complete its study. Ever since the president resigned over a year ago, the college has been in limbo.

I couldn't help discerning the mood of the interview of the candidate from Washington. Because he apparently knew nothing of the district, he asked leading questions which allowed the board to respond in a manner which did not reflect negatively on the college. Naturally, he became more enthusiastic as the interview went along because it does have tremendous potential. It is in a large metropolitan area, will have at least three campuses, and the salary, in excess of $30,000, is certainly competitive. These alone are enough to whet the appetite of many potential college presidents.

During my interview I could not help noticing a difference in attitude. In his opening the chairman of the board said, "Your being from the Midwest means that you're quite aware of our problems." When I concurred, the interview proceeded in a rather tense atmosphere. And, as you know, when I probe, I really probe. I suppose my searching questions did make some of the board members feel rather uncomfortable. I wanted to know just how committed the faculty were to the comprehensive

72

community college philosophy, which includes vocational and technical courses and remedial work. I can understand how a faculty who has become accustomed to denying admission to students who are unable to succeed in college might reject an "open door" philosophy.

At any rate, the interview ended after a rather tense forty minutes or so. At this point I'm not really certain whether I'm still in the running. I talked with the state director for junior colleges and he is rather upset that most of the candidates are not comprehensive community college oriented. They're either four-year college faculty members or in state department positions. He told me that he certainly hoped I would continue my interest in the job because he would like very much to have in the position someone who has had experience in a large metropolitan comprehensive community college. Well, we'll just have to wait and see.

Hold on to your hat, Fisher! Jeanny just returned from her sorority meeting and gave me a bit of news. One of her girl friends just received a letter from a sorority sister who lives in Clearwater. She closed her letter with "Isn't it great that the Grahams are coming to Florida. I just heard on television that Bill will be the president of the new college in Hillsborough County." What do you know about that! There is only one problem— somebody forgot to tell me!

I'd better close for now. Jeanny has lots of news to tell me, and I want to fill her in on the conference in Boston. Regards to all.

Bill

St. Louis
Saturday
March 9, 1968

Dear Fisher:

This business of job hunting is beginning to assume the characteristics of a "who-dunit." I wrote a letter to my friend Lee Henderson, who is head of the state department for junior colleges in Florida, concerning the announcement on Tampa TV. He assured me that all presidential appointments must have his endorsement and that the president would be the first one to know about it.

Last Thursday we had a session with our attorneys concerning labor negotiations. (They suggested we employ a vice-president for personnel who has background in negotiations.) After the meeting, several of us stopped at the Chesire Inn on the way home. We had hardly sat down when I was paged. It was a telephone call from KXOK, one of the local radio stations. The man on the other end of the line informed me that he had been asked by their Tampa affiliate to find out if I had accepted the position as president of Hillsborough County Junior College. I, of course, assured him that I knew nothing about it. At this point I sincerely wish that I did know something. The suspense is killing me.

Yesterday morning I received a call from a Dr. Wilbur Billington, who is chairman of the board of trustees in Johnson County, Kansas—the new district I told you about near Kansas City. They want Jeanny and me to spend the weekend with them after I get back from a computer seminar at the IBM Center in San Jose, where I intend to learn all there is to know about data processing.

Several hours later the chairman of the board of trustees for the new junior college in Waukegan, Illinois, invited me to come up when it is convenient to talk with their board. Doubtless, the national reputation of the St. Louis Junior College District has made me easily one of the top five or so candidates for most of the new jobs in which I am interested. Just keep your fingers crossed for me and hope that I select the best one.

I didn't mean to mislead you into thinking that *all* professional educators do when they attend a national conference is to look for jobs. Admittedly, some of the sessions in Boston were extremely fruitful. One such session was a discussion of future developments in labor negotiations both with teachers and with non-teaching personnel—a problem-area with which neither my college preparation nor my experience has prepared me to cope. I am firmly committed to the concept that the professional teaching staff should be concerned with and should influence educational policy, but when confronted with a situation such as is now found in New York State, where more than a hundred items must be formally negotiated, I confess I find it difficult to consider this a professional relationship with faculty. In St. Louis we have been talking at length with our attorneys as to how best to face up to the crises we know are in the offing. As you may recall, the St. Louis District probably would not have been formed at all had it not been for the efforts of organized labor. Under no circumstances, therefore, can we afford to alienate this group. Yet, no matter how you stretch it, those of us in executive positions do assume the role of management.

While in Boston, I attended another interesting session on developments in remedial programs especially designed for the educationally disadvantaged. Providing for the educationally disadvantaged is a vital concern particularly to administrators in open-door institutions which admit students who are completely unprepared for college-level work, even though they have earned high school diplomas. Further, in many of the *de facto* segregated areas, promotion is automatic and success in high school depends more upon conformity to the rules and regulations than upon academic achievement. Consequently, to the junior college come many students who read at the third or fourth grade level and who are completely ignorant of the fundamental processes in arithmetic. It does no good for us to decry this fact and blame the secondary schools; instead, ways must be found to make the college experience profitable for these young men and women.

I was somewhat disappointed that the thrust of the presentation was more upon the philosophy of the open-door college and the desirability of making education available to all students than upon what should be done with them *after* they are admitted to college. The discussion got a bit heated during the question-and-answer period when the audience insisted on concrete proposals for transforming these unqualified individuals into *bona fide* college students. I was inadvertently put on the spot when AAJC consultant Dorothy Knoell suggested that I explain part of the program which is being supported by Danforth Foundation on my

75

campus in St. Louis. I talked very briefly about our General Curriculum, with its core of general education classes taught by a team of teachers, and our open laboratory, which utilizes programmed instruction and teaching machines to upgrade the reading, writing, and arithmetic skills.

In case I failed to mention it to you, when I transferred to St. Louis, over half of the students enrolled at Forest Park experienced some sort of academic difficulty and almost twenty percent of them were academically disqualified at the end of the first semester. Our staff felt that only a bold approach would salvage the weaker students. When we began the General Curriculum, we divided an experimental group of 200 students into two categories: those who took economics and modern math, and those who chose sociology and biology to supplement English literature, communications skills, and counseling psychology. In addition, the students spent an average of six hours a week in a programmed materials learning laboratory studying the basic skills.

The objective of the experiment was to identify the students' potentials and eventually place them in technical or transfer curricula, community training programs, or help them find jobs in the community if they decided that they could not achieve at the college level. At the end of the first semester we were pleased that all but ten students completed the program. Our phenomenal success in St. Louis does not mean that we have all the answers, but it certainly seems to indicate that we're doing as much as any one in the country to find them. In any case, no matter where my next job is, I intend to borrow freely from the things I have learned in St. Louis.

In my last letter I forgot to mention that I applied for a presidency in a newly organized district in Los Angeles County. Several things about the job appeal to me. In the first place, the Santa Clarita District encompasses the Newhall-Saugus area, one of the fastest growing sections in Southern California. Also, classes are not scheduled to begin until the fall of 1969, which would give a full year for planning. When a college is started overnight, the administrative staff is kept occupied by the day-to-day and minute-to-minute problems which need immediate solutions. It is very difficult to give adequate attention to the long-range planning which is necessary if the college is going to develop in a viable manner. Of course, one of the main inducements to me is to be able to get back near the relatives and once again be able to participate in the California retirement system. You are right; if I return to California at a considerably higher salary than when I left, I will probably double my retirement. This in itself makes California quite appealing to me.

I talked with Fred Kinser from UCLA when I was in Boston, and he said he thought the appointment was pretty well decided. This sometimes happens when a board already has a local man in mind; but to inflate his ego and to prove to the people in the area that they have a top man, they often publish a national announcement without really giving serious consideration to the out-of-state candidates. Also, under California state law the board cannot pay travel expenses for a candidate to interview. Fortunately, throughout the rest of the country expenses for presidential candidates and their wives are usually reimbursed by the interviewing college.

At any rate, I asked USC to send my professional papers and recommend me as one of their candidates for the Santa Clarita job. I also wrote to the chairman of the screening committee, indicating that I would be in California the weekend after the cut-off date for applications. Knowing I will have to pay my own travel expenses, I asked if I could combine this interview with my trip to San Jose. It is little out of the way to stop in Los Angeles and I could easily take a day's vacation to interview. In about three days I got an answer stating that it would be impossible to deviate from the procedure which had been set up. Well, we'll see how hungry I am for the job if I am offered the opportunity to interview.

The family is in good spirits, but would certainly like to know when and where we are going to be resettled. Ken is really upset about the possibility of not being able to remain in St.Louis. He so fully enjoys playing with his rock 'n' roll group that I am sure he would like to stay here and attend college. I talked with him the other day about making some sort of definite plans, but it's

77

difficult for an eighteen-year-old to make this sort of decision. Jeanny and I would feel much better about his living in a college dormitory than his sharing an apartment with one of his buddies. Unfortunately, the fellows in his group all live in apartments, and the idea is rather appealing to him. If we do leave the area at the beginning of summer, I certainly hope he will remain in St. Louis rather than try to come to a new town and make friends before school is in session.

Robin and Dave are still rolling along. Dave is completely engrossed in Dubussy's "Clare de Lune," and Robin is still enjoying being a Brownie. It seems that one of these weekends in the not-too-distant future, I have the privilege of attending a father and daughter cookout. I am certain it will be great fun eating whatever appears on the table. Perhaps you should cross your stomach for me on this one.

Things are moving along smoothly enough at the college here in St. Louis. We are trying our best to prepare the educational specifications for the final phase of construction which houses our heavy technology programs. Our automotive technology instructor is overwhelmed trying to write specifications for the equipment in his area. As a public-supported institution, we are required to put all of our equipment out for bids on an "or equal" basis. This causes considerable confusion when the architect attempts to design utilities for an unidentified brand of equipment. In fact, the other day we were planning for washers and dryers in the physical education building and couldn't decide whether to specify electricity or natural gas. I suppose if you're talking about getting clothes dry, gas is equal to electricity. But it certainly does make a difference which utilities are specified on the drawings.

We are again approaching a very difficult time of year—the time to recommend faculty members for retention or termination. One case which is extremely difficult this year involves one of our male teachers. It seems that a year or so ago he was arrested on a morals charge, but was not convicted. In fact, he was not really formally charged. We became aware of the situation when one of the local school administrators asked why in the world we

78

would hire this man. Upon checking through the police records, we are convinced that there is enough smoke to have been a real fire. However, because the police used an entrapment technique, they felt they could not make a case in court and dropped the charges.

Now I'm in a dilemma; the police tell me that they firmly believe that the man is a homosexual, yet there is absolutely no specific court evidence to the fact. I'm torn between being an understanding humanitarian in a society where social values are rapidly changing and giving the man the benefit of the doubt, throwing myself wide open to severe criticism if one of our board members happens to stumble onto the story as it is circulated through the community. I have a feeling that I have only one choice—to replace him.

Give all our love to the family. Boots spent the weekend away from home. You can imagine my reaction when about noon last Monday I got a call from the Webster Groves Police Department. My first thought was: "What has Ken or Dave done now?" However, it was Boots who was tied up behind the police station, and the police were calling us to come and get him. Just what do you do with a lovesick beagle?

Bill

St. Louis
Thursday
March 28, 1968

Dear Fisher:

Last Thursday I beat a hasty retreat home from the IBM Computer School at San Jose. You recall I told you I was to spend a week out there. No, the weather wasn't bad; I simply lost my power to concentrate. Let me tell you what happened.

For the first three days the school was fascinating. I learned something about how to write a computer program and a great deal about computer terminology. I even learned that there were such things as bits, that two bits make a byte, and that two bytes make a gulp. How about that! Then Wednesday afternoon after class was over, Bob Fahl, president of Monterey Peninsula College, and Knute Rochte, dean of the junior college section of the University of Toledo, and I decided to play a short round of golf on the small course next to the IBM School.

When I got back to my room to change clothes in preparation for this great tournament, I noticed that I had two telephone messages—one from Ken Hardcastle in Tampa, and another from the secretary to the Johnson County Board in Johnson County, Kansas. Even without returning the calls, I knew what they wanted. Hardcastle was going to offer me the position in Tampa, and the secretary of the board from Kansas was going to confirm my interview for the following weekend. You can imagine what a game of golf I played, even on a small par-three course. Fortunately, we did not count over seven strokes per hole because I shot an absolutely flat score—seven strokes on each. (I even lost three balls in a waterhole.)

Because I couldn't contain myself, I confided in Bob and Knute, asking them what answer I should give if I were really offered the job in Tampa. As we played the round, they helped me to evaluate the relative merits of the potential positions. After we had talked for an hour or so, Bob looked up and asked me what I was waiting for. As far as he was concerned, I had already decided I wanted to go to Tampa. So with that I returned the call to Hardcastle. His offer included a salary equal to that which I now earn in St. Louis, but he also gave me his assurance that the board would approve attractive salaries for key administrative staff members who, because of our getting started so late, will have to ask to be released from their contracts.

I really did try to go to classes the next day but, finally, I could stand it no longer. Instead of taking notes on computers, I devised curricula, class schedules, calendars, etc. I called Jeanny and told her I was coming home. I also called Joe Cosand and told him that I wanted to take the job. Naturally he gave his blessing, and we agreed that I should ask Hardcastle to coordinate the public announcement with him so that both boards would make the simultaneously.

And wouldn't you know! I had no sooner gotten in the house from San Jose than the phone rang. It was the chairman of the board of the Santa Clarita School District in California. He informed me that I had been selected as one of the candidates to be interviewed. I really don't know if he was disappointed or not when I told him I had already accepted a position in Tampa, but at least he offered his congratulations on my new position. Well, that's the way things happen. If I had waited and not taken the Tampa job, I might have had the chance to live close to the family. But, then again, I might have been a bridesmaid rather than the bride.

Once a decision like this is made, it is extremely difficult to keep it to yourself. Jeanny and I mentioned it to no one until Tuesday, the night before yesterday's board meeting. Then I found out that Joe had already told the other vice-presidents. I guess he found it difficult to keep, also. I did tell my deans late on Tuesday, and put memoranda in the faculty boxes so that they wouldn't have to learn about it from the newspaper. At the board meeting last night the official announcement was made, and I gave the usual "it is with mixed emotions" comments. I'll have to admit that a lump did rise in my throat at the thought of leaving St. Louis. Believe me, I have plowed a good portion of my life into this college without waiting to reap the fruits of my efforts. But I suppose that's the way it is with all pioneers.

This morning many of the college faculty came to my office to offer congratulations and say they were sorry I am leaving. It's amazing that you never know how much people like you until you plan to leave. Or maybe that's why they like you—because you are leaving.

Robin is bursting with the news and has announced to all of her friends that she is going to live in Florida. I'm certain she doesn't quite know where Florida is, but it sounds very glamorous to her. Jeanny is apprehensive about getting the house in a condition to sell. Oh, but this is a worry period. We look at our house, we like it, and we think it should sell; but will other people like the house as well as we do? I can't help remembering that it was on the market a year before we bought it. I certainly hope we don't

81

have to hang on to it that long. Dave and Ken are really non-committal about making the move. Of course, neither of them has ever been in Florida; how are they supposed to know whether they will like it any better than St. Louis? Boots is really the only indifferent one.

I'd better close now because there are many, many, many things to do. Give our love to all.

Bill

CHAPTER III

Lame Duck

St. Louis
Wednesday
April 4, 1968

Dear Fisher:

About 10:00 last Friday morning the phone rang and I was greeted by a Tennessee drawl. "Congratulations, you are now officially the new president of Hillsborough County Junior College! The school board has now put its stamp of approval upon your appointment."

In my conversation with Hardcastle we agreed I would work in Florida on weekends and as many weekdays as I could. I intend to finish my contract in St. Louis which expires on June 30. However, over the past four years I have accrued fifty-two working days of vacation. Therefore, I hope to be able to put considerable time on the new job, yet not have to ask the board to release me from my contract early.

Later in the day Lee Henderson, the State Assistant Superintendent for Junior Colleges in Florida, called and asked if I could come to Tallahassee on Monday to be sworn in by the State Board of Education. He said it wasn't a command performance, but he liked the state board to meet personally all of the presidents of the Florida junior colleges.

I tried to make plane reservations and found that during the tourist season it's extremely difficult to get from St. Louis to Tallahassee because of a bottleneck in Atlanta. Finally, I arranged to fly from St. Louis to Atlanta to Jacksonville and then back to Tallahassee. Exhausted, I arrived in Tallahassee on Sunday evening, the 31st.

On Monday morning Lee picked me up and drove me to his office. After an hour and a half discussion, I was thoroughly confused. While I have been a college president in California and Missouri, every state system is different. They all have their little idiosyncrasies, rules and regulations. I finally got one thing through my head, though; 88 divided by 15 gives the instructional units which are determined by the 6 mill equivalent of the county-assessed valuation, and what one-half of .3 mills (or something like that) will bring in gives you your operating money divided by 24. Oh me, I must have dropped something some place. Well, what do you expect after an hour and a half on the job?

I spent some time in the afternoon with Dr. McGuffey and a number of his consultants, the group that nominated me as one of the candidates for the presidency of Hillsborough Junior College. Hardcastle suggested we hire them to do some of the staff work necessary to open college this next September. The job facing me over the next four months is staggering. Therefore, Mc-Guffey and his group are going to prepare rough drafts of much of the material which normally I, as a president of a new junior college, would develop with my own staff. While most colleges provide at least a year's lead time for staff planning before they open classes, I will have about four months. The initial curriculum will be a cut and paste job. That is, we will simply lift from various catalogs curriculum patterns which appeal to us and call them our own. Fortunately, we can change the original decisions at will.

That evening, Lee invited me to dinner with his family. There, we had an enjoyable time discussing some of the problems of the junior college system in Florida. Florida now has begun operation in twenty-seven of the twenty-eight junior colleges which will complete its overall master plan. This plan provides for 98% of the students in the state to be in commuting distance of a cummunity junior college. In other words, Florida intends to make higher education available at public expense to virtually all of its citizens.

The plan is similar to the California, Illinois, and Pennsylvania

84

plans which have been implemented in recent years. These plans provide for the universities to do the graduate work, the state colleges to offer some graduate degrees, but to emphasize primarily the baccalaureate degree, and the junior colleges to serve as the lower-division training grounds within the higher education system, in addition to offering technical-vocational education and community service courses for the public. While the Florida junior colleges are controlled by the local school boards, there is considerable direction at the state level. For example, Lee chairs a president's council which meets on a monthly basis. Here state-wide problems are discussed by the presidents of the various junior colleges. Because state rather than local funds are used for the most part, the state has a much greater voice in what curricula are offered.

While I am not particularly an advocate of state domination, it would appear to me that any sensible school administrator would not want to proliferate the offerings needlessly. Certainly there is enough for each of us to do without needlessly duplicating curricula. Therefore, even though I'm a strong advocate of local control, I do not find this level of state intervention objectionable. Anyway, twenty-five of the fifty states have state junior college systems rather than splintered, complete local control, as in California, where the junior colleges are coordinated by a state director who has no control over the curricula. However, because there is no equalization of state monies, there is a great difference in the quality of offerings in the colleges. I don't believe this is quite so marked in Florida, where all of the money is supplied at the state level on an equalization formula.

Early Tuesday morning I met with Governor Kirk's cabinet. An interesting group politically, they are all independently elected cabinet members and, as such, have no direct indebtedness to the Governor. In fact, the Governor only meets with his cabinet every other meeting. Apparently he told them that he didn't have time for a weekly meeting, so they decided to go ahead and conduct business without him. So I did not get to meet him. I did, however, meet the rest of the cabinet members. They were very cordial and I had the feeling that I was really in a meeting of a cabinet in Georgia. The southern drawls of these officials fit in beautifully with the dogwood which was in bloom all over the Capitol grounds. There was considerable by-play during the proceedings when every so often one of the men would interrupt a speaker and ask him why something hadn't been brought about. The speaker would then reply that the Governor had vetoed that bill. Of course, the cabinet member knew this before he asked the question, but he hoped that one of the newspaper reporters would report that progress had been stopped by the Governor's veto.

I also learned a great deal about poaching activities off the Florida coast and about the crawfish market. In fact, I learned an hour and a quarter's worth while waiting to be introduced. At one point I even considered the possibility of setting up a junior college curriculum in crawfish technology. We could include a course in rifle practice which should certainly take care of the poachers.

Immediately after being introduced to the cabinet, I was squired to the basement where a battery of television cameras were set up. The first question I was asked was how was I going to provide overnight facilities for a new junior college. I replied that that would depend on the kind of a sale Sears might have on tents. This was just the kind of comment that the media were looking for, so the next day's papers in Tampa played up the tent college to the hilt. Realistically, though, right now the only image I care to portray is one of complete confidence. I may fall flat on my face as the new president but I would just as soon people not find out about it until school fails to open next September.

Later in the day I met State Superintendent of Public Instruction, Floyd Christian. While waiting in the anteroom to see Mr. Christian, Lee dropped a bomb in my lap. He said, "There is something you ought to know—you are not the first person to be offered this position." When I asked him to explain, he informed me that another man, the president of a small community college, had been offered the position, accepted it, and was approved *in absentia* by the State Board of Education. Then the next day he changed his mind. What do you know about that?

Upon thinking about it, I suppose the only thing hurt is my ego. I would like to think that I was the first choice, the most qualified, the most outstanding candidate for the position. However, I know that a lay board has absolutely no way of comparing professional experiences and determining how these experiences relate to the new position. Therefore, I am not surprised. Most interviews really end up as popularity contests. Also, you will recall when I left Palo Verde College, having been president of an institution with fewer than 300 students, I was represented by inference as a president of one of *the* comprehensive California community colleges. Consequently, I was considered for much larger positions than my experience actually warranted.

Lee told me that the committee had asked Dr. Shelton to give them his opinion as to which type of éxperience would be more beneficial—working with a board as president of a small college or working through the president of a large multi-college district and being responsible for a large urban college. I can understand how Shelton, having come from the superintendency of a Nebraska school district where junior colleges aren't really in the picture, might feel that direct board experience was more important than relevant community college experience. Further, he would have no way of knowing how I have been involved with the board in St. Louis. So I repeat, the only thing that is hurt is my ego.

Being the second man hired for a job is becoming a habit. You will recall prior to my St. Louis appointment another California administrator had been named to head the Forest Park campus but left almost immediately. He had been interviewed in St. Louis in the fall and brought his family to the city during the Christmas vacation to look for a house. In March he reported for work. A day and a half later he departed, leaving a note for Dr. Cosand saying that during the past day and a half he had made more decisions than he had in the past five years. He said that night classes in temporary buildings were not his cup of tea. Therefore, on the day that the district had planned a formal re-

87

ception with complete television coverage he was on his way to California. You can imagine the embarrassment to Dr. Cosand and the staff when everybody showed except the guest of honor.

Jeanny, Dave, Robin and I plan to drive down to Tampa next week and spend our Easter vacation looking for housing. Ken prefers not to come because he has three band jobs and doesn't want to let the group down. I suppose we'll take the little car because the big Buick station wagon is not too dependable. I should sell it since it is four years old.

Bye for now—I'll write again when we get back. Love to all.

Bill

P.S. I just saw a newspaper clipping from the Los Angeles *Times* indicating that my friend Bob Rockwell, president of Santa Barbara College in California, has accepted the position as president of the new Santa Clarita District in Newhall. It is interesting to know who my competition would have been had I remained a candidate for that position. At any rate, Bob is a good man. Further, I am not sure that I could have competed with his level of experience. However, now starts the game of musical chairs. I'm certainly glad I made a choice which ended the suspense. Had I passed over the Tampa position, I might have made several trips to California interviewing for positions as they occur one by one when each president moves up the hierarchy. It's quite a relief to be out of the game and on the bench again.

St. Louis, Missouri
Sunday evening
April 14, 1968

Dear Fisher:

We just returned from a frantic Easter week in Tampa. I worked late on Friday evening to get all my work caught up on the Forest Park campus so that I could be gone a week without the local operations suffering. So we left on Saturday morning about nine o'clock.

We had a difficult time deciding whether we should drive south through Memphis or go through Nashville and Atlanta because this was the weekend immediately following the death of Martin Luther King. Normally on a trip like this I would drive at night, but under the circumstances I didn't want to risk being stalled out on a lonely highway around Nashville in the middle of the night. Although we were a little startled to see the National Guard surrounding the Capitol as we drove through Nashville, we did have a nice drive during the day before stopping in Chattanooga for the night, too late to take Robin up to the top of Lookout Mountain. We'll have to do that some other time. We had an uneventful drive into Tampa on Sunday; the roads are excellent. It was delightful to watch the foliage change from winter to summer as well as the beautiful dogwood blossoms in southern Georgia.

Monday morning I drove to the county school offices in the courthouse, where Frank Farmer showed me my temporary office—two small rooms one for a receptionist-secretary, the other for my office. While the furnishings are austere, Farmer was able to dig up a desk and three war-surplus chairs. I don't have a file cabinet but was able to beg paper and pencils. I even had to purloin some paper clips. Thank goodness I brought my own pen. I do have a temporary secretary to answer the phone. Believe me, it practically rang off the hook while I was there. We got at least fifty job inquiries every day.

That afternoon I held the first formal press conference of my career. The board room was set up with flood lights and two TV cameras. Eight or nine reporters showed up to fire questions at me. Of course, the first interrogator wanted to know if I had found any tents as yet. I was asked the obvious questions about physical facilities, initial enrollment, curriculum, etc. I could very honestly tell them that I didn't have any idea what we would do with physical facilities, but that I had been assured that there were facilities available. I told them that limitations on size of our initial student body would have to be decided by the board of trustees. While I have my own ideas about an initial enrollment, the board must decide the actual numbers and the manner in which the students are selected.

89

When asked whether the NEA sanctions on Florida teachers and the recent walk-out would affect recruiting of teachers for the junior college, I gave the only answer which I could give the media. I said I thought there was enough thrust in the community college movement nationally to overcome our teacher recruitment problems. The fact that we received 250 applications the week I was in Florida is an indication of the interest people have in teaching in the junior college. Further, at least a third of these applications are from out-of-state teachers. However, I have found that many teachers will indicate an interest, then refuse a firm offer when it is actually made. Consequently, we will have to wait and see just how easy it is going to be to recruit. I am most concerned about attracting top level administrators. It is extremely important that I not make mistakes in hiring a dean of instruction, dean of students, and dean of business affairs. Each of these staff members is in a position either to make or break me before I find out if he can handle his job.

Throughout the week I appeared on television every day on the short news spots. In fact, I was on so much I couldn't even get the family to let me watch the TV to see how I came through. However, while seeking housing, Jeanny found that the people she talked to thought that I was delightful and charming on the boob tube. How about that!

Jeanny spent every day looking for a house to buy. It is certainly confusing when you have an area of 900 square miles in which you may live. Each section has many advantages and disadvantages. Every home seems to have some points that must be compromised, such as size, layout of kitchen, location, proximity to schools, individual school conditions, etc.

Anyone who tells you house hunting is fun hasn't moved as often as we have. Jeanny would line up three or four houses for me to look at, I would sneak away early in the afternoon (about 6:30) and try to see them before dark. We finally focused on two areas: on the bay near the Clearwater causeway, and slightly north of town in a tract development on Lake Carroll. On Friday we decided to make an offer on the only home that the entire family agreed was the place we should live. Unfortunately, the house is too small, has no basement, and, because it has a carport, we will immediately have to spend $600 to $800 making it into a garage so there is a place to store the airplane. Other than that, it is delightful.

It is located on a small lagoon, with a small sea wall in the back yard. From the master bedroom you look directly down the lagoon into the main lake which is about a mile long and three-quarters of a mile wide. From the family room you can see a small palm-tree-covered island in the middle of the lagoon. It was the location and the back yard which made us agree this was the home we had to have. Though we have made an offer and will begin horse trading, I have a feeling that because we all like it so much I will pay full price if I have to. I certainly hope that I can find someone who likes our house in St. Louis as well as we think we will like the one in Carrollwood.

My five work days in Tampa must be described as frantic. Townspeople dropped in to welcome me to the city. All of the bankers in town appear to want our business and most of the realtors would like us to live in their neighborhoods. At any rate, it's nice to be wanted.

I visited the two temporary sites—Hillsborough High School, near the north central part of town, and Leto High School, in the northwest section—which has been recommended by Dr. McGuffey, the consultant. Talk about a contrast! While Hillsborough High is attractive from the outside, it is very old and much in need of repair. (I walked through a chemistry lab and mistook it for a physics lab.) The rooms are crowded and the furniture is old. Leto High, on the other hand, is about two years old and well-equipped. Because of a quirk in the state law, when a new high school is built, capital funds are provided, but the equipment purchased can only be used in the new building. Therefore, even in the same school system you will find some well-equipped modern schools alongside some ill-equipped and antiquated ones.

Several members of the Plant City Chamber of Commerce attended the press conference on Monday specifically to meet me. I had heard rumblings that there was a strong movement afoot

A quiet cove in Carrollwood, open Lake Carroll beyond.

to locate the first temporary site for the junior college in Plant City. Therefore, even though McGuffey's recommendation did not include a Plant City location, I felt that before I made a recommendation to the advisory committee I should at least look over the situation. So on Wednesday afternoon Jeanny, Dave, Robin and I drove east some seventeen miles to Plant City. We were met by Horace Hancock and Frank Moody who wined and dined us even without benefit of drink or food. They drove us around the community and showed us the buildings we could use. They offered the college a two-story home which would be adequate for administrative offices and took us through a fair grounds building which they would remodel even though it would mean discontinuing the Strawberry Festival while the college was using the grounds. How's that for a commitment to the junior college? They even offered interim housing for our family while we get settled and buy a home. As the *coup-de-grace*, they gave us a flat of strawberries and the smallest berry in the flat was the size of a golf ball!

Plant City, as you probably do not know, is the strawberry capital of the world. At this point I would not be one to take exception to that fact; I wonder, however, if it makes sense to place the first campus of a new college in an area that serves a population of 12,000 and ignore Tampa with 350,000 people. I, therefore, decided to concur with Dr. McGuffey's recommendation and suggest our first operation be at Leto High School.

On Thursday afternoon I had my first official meeting with the advisory committee. I'll have to admit I was a bit nervous, in spite of my years of administrative participation in board meetings. After all, this was my first meeting as head of a school district. It was difficult to accomplish, but I managed to put together a fairly decent-looking agenda. It had a place for roll call, reading of the minutes, introduction of guests, presentation of petitions by citizens, etc. I wasn't able, however, to give the detailed background material which I feel is essential if a board is going to be knowledgeable. Under no circumstances do I feel that the board should administer the college, but if the members are going to make intelligent decisions concerning policy, they

93

certainly have to understand the administrative problems of a college. Therefore, I believe in explaining in detail the rationale for all administrative recommendations. But, in an open meeting with the press in attendance, it is not always possible to include the little subtleties which may influence your recommendation. In the future I plan to write a letter of transmittal to the board. At this meeting, however, we had nothing but a printed agenda with the subject headings. I had hoped to go over the agenda with Hardcastle, but he arrived about three minutes after the meeting was supposed to begin. I simply handed him the agenda and we went into session.

There was a very interesting group in attendance—the five members of the advisory committee, three members of the school board, a contingent of seven persons from Plant City, Dr. Shelton, Mr. Farmer, Dr. McGuffey, who had flown down from Tallahassee, and several members of the press. The meeting began as if we knew what we were doing. I had asked Frank Farmer's secretary, Betty Benson, to serve as secretary and take minutes. She had agreed, saying she had been the secretary for the previous committee meetings. But when we came to item #2, the reading of the minutes of the last meeting, there were none! I had forgotten to ask Betty to bring them to the meeting. After an embarrassed pause, I suggested perhaps these could be deferred until the next meeting.

After we established the official meeting day and time for the committee, we came to the items on personnel. In Florida there is a "government in the sunshine" law which, as in many states, makes it illegal for a board to take action behind closed doors. However, because they can consider matters of personnel in private, I asked for an executive session. Further, because the advisory committee is advisory to the school board rather than a legally constituted board of trustees, I suggested perhaps the rest of the meeting should be closed to the public. I should admit that because this was my first official board meeting, I wanted to discuss the working relationships between the committee and me without the press around. Hardcastle wasn't quite sure who

94

should be excluded, but it was finally agreed that the contingent from Plant City and the press should leave the meeting.

The first item under personnel began with "The President recommends," followed by a blank space because somehow I had failed to dictate the rest of it to my secretary. And in the confusion I couldn't remember that the incomplete item was the approval of *my* contract. Consequently, I didn't even get my own contract approved! The committee did approve an administrative salary schedule which I'll have to admit was constructed virtually off the top of my head in ten minutes. But my first order of business is to secure a qualified administrative group to assist me. Therefore, I had to have a good salary schedule approved so that I can discuss salary as I attempt to recruit my staff.

When we got to the section on physical facilities, I recommended that Leto High School be secured for temporary facilities for the college. I further stated that while I was impressed with the enthusiasm of the group from Plant City, I did not think that the offer was a sound proposal. (Perhaps I should have told you that both the Mayor of Plant City, Dick Elston, who is a member of the advisory committee, and Carl Carpenter, a member of the school board from Plant City, were in attendance.) Carpenter became more and more agitated as the discussion went on, insisting that if we were going to consider the proposal pro and con, the contingent from Plant City should be allowed to hear the discussion. A vote was finally taken and the advisory committee decided the issue could best be discussed without the added pressure of a group of citizens in attendance.

Dr. McGuffey supported the Leto site and told why it was his number one recommendation. Finally, after a lengthy discussion, it was agreed that we should call the Plant City contingent into the room and I should explain in detail the reasons for our not accepting their generous offer. This I did. I must admit, however, that while they left the meeting apparently satisfied, they were hardly overjoyed. I did tell them that I would consider holding some classes in Plant City in the fall of 1969 after we get things underway in Tampa proper. I do believe there is a need for a limited offering in the community, and I see no reason why we can't get underway with a year's lead time.

At any rate, no action was taken on the temporary facilities problem. The advisory committee was invited to meet with the Plant City group the next day to hear their full presentation. I suggested we postpone action until next Wednesday's meeting, even though I wouldn't be there. I realize that I am sticking my neck out by allowing the committee to meet without me, but under the circumstances there is not much I can do. Further, they have already heard my recommendation, and I assume that they will be hesitant to veto the first recommendation of their president.

By the way, the official name of the new college is Hillsborough Junior College. We plan to retain this name until we have more than one college, whereupon it will become the Hillsborough Junior College District, each college having a separate name.

This organizational structure will be new to Florida because the existing two-college systems are really multi-campus organizations. For example, St. Petersburg Junior College has two campuses: St. Petersburg and Clearwater. Under this type of administration the central office tends to have considerably more authority than under a multi-college approach as in St. Louis. There the entire district is called Junior College District of St. Louis—St. Louis County; each college is then given a definitive name—Meramec, Florissant Valley, and Forest Park and has a head who reports directly to the president of the district.

Under a multi-campus organization, however, there is usually a president with district-wide deans for instruction, business, and student personnel. The diversified approach, I feel, produces a more dynamic institution than does centralized control. The important difference lies in where the individual decisions are made, on the campus or in the central office. At any rate, we're going to give the multi-college approach a try.

It's interesting, also, that in Florida the two-year colleges are called junior colleges, while in California most of the institutions have dropped the junior. Elsewhere in the country there is a trend toward calling them community colleges. Here I believe we can combine the two by calling the entire district Hills-

96

borough County Junior College and by calling each campus a community college.

Other action taken at the meeting limited our total enrollment to the equivalent of 750 students. If we hold our classes after 4 p.m., it will be "touch and go" whether we actually enroll that many students because it will require a head count of approximately 900 students. If we were in temporary facilities where we could offer day classes, I would have no reservations about our enrolling even more students. However, most freshmen don't equate an afternoon and evening program in a local high school with "college."

We are also going to attempt a rather unique program for year-round operation. I borrowed directly from Santa Fe Junior College in Gainesville an idea which we plan to modify slightly. The universities in Florida are on the quarter system, offering three twelve-week terms over the nine-month period. On the other hand, the junior colleges are operating on two shortened semesters within the nine-month period. In comparing the credits for the two systems, registrars equate one quarter unit to be equal to two-thirds of a semester unit. Therefore, a student on the semester system will earn approximately thirty semester units during an academic year while under the quarter system he must earn forty-five quarter units.

We intend to mix the two systems. That is, we will offer three twelve-week terms but structure our courses to include the same number of minutes of classroom instruction found under the semester system. In order to do this, each one of our classes will be lengthened from the usual fifty minutes to seventy-five minutes. Also, we plan to hold classes on Saturday. A student may take a course on Monday, Wednesday and Friday or on Tuesday, Thursday and Saturday. Several educators in the area have told me that Saturday classes will not work in Florida, but I believe we can fill our classes.

There are several advantages to the new system. Most instructors have received their academic preparation under the semester system; therefore, they tend to teach their courses under a semes-

97

ter organization, whether they're on the quarter plan or under the semester plan. For example, two years ago when I taught at the University of Minnesota, I wondered why my students complained so violently about the work I poured on them. I chalked these complaints up to the lazy youth of today, until I found out that they were on the quarter system whereas I'd always taught the course on a semester basis. I'll have to admit that I was a rather poor teacher because I should have paid more attention to the mechanics of the system.

Under our plan the instructors will have more than an hour to present material to the class. We justify shorter classes in the secondary schools because of the short attention spans of youngsters, but college students should be able to devote full attention to a class for seventy-five minutes. Further, each student, instead of taking five three-credit courses per term, would only take three. For freshmen students this should be a distinct advantage in that they can concentrate on fewer subjects while becoming acclimated to college-level work.

Also, the full-time teacher will only teach three classes. Under a two semester system, if the average class size is twenty-five students, a teacher must arrange conferences and have interaction with 125 students each term. Under our system he will have contact with only seventy-five thus allowing him to work more closely with individual students. Over the entire academic year the students and teachers will have accomplished the same objective, but I feel that our new system will do the job better.

I would like to explore the possibilities of even further fragmentation of the semester. In an urban setting whether a student actually enrolls in college may depend upon whether he has a job the day school opens. Many of our students in St. Louis, for instance will come to school one semester, then remain out a semester to work, and back and forth, depending upon their personal financial circumstances. I would like to develop a system whereby new classes would begin every six weeks for the student who must miss a term. This would mean a smaller outlay for fees and a shorter break in his education.

Yet, it is very difficult to articulate with four-year colleges. In

98

a comprehensive community college there is traffic in both directions between the senior institutions and the junior college. While many of our students will transfer to the University of South Florida upon completing their freshman and sophomore years, many USF students will transfer to us after they have found that they are not prepared to do university-level work. Because of the time necessary to receive transcripts and give the students preregistration counseling, it may not work to match identically our calendar with that of the University of South Florida. With six-week terms students who wish to transfer probably would not have more than three or four weeks to wait.

After the committee meeting, I held my second press conference. Even though the press had been excluded from a portion of the meeting, there appeared to be a good relation between us during the interview. Yet, Channel 13's eleven o'clock news commentator was careful to indicate that the press had been excluded from a portion of the meeting. Oh well, you can't win them all.

I spent Friday morning frantically trying to get on top of the paper work and acknowledging the letters of welcome which had come from all over the county. Ken Hardcastle called late in the morning and asked if I could meet him for lunch at the Chamber of Commerce meeting. We arrived after the lucheon had already started and were quietly escorted to the head table. I had anticcipated being introduced; but just before the introductions began, the toastmaster leaned over to me and said that they had no speaker for the day and they would appreciate my saying a few words about the junior college—just limit my remarks to twenty minutes.

Therefore, with a full fifteen seconds' preparation, I became the featured speaker. Of course, I really have no trouble talking extemporaneously about my favorite subject. I long ago discarded the practice of using notes because I find I do a better job if I simply let it pour out. Further, I seem to have a built-in time clock and can pretty well hit on the nose ten, fifteen, or twenty minutes without ever glancing at my wristwatch. So with no further fanfare, I launched into my usual presentation interspersed with a few corny jokes.

Leaving the Chamber of Commerce meeting, I barely had time to get to the studios of WTVT for a half-hour interview on video tape which was to be broadcast the following Sunday. The program is moderated by News Director Hugh Smith and by another staff member, Cy Smith (no relation). The first question Hugh Smith asked me would have been easy to answer if I had had an hour and a half to devote to it. He wanted to know if I could describe the comprehensive community college and its functions as it would relate to the Hillsborough situation. I gave him my brief "cocktail party" reply about the five main functions of the community college: College Transfer, Vocational-Technical, Continuing Education, Remedial, and Guidance.

Then he began to get tricky and asked how I felt about the teachers on my staff belonging to a militant organization and whether or not I approved of the recent teacher walk-out. I replied that I really had nothing against teachers belonging to any organization designed to promote the best interests of education; but the walk-out I could not condone because I felt that it did not profit educational programs in any school system.

After the interview I had a chance to chat with Hugh for a few minutes before I caught a cab back to the office. He was very interested in our projected use of advisory committees for the vocational-technical areas. I explained to him the St. Louis system, which has three levels of advisory committees.

An overall advisory committee made up of chief executives of large industrial firms and service agencies—presidents of corporations, directors of hospitals and the like—provides the general guidance. Then follows the breakdown into four distinct areas: business, public service, health and engineering.

Committees represent each one of these areas and, once again, paint with a rather large brush because their representation is rather diverse. For example, the health occupations advisory committee consists of a director of nursing, a hospital administrator, a practicing physician, the head of the dental association, a radiologist, etc. The third level committees get down to the

100

"nuts and bolts" of evaluating our curricula and determining the employability of our graduates.

In addition, there is a Dental Assisting Advisory Committee and an Automotive Technology Committee as well as committees for many other specific programs. For example, on the Automotive Technology Advisory Committee we have the owner of a Ford agency, a representative of the mechanics union, a representative from General Motors, etc. Thus we are able to get continual feedback from the business community as to the development of our two-year career programs.

Late Friday evening Jeanny picked me up at the courthouse and we went out to Carrollwood to make a firm offer on the house on the lake. It's interesting to see how the business community reacts to us as clients. Several of the banks and loan companies have indicated that they would "throw the book away" when it comes to interest rates because I am president of the new college. While it is flattering to feel that you are wanted in a community, you soon begin to wonder whether people want you for yourself or for your position. In any case, I don't think I will insist on paying half percent extra interest just to soothe my conscience.

We left Tampa on Saturday (6 a.m.) for an uneventful trip back to St. Louis. That night we stayed in Chattanooga, leaving the next morning in a fog. Because the visibility was rather bad as we approached a construction area, we fell in line behind a string of cars. You can imagine our chagrin when one by one we followed the lead car right off the road into a muddy field. As we all plowed back onto the main road, sheepish grins were a dime a dozen.

Love to all. I'll write again soon when I get caught up on the pile of paper work which accumulates every time I'm away from the office for a few days.

Bill

Tampa
Sunday night
April 21, 1968

Dear Fisher:

I was back on the job in St. Louis Monday morning after being away a week. Even though no major problems had arisen, it took almost a full day to get on top of things again with so many administrators on my staff who have to brief me. In the afternoon the college council met to discuss the rights of faculty members. We are considering placing in our policy manual the statement that any teacher who is charged with a felony will be suspended (not discharged) until the case is decided. The faculty, however, feel that this is an impingement upon the faculty member's civil rights and suspension should be only upon conviction. After considerable discussion of the topic, they asked to have our attorney meet with them to iron out the fine points of terminology.

This problem of college governance is a critical issue in higher education. Our college council is so structured that faculty always outnumber the administration two to one, but some of the younger faculty members still feel that the administration is in a position to intimidate the faculty. I keep telling them that over the past two years I had never had to veto any of the council's proposals. Perhaps after we have operated four or five years, they will believe that I truly have confidence in the integrity and responsibility of the faculty.

While I was away one of our part-time philosophy teachers wrote an article in the school newspaper lambasting our physical education program. He claimed that it was strictly a high school program with a "throw out the ball" philosophy because of the physical education faculty are former high school teachers. He proposed that we offer courses such as scuba diving, golf, tennis, camping, canoeing, etc. He further established his credentials as a former physical education instructor at a large Midwest university. Frankly, because he is a part-time instructor, I had never met the man. Upon examining his credentials, however, I found that he has two degrees in philosophy but not one professional course in physical education, although he taught one-fifth time for one semester in the physical education department at the university. To find out what he was trying to prove, I arranged for him to come to my office.

Our interview was quite interesting. I must admit that both of us became emotionally upset during the initial part of the interview. However, we were able to straighten things out objectively after about an hour's discussion. I contended that as a college instructor it is his responsibility to prove through his actions that he is capable of operating within a scholarly environment. And one of the prime requisites for scholarship is to ascertain facts before jumping to conclusions. I contended there was no factual basis for his statements. In the first place, what he is advocating as something new in the curriculum has been on our drawing boards for two years. Lack of staff is the only reason we haven't implemented the courses. He claimed that he had checked his data by asking the student editor of the newspaper to talk with the dean of instruction. However, because the student editor was himself busy writing an editorial against varsity athletics at the college, the information the instructor was given pertained to varsity athletics, not to our physical education program. His accusations were thus completely without foundation.

I asked how could he really convince our students that they were studying with scholars when he so flagrantly violated the rules of scholarship by jumping to conclusions before ascertaining the facts. After a while he admitted that his prime motivation was to secure a job for the summer. I told him that had he come through our established channels, we possibly could have made a place for him because he is a qualified scuba diving and canoeing instructor. But because it was late in the year and the budget had already been approved, it was impossible.

I also had to laugh at the student editor's editorial concerning our overemphasis on varsity athletics at Forest Park Community College. Normally overemphasis on varsity athletics means that extensive scholarships are granted to athletes, that academic standards may be lower for athletes than for regular students, and that an extensive recruiting program is the order of the day. At Forest Park we have no scholarships for athletes (anyone is eligible to try out for the teams) and we do not even have a full-time staff member coaching our teams. Further, our basketball team this last year won one game and lost twenty-eight. The baseball team currently has two wins and nine losses. So an editorial concerning our overemphasis on varsity athletics verges on the ludicrous.

Actually, the student editor does have a point worth consideration; he is simply too inexperienced to know how to put his finger on the real problem. There is no denying that varsity athletics are more expensive than the regular instructional program. For example, we pay an instructor as much for coaching a basketball squad of twenty students as we do for him to teach the same twenty students in a two-credit semester course. However, instead of these students paying fees for the course and our getting state assistance, the college itself has to bear the entire expense. Also, the equipment tends to be expensive because wherein students furnish their own tennis shoes for gym classes, most varsity athletes get all their equipment provided. I'm really not certain that the alleged favorable public relations and *esprit de corps* which varsity athletics develop among the students of a large metropolitan junior college are really worth the expense to the taxpayers.

I spent most of the week worrying about houses. Jeanny has had ours cleaned, and people are tramping through giving it the usual once-over inspection. During our weekend in Florida, the realtor held open our house. According to him, several people appear interested. We all can hardly wait to get it sold because Jeanny's disposition is positively miserable while trying to keep the house in a presentable condition. Of course, this is the rainy season, and she sets up a howl everytime any of us boys stomp through the house with mud on our shoes. Further, we all have to get up at least fifteen minutes earlier to clean our rooms before we take off for school or work. Our efforts may not sell the house, but they are making first-class domestics out of us. Even

104

Boots has been relegated to the back yard. And he doesn't even know what it's all about.

We are still negotiating for the house in Tampa. We made an offer; they made a counter; we countered their counter offer. And last Friday we got a counter, counter offer. I'm trying to stall a little bit to see if anything happens on the house here in St. Louis so that we will be able to tell how much money we can afford to spend. Perhaps I shall have good news when I return home from a working weekend in Tampa.

I have spent a good deal of time putting out feelers for key staff members. I will have three key positions to fill—a dean of instruction, a dean of business services, and a dean of student personnel. There are many different titles that these positions may take, and they will probably change over the next three or four years. For example, when we move into a multi-college operation with two to three campuses, I will want to change the title of the dean of business affairs to vice-president for business services. Also, the dean of instruction in many colleges might be called the dean of faculty, or academic dean, or even executive dean.

I only hope the person I hire in this position will be capable of assuming the leadership of the large campus in Tampa. If so, we might call him president of the campus and change my title to chancellor. This is being done in some multi-campus systems in the country. Also, it's possible that the dean of students might be able to assume a similar responsibility in one of the smaller campuses. However, because I'm not certain of the strengths and potential of the people I will be able to hire, for this first year I'm going to call them deans. If I don't feel that the dean of students is capable of running one of the colleges I can have him remain as dean of students and report directly to the president of the Tampa campus without having to demote him from a vice-presidency.

I have been fortunate to stumble across a very qualified man for the business area. He wrote a letter to Tom Baker of the State Department in Tallahassee indicating that he would like very much to be able to consider the position in Tampa. So when

105

I called Wally Nichol, who is vice-president for business affairs for the McComb County Community College in Detroit, he volunteered, at his own expense, to fly to Tampa for the weekend as an excuse to take a vacation.

I left for Tampa Friday night to meet him Saturday morning. I spent an hour talking with him and his wife and was very much impressed with his background and personal characteristics. He has had extensive experience in running a large two-campus system in an area where there have been considerable problems. He was responsible for union negotiations, both in the classified and teacher areas, which would certainly compensate for my inexperience. Also, he has been involved in a large building program with responsibility for liaison with the architects.

Over the next few years much of our effort will be directed toward a building program which must be sandwiched in with the day-to-day operation of the college. In many respects, the pattern usually followed by state colleges and universities, whereby the buildings are virtually completed before a teaching staff is hired and students are accepted, certainly has its advantages. In St. Louis it took us approximately five years to get into our first permanent building. I feel that this could easily have been accomplished in three years had we not grown to 10,000 students on temporary campuses during this period.

Wally is also experienced in data processing. We have had a frustrating experience in St. Louis because initially we installed an inadequate data-handling system which, for financial reasons, became completely inflexible and was not able to be changed as the needs of the college changed. Because I am determined not to repeat this mistake, I offered to J. C. Lasmanis, the young University of Minnesota intern who worked on our campus last fall, a position as my assistant. I would like to have him work with our top administrators in their policy and procedural discussions. With a doctorate in education with special emphasis on institutional research, his main responsibility would be planning data collection systems which may be used five years from now to test the validity of the decisions which will be made when Hillsborough Junior College is in its infancy. I'm certain he would also be of great assistance to me in attacking the mass of details which have to be handled in the establishment of the new college. Besides, he is a great guy to have around. With his sense of humor I know he would contribute greatly to the *esprit de corps* of the staff.

On Saturday afternoon I interviewed a dean of students from a liberal arts college whose resumé certainly was impressive. As a former dean at a college in the Tampa-St. Petersburg area, I assumed he would have an insight into the characteristics of the students in the community.

I met him—a very pleasant, good-looking man of about thirty-seven—at the motel, then took him through Leto High School to show him where our temporary facilities will be located. On the way I casually asked him about his background in data processing. His immediate response was that he didn't know anything about data processing because he had never used it. Normally I carry an interview fairly smoothly, but his response left me speechless. In an age when even relatively small colleges can and do justify the use of data processing equipment, I feel that it is absolutely necessary for the student personnel dean to have at least a minimum working knowledge of data processing systems.

After visiting Leto we returned to the hotel and, for forty-five minutes, discussed student personnel services. I asked what he felt was the difference between academic advising and counseling at the junior college level and how he would foster dialogue between faculty members and counselors. (You recall the trouble that we had in Ventura convincing the faculty members that counselors really earn their salaries. Too many instructors think a counselor has a secretary to do all his work while he simply sits and chats with students.)

I inquired how, as an administrator, he would establish liaison among the area high schools and colleges and Hillsborough Junior College. He said he didn't know; in his college experience he had recruited students on a nation-wide basis and had paid very little attention to the local community. (This simply confirmed my suspicion that liberal arts colleges do not attempt to relate to the local community.)

107

I asked him whether he believed in presenting freshmen orientation in organized scheduled classes or informally before college started. He explained his current orientation program, but admitted that he had never really thought through any other alternatives. I queried him as to how he would suggest organizing student data so that it could be handled easily when we reached 15,000 full-time students. I then asked his philosophy of financial aids and the distribution of the money to insure that the neediest and most worthy students would receive help.

When I asked him, as a representative of a student's point of view, how much tuition we should charge at Hillsborough Junior College, he asked for some time to think through his answer. I told him he could have up to ten seconds because that would probably be all the time he would have to make similar recommendations in our new operation. If we get this school opened by next September, we will not have time to sit back and philosophize in reaching solutions to our problems.

At this point in the interview he was becoming quite uncomfortable because of his inability to come up with clear, concise answers to my questions; so he asked me to give my point of view and to justify it. I told him that I approved of a token tuition in order to insure the students are really serious about going to college. In California, where there are no tuition charges or lab fees, we found that many students went back to school simply because there was nothing else for them to do in September. Besides, most of their friends were going away to college, so they decided to try college too. Therefore, when they enrolled in college without any specific objectives or without realizing the purpose for which they were there, you can understand why the attrition rate was excessive. On the other hand, in St. Louis, where a relatively small tuition is charged, the attrition rate is considerably less. However, I do not feel that we should justify student tuition as a major source of income for running the college. I believe it is the responsibility of the state and local district to provide operating funds.

Later, we discussed tentative admission policies. I asked him how he thought we should select our students at Hillsborough

108

Junior College; if we limit our initial enrollment to between 500 and 750 students, I asked, should we select them on the basis of high school rank, college entrance examination tests, or on a first-come, first-served basis? He admitted that his experience in private liberal arts high-tuition colleges made him lean toward selective admissions. At this point, when it became obvious he really did not understand the philosophy of an open-door college, I pushed my chair back and looked him straight in the eye. I suppose I was pretty brutal, but I reminded him that for the past hour I had been firing questions and for the most part he hadn't had the slightest idea what I was talking about regarding student personnel services in a comprehensive public community college. He admitted he was quite aware of this fact. After an honest discussion of his candidacy, we agreed that, though he had considerable potential, under the circumstances I did not have the time to run a training course to teach him how to handle student personnel services in a comprehensive community college.

He was obviously disappointed when we left, because he had traveled to the interview at his own expense. Apparently he had assumed that if he were qualified to be a dean of students at a four-year college, he certainly could run a student personnel program in a two-year college with perhaps half the effort. It is unfortunate he didn't at least take the trouble to read the brief AAJC publication describing student personnel services in the community college. He could have read it on the plane and answered intelligently every one of the questions I asked him.

In the afternoon I drove out to Carrollwood to take another look at the interior of the house. A leisurely walk-through convinced me that this is the house I want, even though it's not quite adequate for our needs. I'm sure we will have to spend at least $600 enclosing the garage so I can store my airplane and work on it. Of course, I could sell the airplane, but after six years of blood, sweat, and tears, I'm going to finish the darn thing!

After I looked over the house I cruised by Frank Farmer's. He was in the yard putting together a new barbecue set. I stopped because I wanted to see if he thought the advisory committee is really aware of the difficulty in finding qualified leaders in the

109

community college movement. In passing he mentioned that not all of the administrative staff in the public schools are in favor of our using Leto High School. Apparently they think that Hillsborough High would be a much better location and that the facilities are just as suitable. It's too bad I wasn't around at their staff meeting to enumerate the advantages of Leto and point out the difficulties (especially with parking) we would encounter at Hillsborough.

Before I thought about leaving, Frank had a couple of steaks cooked and I was invited to dinner. I really didn't plan it that way, but the Farmers were gracious to invite me to share their fare. About 8:30 I left for the office to remain there until midnight doing paper work. My desire to stay on top of the many details certainly makes me wish I were on the job full-time.

I got back to the office bright and early on Sunday morning. I don't know where the teacher applications are coming from, but we must have had fifty new ones this week. Some are good prospects and some are dreamers—mostly dreamers. In any case I believe we will make out all right, even though most of the people we hire for teaching jobs will probably have to be released from contracts to accept an offer. In this connection, I checked with Hardcastle on the phone about the possibility of offering Wally Nichol the maximum salary with a travel allowance thrown in. He seemed enthusiastic about the possibility of getting top-flight people and gave me the go-ahead.

In the afternoon I went out to Carrollwood to sign the contract on the house. While there, I dropped by the house to take pictures to show Ken in St. Louis. The weather was warm and the neighbors were out on their lawns barbecuing steaks. A little boy in a small pram with a trolling outboard motor on the back of it was racing around the island in the lagoon. This kind of life is going to be tough to take!

I'd better close now. I'll try to keep you posted on our activities in between commuting trips. I intend to work as many weekends as I can in Tampa, but I have a feeling I am going to become exhausted in the process.   Love to all.

Bill

Tampa
April 28, 1968

Dear Fisher:

Will wonders never cease? We sold our house in St. Louis! The man who lives directly across the street has been out of town on a vacation. When he returned, Robin announced that we were moving to Florida. He immediately came across the street to tell us that he wanted to buy our house. Apparently he had tried to get together enough money to purchase it before we bought it but couldn't handle the down payment. In the meantime he has saved his pennies and waited for us to accept a promotion and leave St. Louis. Furthermore, he liked the improvements I put in the house enough to reimburse me for my effort. Even though I did put several thousand dollars in the house, I never expected to have it improve the value of the house. My real intention was to make the house more livable for us and serve the needs of our family.

There is one thing that I can't quite understand. What is a man with a wife and one infant daughter going to do with a house with six bedrooms, two family rooms, two kitchens, three baths, a living room, dining room, and workshop? On the other hand, what are we going to do with the furniture for a house this size when we're moving to a three-bedroom house in Tampa? Jeanny says we're going to throw away many of our things but, frankly, it is easier said than done. At any rate, I feel as though a huge weight has been lifted from my shoulders.

Early last week a man from Iowa called me about the position of dean of business services. I arranged for him to fly into St. Louis and meet me for dinner near the airport. He is about fifty years old, but actually looks old enough to be my grandfather. He had quite a breadth of experience, but I became cagey when he kept bringing the subject back to salary. I got the impression that money is all that's important to him. Also, he told me he has already resigned from his current position. Could it be that he had been urged to resign? Well, before I consider him further I certainly intend to check him out thoroughly.

111

I got a letter from Wally Nichol advising he's not interested in the position because his wife decided she did not want to leave her friends in Detroit. Thank goodness your daughter has never blocked any of my plans or professional aspirations! Instead, she has always been fully supportive, though not to the point of driving me too hard.

On the weekend J.C. Lasmanis phoned in response to my offer of a position as my assistant. I am amazed at the salary offers that young potential Ph.D.'s are able to attract these days. He told me that he had one firm offer at $15,000 a year to work in a research program with a foundation. How in the world can a man with absolutely no work experience really be worth $15,000 a year? I told him frankly that I thought that he would be overpaid at this salary and the best I could offer would be $11,500 or perhaps $12,000 per year. He said that he would think it over and let me know. I can't help but compare his offers with the salary which I made in my first teaching position. Just nineteen years ago with a similar background I made only $3,500. Who says we haven't had inflation?

The latter part of this week I tried frantically to finish up the paper work at Forest Park so I could get away early to fly down to Tampa to begin work over the weekend on the "south" campus. It's been two weeks now since I have been here, and it is not easy to get an operation underway by telephone. The phone has been ringing madly with people wanting to contact me about jobs. I was called out of the president's council meeting last Wednesday reportedly on urgent business in Tampa. When I answered the phone, it turned out to be a woman checking to make sure I had received her application for a position as an English teacher. Today I received the fourth telephone call from a young man in New York. He is most eager to have a position on my staff, but he is becoming such a pest I have just about decided that I wouldn't want him around. It's unfortunate he has created this image because his credentials appear to be adequate, even though they are not outstanding. I don't mind aggressiveness and I certainly want people on the job who are delighted to be there, but at this time I don't particularly like to be bugged.

It is interesting, now that I am in the position of having dozens of people clamoring to fill each of the positions, to realize what a part luck and timing play in professional growth and advancement. As I read through the stacks of applications, each one offering slightly varying experience and background, I am more than bewildered. Over the past years when I have applied for positions for which my background seemed to make me the logical candidate, I have often wondered why I have been completely passed over. Perhaps when I dropped those applications in the mail I should have sung the song, "Luck, Be a Lady Tonight."

Last Friday morning I participated in a seminar at Washington University on problems in college construction. Ben Weese of the architectural firm which constructed the Forest Park campus was one of the speakers. I went along to answer questions about the educational problems which were studied in relation to the building program. Theoretically, the architect is supposed to work from an educational program which is provided by the staff. In the case of the Forest Park campus, however, most of the initial planning was done by the administration before there was a staff to help out. We even received national recognition from our use of the computer in planning the buildings. We made twenty-five computer runs of master class schedules for a college of 7,000 students until we got the most efficient one. Then we calculated the number of classrooms necessary and gave the program to the architect to use in planning the buildings.

But in one instance the building program actually has dictated our educational program. I am referring to our concept of diversified counseling. When we attempted to build a counseling center to house twenty full-time counselors, it looked like a sick bay, no matter how we arranged the offices. Because it is difficult to get students to consult with a counselor, I felt the students would not feel comfortable in a maze of counseling offices. Therefore, we conceived the idea of putting the counselors all over the buildings so that they would be near the students and close to the faculty offices.

We encourage faculty members to refer students with problems to counselors for more intensive guidance. However,

113

if the instructors do not become personally acquainted with the counselors, they have little confidence in the counselors' ability to help the students. Under our physical arrangement the counselors drink coffee with the faculty and get to know them well because their offices are right next to each other. We even went further and put the counseling offices right next to the student lounges where the students spend some of their free time. Also, each counselor is attached to an academic department and, as a member of the student personnel staff, coordinates the counseling activities within the department.

I believe in the "trip" philosophy of counseling. If the students are not inclined to seek counseling assistance, the counselor should be able to stand in the doorway, stick his foot out and trip a student as he walks by. Thus, when the counselor helps the student to his feet, they can discuss any problem the student might have. We don't really go to that length, but our diversified counseling scheme appears to be working well.

On Friday morning one of the assistant deans at Forest Park came to my office to let me know that in the future he would be interested in working for me in Tampa. He said he had appreciated the manner in which I had helped him as an inexperienced administrator, adding that I had never bawled him out in front of people but, instead, had called him into the office and discussed the situation in detail when I felt he had not handled a matter properly. Naturally, I told him that I would keep him in mind but that I had no intention of stealing staff members from St. Louis this year. While we were talking he told me that the faculty members were becoming a little apprehensive about the selection of my replacement. I imagine there are many rumors about who will fill my chair.

Dr. Cosand asked that I set up a committee of staff members to screen candidates for my position. We have a faculty committee from our council who actually recommends members of our committees. They recommended one representative from each department, a dean, an associate dean, and an assistant dean. I suggested they go one step further and include a representative of the classified staff and at least one student representative. It

114

appears to me that if we are going to ask members of the faculty to help with the screening, we should also include representatives of each constituent group. I don't know of any other college where students and classified personnel have been included on this type of a committee, but I see no reason why we shouldn't include representatives from every area.

Just before leaving for the airport, I got a phone call from one of McGuffey's consultants on our master plan report which he is preparing. He suggested that perhaps he should come and spend a day talking with me before he begins to write his report. I suppose I was a bit curt with him, but I told him that I didn't think this was the way to approach the problem. If his report is going to be of value to me, I need a report based on the facts rather than a report which simply mirrors my preconceived ideas of what the problem in Tampa might be. Anyone can read a textbook and project a typical curriculum for an urban community. However, before a report is really meaningful, a great deal of background work must be done. He assured me that he had made some studies in the Tampa area. I thereupon suggested he write the rough draft and submit it to me for my reaction. He agreed to do this; I will await his response.

My weekend in Tampa has been frustrating. I didn't realize it would be so difficult to do business on the weekend. I wasted considerable time attempting to locate auxiliary space near Leto High School. You will recall that in St. Louis when we operated the college at Roosevelt High School, we took over the old Edmonds Restaurant as a headquarters for the faculty and administration. Because Leto High School is so crowded we won't be able to use any of the space in the high school during the day. Therefore, it is essential that I locate some office space within reasonable distance. I contacted a church across the street, and there is a possibility of our using some of their Sunday School classrooms. We would have to use the periphery of the rooms, pushing our desks against the wall. Thus, they would be able to put tables in the center of the rooms when they are used on Sunday mornings for Sunday School classes. It would be a rather awkward solution to the problem; I hope we can do better.

115

After an intensive search, I located the sales manager of a company which manufactures metal pre-fabricated buildings. Lou Rocha agreed to send me some information about portable buildings which could be put behind Leto High School. This might be a good solution for faculty offices, but it seems a shame to spend up to ten dollars a square foot to construct temporary buildings. Furthermore, I'm not certain it is legal to use our funds for this purpose. At any rate, we'll have to see how it comes out. Anyway, if the school board denies our request to use Leto, we will have a whole set of new problems to solve.

I was fortunate to be in the office yesterday to receive a phone call from Bud Gilligan, dean of students at the junior college in Ocala, Florida. I had asked Terry O'Banion of the University of Illinois to suggest a possible Floridian as a dean of students. He indicated that Gilligan was one who could handle the program at our college. I agreed to meet him in the afternoon at my motel rather than at the courthouse because the air conditioning was not functioning.

Gilligan appears to have considerable promise. We talked for an hour and I was favorably impressed. I had to laugh, though, when we got around to discussing student activities in community colleges. Several years ago I wrote an article for the AAJC *Journal* in which I blasted community college student activities pro- ·grams for apeing those of the four-year colleges. In the middle of our discussion Gilligan realized that I was the Graham who had authored the article. After stammering a bit, he asked if he could take the Fifth Amendment. I told him he might already have incriminated himself, and we might as well discuss the problem on an intellectual level.

My main concern with most student activites programs at community colleges is that they are identical with the "rah-rah" concept that usually grows out of a dormitory-oriented college program. It seems rather foolish to make a big deal out of a homecoming parade when you are serving primarily commuting students. After all, who comes home? I have always felt that cultural programs, forums, political discussions, vocational interest

116

groups, and the like are much more appropriate, at least in an urban-oriented junior college.

Gilligan made a valid point when he stressed the fact that his program at Ocala was more closely related to a small liberal arts college program than to a large metropolitan one, because the college is located in a small town. His broad student activities program, therefore, is designed to serve the needs of the students. Even though they live at home, they closely identify with the junior college which has become a focal point of the community. I felt he justified his position, so I continued the questioning.

After a while I offered him the job right on the spot, even though I had not checked his professional papers. I did, however, tell him that I would check his references and then if there was a question in my mind, I would withdraw the offer. He indicated that he first wanted to bring his wife to Tampa for a day to look over the town. I certainly hope he accepts the offer because I need to get my staff hired.

On Sunday I managed to catch Ray Shelton between golf games to discuss our request to use Leto High School. Frank Farmer had informed me that there was concern on the part of the professional staff that there would not be room for the college to stay at Leto more than one year. It does not make sense for us to have to find another home for the college in the fall of 1969. If there is room for us to have evening classes this year, there is no reason why we can't stay for two more years at least, even though the total number of classrooms we would use after the high school was through with them in the afternoon might be increased.

Shelton told me that Dave Erwin, the assistant superintendent for Vocational and Adult Education has been trying to build a night program at Leto and feels there would not be room for both programs. I told Shelton I had no intention of hampering the public school effort. Also, we certainly hope to make use of several other high schools in the coming years. Therefore, I don't see how our program could conflict with the small adult program this year and next. Erwin rightfully thinks that many adults will

117

prefer to attend the college rather than the adult high school. Let's face it—there is more prestige in attending college than high school. I feel that the two programs must be correlated or both programs will end up looking very foolish and wasting public funds through unnecessary duplication of effort.

I had better close this letter now because the plane is nearing St. Louis. It will be good to get back and see the family. Even though I have only been away for two days, the pace I'm keeping makes it seem like a week.

Love to all,
Bill

Tampa
May 13, 1968

Dear Fisher:

I arrived at the airport a little early on my way back to St. Louis; so while waiting to board the plane I will start this letter. The whole family has been extremely busy since I last wrote to you, but my mind is almost entirely on the job facing me here in Tampa. Let me bring you up to date.

I flew into Tallahassee last Wednesday evening and registered at the Duval Hotel. I was exhausted and looking forward to a good night's sleep. However, a dog howled outside my window for over an hour right in the middle of the night. So on Thursday morning I entered McGuffey's office bleary-eyed, begging for a cup of coffee. I did put in a productive day, however, finalizing with his staff some of the materials he was preparing for printing. (I certainly could use student and faculty application forms and instructor contract forms as well.) We also studied proofs for brochures to be used as advertising material. McGuffey feels that we will be so inundated with applicants that we will have to cut off student recruitment early in the summer. I wish I shared his optimism.

I cannot help but recall my first summer in St. Louis when we were holding classes in the afternoon and evening at Roosevelt

High School. We had staffed for 1300 students and by the middle of August had less than 600 applications. We finally made our estimated enrollment, though only after some excessive last-minute advertising. Therefore, I believe it's essential to get applications and brochures in the hands of the high school seniors before spring term ends. I wish we could tell them where classes will be held and what courses will be offered, but we can't hold up the production schedule.

Thursday evening I caught a plane to Tampa so that I would be fresh Friday morning to prepare for my second official meeting with the advisory committee that afternoon. The need to organize the committee became evident when Ken Hardcastle arrived late for the meeting. The committee does not even have a vice-chairman to preside when the chairman is not there. Therefore, I presented a policy manual which I asked the committee members to study and approve at our next meeting. Joe Cosand gave me permission to borrow quite liberally from the manual we use in St. Louis. I was especially interested in having a guide for the committee to follow as we develop a working relationship. I would like to have prepared an original policy manual, but I just didn't have the time.

At the meeting we discussed the role of the committee and I passed out some material that was sent to me from Lee Henderson's office which I thought you might be interested in looking over. It is called the ten commandments for trustees.

Ten Commandments for Trustees

1. Don't conduct board meetings without the college president.
2. Don't have more than one person, the president, directly responsible to the board.
3. Don't solicit or encourage faculty gripes.
4. Don't become an advocate for someone seeking a job at the college.
5. Don't conduct personal investigations into charges of unfairness in some student's failure.
6. Don't act like a trustee except when you are meeting as a board or as a committee of the board.
7. Don't speak for the board except when authorized to do so by the board.

119

8. Refer questions pertaining to administration to the president of the college.

9. Don't form standing committees of the board.

10. Insist upon written policies.

The committee seemed quite pleased with the manner in which I presented a proposed faculty salary schedule for next year. I told them I would be pleased if they wanted to study it and react at our next meeting. However, after a brief discussion, Ray Thompson said he understood the proposal and thought they should approve it as recommended.

In explaining the rationale which I had used in developing the schedule, I emphasized our need to recruit and retain a wide range of competencies which would require differentiation in formal preparation or experience. I also pointed out that the master's degree or its equivalent was used as the base line, as the minimum satisfactory preparation for a junior college teacher. You will recall that I have always contended the Ph.D. is the union card for college teaching, especially at the university. In the junior college, however, the master's degree in a subject field gives sufficient academic background to prepare a superior teacher. I did point out, however, that I wished to reward and encourage instructors to take additional course work beyond the master's level.

The salary schedule I recommended provides for twelve experience increments. In the secondary schools annual increases in salary are virtually automatic. In fact, in most schools you either receive an annual raise for twelve to fifteen years or you can expect to be fired. At the university level, however, there are usually quotas within the various academic ranks. That is, each department may be authorized a given number of assistant, associate, and full professorships. Each rank, then, has its own series of salary schedule steps. At the junior college, though, a teacher with a master's degree and no experience can expect to progress to quite a respectable salary without markedly increasing his subject-matter proficiency.

The schedule which I suggested modifies this concept to include specific percentage increases each year. Moreover, it includes an increase for the teacher who earns thirty semester units in the subject field beyond the master's, an additional twenty percent for the person who receives the Ph.D. degree, and a merit system which would include a five percent bonus for ten percent of the teachers each year. Most school systems hesitate to implement merit evaluations because it is so difficult to identify the top teachers. I believe, however, that it is philosophically sound to reward those who produce and are most creative and effective in the classroom. Therefore, as professionals, it is up to us to find ways of satisfactorily identifying those individuals.

For part-time teachers I recommended a pay scale which is approximately two-thirds of what a full-time teacher would get for teaching the same subject. My reasoning is that a full-time teacher is required to spend a great deal of time in student advisement and faculty committee work. Because the part-time teacher is held responsible only for teaching the students in his classes, I don't believe that we should pay him the same rate.

On Friday evening one of the staff members of the public school system invited me as his guest to attend a play at the University of South Florida. I readily accepted the invitation as I was desperately in need of a change of pace to take my mind off the multitude of problems which I face. It was a Eugene O'Neill play produced by one of the drama classes in the university. The play itself was adequately performed, but I was most impressed by the facilities. The hall was a small teaching theatre, but the equipment and design were excellent and the appointments verged on the plush. It always amazes me how, without fear of criticism, a state college or university can spend quite freely for buildings, whereas the locally controlled and locally scrutinized junior college cannot.

Over the weekend I interviewed a number of applicants and hired a person to head our program for remedial students. Plano Valdes is in the Upward Bound Program at the University of South Florida and is committed to a completely integrated program for remediation of basic skills and general education subjects. He has some very creative ideas and I'll be interested to see how our program develops.

At noon I met Allen Brown and his wife Sally, who came to Tampa to look over the city. Before leaving St. Louis on Wednesday I met Brown at the airport and interviewed him for the position of dean of business services. He is vice-president for business services at Metropolitan Junior College in Kansas City. Al has an excellent reputation among the business officers in the junior colleges in the Midwest and has a very pleasing personality. So on Friday I got the advisory committee's approval to offer him a contract and invite him and his wife to fly to Tampa to see if they would like to make their home in this area.

At the board meeting on Friday I casually mentioned that I had lost two potential deans because their wives did not like Tampa. (Gilligan turned down my offer because his wife didn't want to leave Ocala.) Hardcastle asked how the board could help. I suggested that perhaps these out-of-town candidates could be shown the better side of Tampa and made to feel welcome if the board took an active interest. They immediately volunteered to wine and dine the Browns royally at a Tampa Yacht Club party. Frankly, we all had a wonderful evening. I was disappointed that Jeanny was not able to participate. After we move down next month, it will be much easier for us to welcome the staff and make them feel at home.

Before I left home last Thursday, Jeanny struck a low blow. Realizing that I probably was unaware that I was going to be away from home on the weekend, she innocently asked if I thought it would be all right if she took the children out to dinner for Mother's Day. (She really knows how to hurt a guy.) Yesterday, when I called home to wish her happy returns of the day, she told me that I had received numerous telephone calls from job applicants while I was away. And there certainly are a lot of aggressive people with bloodhound-like noses who didn't hesitate to chase me down at my motel in Tampa. I must have talked to half a dozen candidates from all over the country. Well, until I find my staff I hope the calls keep coming.

I did most of my work at the motel on the weekend because it is difficult to operate from the courthouse. The air conditioning is turned off over the weekend, and alarm bells ring constantly. Furthermore, because the doors are locked, I have to meet all the people I interview at the door and escort them up a non-moving escolator, talk to them in my stuffy office, then escort them back downstairs to let them out the door. I find it much more pleasant to interview them at my motel. I suppose however, that I am a bit prudish. I get embarrassed when I talk over the phone to a woman whom I have never met and invite her to meet me at my motel.

The desk clerk called me about 10:15 yesterday morning and announced that there was a very attractive young woman asking for me in the lobby. I suppose I blushed all the way down the hall to interview Yvonne Pierce. She is a very attractive divor-cee who is interested in becoming our librarian. I'm not sure whether I'll hire her or not, but it was a pleasant chore to interview her, even in the lobby.

I drove out to Carrollwood for my weekly check to make sure that our new house is still there. The neighbors were lounging on the beach while the kids swam in the lagoon. Tough life! On the way back to the motel I stopped at a Pontiac dealer because, as I told you, we have decided to sell the Buick station wagon. I must confess I sometimes enjoy playing the role of an eccentric. I walked into the sales manager's office, which had walls plastered with "wide track Pontiac" posters, and informed him that I didn't particularly care what kind of an automobile I bought as long as it was very narrow. I went on to explain that because our new house has a very narrow driveway and I must store my airplane in the garage, I must park two automobiles outside on the driveway. He informed me quite indignantly that Pontiacs were full-size automobiles and were in no way competing with the Volkswagen.

After casually brushing me off, he asked if I was Bill Graham, the insurance salesman. When I confessed that I was the new president of Hillsborough Junior College, you should have seen the change in posture. Anyone in my influential position certainly should have a Pontiac LeMans parked in the driveway. He insisted that I meet the owner and allow him to make the best deal that anybody had received in the Tampa area. He squired me around to the other salesmen, reminding them that I was the person they had all seen on television recently. Well, that's the life of a celebrity I suppose.

Last night Al Boulenger, who was the assistant administrator at Barnes Hospital in St. Louis when we planned the initial phases of our health program at Forest Park, invited me to see his home. He is now the administrator of Tampa General Hospital. We had a great time reminiscing about St. Louis before we began discussing the health needs in the Tampa area. He is attempting to coordinate the educational programs in his hospital with the graduate and bachelor's degree work in the health field at the University of South Florida. Of course, he is a strong advocate of the junior college and would like us immediately to fit him into our slot.

The Hillsborough County School's adult education program trains vocational nurses in a one-year program. These nurses work under close supervision and are really high-level aides. The university trains nursing supervisors and nursing educators, while the bedside registered nurses are trained in a hospital diploma program. This program takes three years and involves considerable service to the hospital in return for the training the nurses receive. Al told me that out of his eighteen million dollar budget for this year, over a million dollars was going toward his education programs. Inasmuch as this cost is passed directly on to the patient, Al enthusiastically endorses public institutions taking over these responsibilities to keep in line the cost to the individual patient.

The Associate Degree Nursing Program in the community college is designed to serve the same function as the diploma program—to train bedside nurses. The girls take the same state board examinations for registry and, as far as credentials are concerned, are equal to the graduates of the three-year programs, even though the junior college only gives them two years of training. The junior-college trained nurses take classes at the college

124

but also get experience in a hospital under the supervision of junior college instructors whose main function is to insure that every experience the nurse has adds to her training. On the other hand, because of the large investment the hospital has in training its nurses in a diploma program it is necessary that the girls give service in return for their training. As a result, the nurses in the three-year course repeat many more times tasks at which they have already developed sufficient skills to operate effectively. (Or, how many times must you empty a bed pan before you become an expert?)

Al is also involved in training laboratory technicians and radiologic technicians. (I used to call them X-ray technicians, but in this business you have to keep up on the "in" words.) Because most of the medical training programs have in the past been completely hospital-oriented, they have tended to develop around an apprentice philosophy. That is, the student works directly with a full-time employee who is a laboratory specialist rather than a teacher, but who devotes part of his time to giving on-the-job training to the student.

The American Medical Association has established quite rigid rules for accrediting these programs. Al and I agree that the rules are completely unrealistic when applied to a junior college setting. For example, in the cyto-technology program the AMA insists that the student-teacher ratio be no larger than 4 to 1. There is absolutely no provision for classroom instruction or college-level laboratory experiences for the students.

There appears to be a great need for medical education programs in the Tampa area, and with the tremendous expansion program projected, it is doubtful that sufficient staff can be trained unless all segments of education exert every effort in this direction.

Ray Shelton asked me to meet with his staff to discuss the Leto High School recommendation before it goes to the school board for action. So this morning I went to the office early to clean up some of the paper work before the meeting. I had a short conference with Don Taylor, who is working with the Tampa Model Cities program and is anxious to see that the junior college has a proper role in the educational segment of the proposal. It's unfortunate that I don't have more time to spend in this type of endeavor, but at the present time most of my efforts are directed toward getting the college open in September. Such is the case when we don't allow time for the tea to brew, but insist on the instant variety.

At Shelton's staff meeting I presented my reasons for concurring with McGuffey's recommendation that the college hold classes in Leto High School. Dave Erwin openly opposed our operating in a building where he had adult classes. He contended that the adults simply would not remain in school if they had to walk up and down the halls with "those kids" tearing around the place. I told him that in a junior college which holds late afternoon and evening classes, the average age of the students will be higher than in a day program. Furthermore, the general attitude is more serious and subdued than in a day college. At Forest Park we even had difficulty developing school spirit among the students. In fact, one semester we couldn't get enough students to run for the student parliament to have a quorum.

I suppose it's natural to expect Erwin to fear for the development of his own program. I am certain that you are aware that in California almost all post-high school education is handled by the junior college. Consequently, there is no conflict between the junior college and adult education, since it's all administered under one segment of education. I tried to point out that under no circumstances do we want to interfere with the ongoing program in the schools. However, Erwin was still very apprehensive insisting his adults would quit because by the time they arrived at 7 o'clock in the evening all of the parking places would be filled. Naturally, I suggested that one parking lot be reserved for adult education students. When Frank Farmer supported my arguments right down the line, I had a feeling the administration would recommend Leto High School for our use.

I had a luncheon appointment with Al Boulenger to look over a hospital complex which is being renovated, a portion of which he thought we might be able to use for administration offices. When I got back from lunch, the noon meeting of the public school

126

board had just ended. For the next hour and a half I was in a state of shock. Shelton told me he and Farmer had both strongly recommended the junior college be allowed to use Leto High School, but after hearing arguments pro and con, the board had unanimously rejected the recommendation. Apparently some board members felt that in the future Leto would be overcrowded and others simply did not want three segments of education— high school, adult school, and college—in one building.

I called Ken Hardcastle and broke the news to him after assuring him that even though I was upset I had no intention of resigning. I realize this is just one of those setbacks you must expect. I want to be proud of Hillsborough Junior College. But unless we offer our program in a modern, well equipped facility, it may be difficult to convince the community that we have one of the finest colleges in the state. At any rate, here we go again. We've lost one month of the five months lead time we had, and we're right back where we started, looking for temporary facilities for the junior college.

On my return to St. Louis, I arrived at the airport with a little time to spare and thought I would have some refreshment to ease the pain of the Leto announcement. I had no sooner checked my bags than I heard my name announced over the public address system. When I reported to the Eastern Airlines counter as requested, a man stepped up and introduced himself (so help me I can't remember his name) and said he was passing through Tampa and had heard that I was looking for a dean of instruction and would like to talk to me about it. Well, since I had a half hour to spare, we discussed his candidacy over a cup of coffee. He was another academic dean from a liberal arts college. Because I had so little time to talk with him (less than twenty minutes altogether), I was quite probing with my questions.

Like so many other candidates, however, he did not have the slightest idea of the difference between the highly selective, high-tuition liberal arts college at which he was academic dean in Ohio and the comprehensive college which we are starting in Tampa. He had had no experience in a large institution which used multi-media teaching techniques and the new teaching technology; he

127

had never heard of Sam Postlewaite and the audio-tutorial method; he felt that it was necessary to have a remedial program, but only to help some of the skills that would make a student successful in a liberal arts college. He admitted he knew absolutely nothing about any of the vocational areas. I told him, as I have told the other unqualified candidates, that I did not have time to give him a training course in the philosophy of the community college.

I'd better close for now and finish this letter before I get off the plane in St. Louis. Getting the blow about Leto High School and returning to St. Louis in time for a board meeting tonight have made my day rather hectic. This commuting a thousand miles each way is killing me. I hope the board meeting in St. Louis is a short one; I will have lost an hour's sleep because of the time change as it is. Give our love to all of the family.

Bill

St. Louis—11:30 p.m.

P.S. Before mailing this, I thought you might be interested in one of the problems we are facing here in St. Louis which was discussed at the board meeting this evening. While I was president at Palo Verde and an administrator in Ventura, we paid very little attention to campus security problems. However, over the past few years the problem has been magnified completely out of proportion. While a custodial force around the building used to be sufficient, we are now considering a full force of armed guards inside the building and outside. On the Forest Park campus we have had cases of assault in the parking lots and even in the hallways. A great many felonies occur during the daylight hours. A girl who leaves her purse on the cafeteria table while she goes to the vending machine to get a coke might as well kiss the purse goodbye. And because it is a metropolitan campus, it is very accessible to non-students.

I don't want to create a prison atmosphere by placing guards at each entrance to check the identification cards of every person who enters—hence our open campus. But it has become known

128

very rapidly within the criminal society that Forest Park is a soft touch for petty theft. Also, if we lock all the audio-visual equipment up in tool-room fashion, then ask the faculty to walk several hundred feet and climb three stairways to check the material out, it simply will not be used. Therefore, I think it is better to lose a few pieces of equipment than to try to save a few dollars and lose the educational benefit from its use.

Tampa
Sunday
May 19, 1968

Dear Fisher:

Last week Betty Benson, Frank Farmer's secretary, sent a clipping to me in St. Louis reporting the rejection of the Leto site. The lead sentence began, "Second Choice appears to be the pattern for new Junior College." Of course, they were referring to the fact that I was the second choice president, but by golly, I wish they wouldn't rub it in. The more I think about it, the more disappointed I become about our inability to secure Leto High School.

I recall the statement by one of the accreditation team members who visited St. Louis last year when we were in Roosevelt High School. He admitted that Forest Park Community College would not have received accreditation had it not been accredited as a part of the St. Louis Junior College District. He said under no circumstances could a college using facilities as inadequate as Roosevelt High School's be given formal accreditation.

McGuffey called from Tallahassee to tell me he had talked with Everett Prevatt, chairman of the school board. Prevatt is willing to see if the board will discuss the topic again. I certainly hope we can take a new look at it. Mac said he didn't mention in his report that the Hillsborough High science labs are far below standards even for a high school, because he didn't want to embarrass the board.

Also, the Iowa candidate for dean of business services I told you about called to inquire about his status. I told him that I had

129

just written to let him know I had hired Allen Brown. He sounded quite disappointed and asked me to tell him where he had failed in the quest for the job. I am afraid I fibbed because I could see no point in being brutally honest over the telephone. I told him that his previous experience was not as appropriate as Mr. Brown's, which is true. I did not add that had they had exactly the same experience, I still would have hired Brown. You will recall, he was overly anxious about salary during the interview; I believe his asking me this indiscreet question on the telephone proved he is not smooth enough to handle the position. He further asked how he should go about applying for Brown's job in Kansas City. I appreciate his interest in following up on a job; I don't, however, feel that it was my place to tell him how to go about getting a job. Were he a personal friend, I would have been delighted to do so.

With so much to do in Tampa, I arranged with Cosand to leave the St. Louis president's council meeting early to go to the airport to talk with a candidate from Texas whom I had asked to come interview for the position of dean of instruction in Tampa. To reduce travel expenses I have been interviewing in St. Louis most of the candidates who live outside of Florida.

I was amused after having selected the top candidate (on paper) for dean of instruction to discover that he was also a candidate for my job here at Forest Park. Furthermore, Dr. Cosand had already arranged for him to fly to St. Louis Thursday, the day I was supposed to be in Tallahassee working with McGuffey and his crew. So I called Joe and asked if he had any objection to my bringing the man in a day early to talk with me about the Florida job, if I were to pay the cost of his extra day's stay. Joe said of course not and, because he had contacted the man first, agreed to pay the whole cost of air fare. I didn't feel he had sufficient experience in a large urban college to be seriously considered for the St. Louis position, so I interviewed him with a clear conscience.

I am sorry to say that it was a very disappointing interview. In addition to presenting a rather folksy image with his Texas drawl, I had the feeling that he had in his various positions been a very mechanical administrator. He has had experience as dean of a rather large college in New England, but when I queried him about specific programs, I had the feeling that he had simply moved into an ongoing situation and had never questioned the rationale for any of the decisions which had been made. Also, he obviously was not prepared to accept the level of faculty involvement in policy decisions that we are used to here in St. Louis. His attitude was completely paternalistic: let the faculty give advice, but the administration has no responsibility for responding or justifying to the faculty any recommendations rejected.

I do not believe that an administrator is required to accept the recommendations of the faculty; but under today's scheme of things, if you do not give a detailed rationale and spell out the reasons why the recommendations are not feasible, the faculty may get the impression that the whole procedure is a sham. Unable to make him an offer, I left for Tallahassee rather disappointed. Further, I had the feeling that our faculty screening committee at Forest Park might make this candidate rather uncomfortable with their direct and probing questions.

Thursday morning I met with McGuffey and his crew to find out how they were doing with the assignments I had given them. We discussed a great many problems, and I made key decisions on the basis in a staff meeting which included only myself. I decided, for example, that a fee of $7 per credit would be charged (including $1 per credit for a student activity fee), although there really is no logical reason for establishing such a fee. The amount of income is certainly inconsequential when the entire budget is viewed as a whole. I do feel, however, that there is a certain advantage in the student's having a financial stake in his education. On the other hand, I would hate to feel that the small fee denied any student the education he deserves. There is a great deal of federal money available for hardship cases, but I'm not sure how it is distributed in Florida. In St. Louis funds from a Work-Study Grant make part-time jobs or even out-right grants available to students. There are also the NDEA Loans which allow the student to borrow money interest-free until he has finished college, then to repay the money over a ten-year period at three percent interest. The decision I made was a compromise. I wanted a fee structure which would be fair to the student and, at the same time, provide a reasonable income to the college.

Another small point we discussed was the possibility of a $5 application fee. Here, again, the $5 fee has little to do with the financial needs of the college, but many students make multiple applications and some apply on a whim. Unless there is some reason to hire a staff to teach the classes. On the other hand, if we assume all applications are *bona fide,* and then students don't enroll, we end up with extra teachers hired and no income to pay salaries. The $5 fee thus tends to make a student more serious about his application. Also, a late registration fee of $1 per credit is going to be charged if the advisory committee follows my recommendation. This fee will encourage students to file their applications early.

I flew on to Tampa Thursday evening, then dashed to the office Friday morning intent upon unsnarling the paper work. The poor little clerk-typist we hired is completely bewildered by the inquiries she receives. And Gilda can't even get an intelligent answer from me as to where the college will hold classes or what courses will be offered. Further, I am amazed at the number of applicants for teaching positions who apparently try to keep secret their fields of specialization. Most of the time you have to read a letter to its very end before you find out the interest is in a position teaching history.

I called Ken Hardcastle to find out if he had been successful in getting the school board to reconsider our use of Leto High School. He said he was hesitant to push them, not wanting to offend our benefactors. So I set out in the early afternoon to see if I could discover suitable off-campus office space fairly near Hillsborough High School, on the assumption that we will hold our classes there. I found one facility which would work, but it certainly would not provide an inspiring environment in which to house our staff. I looked at two other office buildings downtown which also would serve, but they're located four miles from the high school. None of them are ideal solutions.

When I got back to the motel I had a message from Plano Valdes, the instructor I hired last week. He wanted to know if I had considered Tampa Catholic High School as a possible site. From his description of the physical plant, it certainly seemed worth investigating. So, bright and early on Saturday morning I went out to look it over. Much to my surprise it has far more potential than Leto High School. It is a brand new building with a new gymnasium and a theatre which has yet to be put in use. Furthermore, Tampa Catholic is located near public transportation (approximately one-half mile from Hillsborough High School). It is definitely in the center of population, yet has new equipment and buildings. I was so enthusiastic that I arranged to meet with Monsignor Scully that evening. During the afternoon I looked for possible office space in the vicinity for our headquarters. Almost immediately I located two viable facilities within half a mile of the high school. With a little luck, we may have hit pay dirt.

I spent the rest of the weekend checking all of the possible stumbling blocks which might frustrate our efforts. At this point, prospects look very good. Ray Shelton's staff sees nothing wrong with our using the Catholic school; the advisory committee is enthusiastic. In fact, everyone feels that it would be an excellent solution. The only real drawback is that it is not a comprehensive high school; therefore, it has no vocational shops. I believe, however, we can rent off-campus space for shops and labs as our curriculum develops.

So you won't think all has turned rosy, we still have a real problem with our budget. A complicated equalization formula is used to determine the funds provided for each full-time student. Up to the maximum tax levy the state and local districts share on a 50-50 basis. But the formula prohibits a school district from raising more than $625,000 this year for operating a junior college. Any money in excess of that amount is provided by the state. Because our initial enrollment is small, the school board will not be required to raise more than $250,000, even though

133

they have indicated they are willing to levy the full amount. In other words, they generously agreed to levy a local tax which would provide almost $400,000 more than they are required to raise by law. But Tom Baker doesn't think it's legal for them to tax themselves more than the minimum amount. As a brand-new junior college, however, we need more than the minimum support.

Problems such as this separate the cookbook administrator from the shrewd executive. It is my job to secure the necessary operating funds and, at the same time, stay out of jail. I suppose we could change our projected student enrollment and pretend that we will have 1500 to 2000 students. Then Baker could inform the school board that the law requires them to levy the full amount. There's not a Chinaman's chance that many students will show up, but if they did we would have the money in hand. Of course, we might run the risk of a taxpayer's suit, but as with most school laws, the worst that could happen would be that we would have to pay the money back. We'll have to play this one close to the vest. But enough of school business.

I wrote a letter to the president of the local Experimental Aircraft Association chapter and received a very friendly reply. The fellows are going to do what they can to find a temporary storage location for my airplane until I can get the carport enclosed into a garage. These groups are always very helpful to the aircraft homebuilder. In the East, where you are almost forced to build your airplane in a basement, many of the builders eventually have to face the problem of getting a fuselage two to four inches wider than a door from the inside to the outside. Therefore, the EAA chapters sponsor "coming out parties." The home-builder furnishes the beer and the members take sledge hammers, pound a hole in the basement wall, roll the fuselage out and then cement all of the bricks back in place.

The other night I got home from work and almost blew my stack. Ken has been working quite often with his band during the past month. When Jeanny informed me that Ken and Dave had left pulling a trailer full of electronic band amplifiers to Rolla, which is about 110 miles from St. Louis, I wasn't surprised. I knew Ken was scheduled to play at fraternity parties on Friday and Saturday night, but what upset me was that he was scheduled to take the College Entrance Examination Board (CEEB) in St. Louis on Saturday morning at 8 o'clock. Jeanny said Dave had gone with Ken so that he would not have to drive back at 2 o' clock in the morning by himself.

Well, at least in education circles, I sometimes have influence. I got on the telephone and contacted Rolla information. Fortunately, Rolla is not a very large town because when I asked the operator to locate the telephone number of the person who would be most logically scheduled to administer admission tests in Rolla, the call was put through. The operator, who has a daughter in high school, left me hanging on the line while she checked the details out with her daughter. I called the counselor in charge of testing at the high school and explained the situation to her. She said she was administering the test and Ken could take it there instead of driving back to St. Louis. I then asked the operator to locate the frat house where Ken's band was scheduled to play. The automated dial telephone system in a large metropolitan area does not provide this level of service.

I was anxious for Ken to take the test because a great many colleges use it as a screening device for admissions. Naturally these are the selective colleges, most of which are four-year universities. While an open-door junior college will usually administer examinations, they are used only for counseling purposes and do not affect admission to the college. The tests provide data which are useful for counselors and faculty members when advising students about career choices or study problems.

Jeanny and I hope Ken will want to come to Florida to attend college, but for him I can't recommend Hillsborough Junior College. I don't think it would be fair to him to be a student in a college where I'm president. Anyway, the University of South Florida is an excellent school with a wide choice of curricular offerings.

If you have any suggestions for getting Ken to cut his hair, let me know. He and I had a father-and-son discussion about the length of it the other night. I suppose I insinuated that he looked

135

like a hippie. He insists, however, that his is not. He says he keeps his hair clean and doesn't think like a hippie. Further, he says he is not rebelling against his family and that he really doesn't want to leave home. He claims the long hair is a part of his band uniform. If he could even grow a goatee, a mustache or sideburns, he would. However, he says all he can grow is hair. I tried to explain to him why it bothers me to have him looking this way. I pointed out his responsibility as the son of one who is in the public eye. I went on to say I wanted him to assume a role in a middleclass Caucasian society. At that point, his eyes lit up. Ah, I thought, I'm finally getting through. Then he replied, "What a great name that would make for a group, The Middle-Class Caucasians!" With that, I gave up.

That beagle of ours should never have been named Boots. Snoopy would have been much more appropriate because he loves to sleep on his back. I've been thinking of building him a dog house in the back yard so he can really be in character and sleep on the roof. He lies in the middle of the floor in this grotesque position by the hour, his four feet straight up in the air. When you come in the room, he tries to wag his tail. I suppose if he would sleep this way on the fireplace hearth he would keep it neat as a pin.

I'll close for now and write again when I get back to St. Louis. I have to get back tomorrow evening for our board meeting, so I'll catch a plane at 4:15 p.m. and arrive just in time to take a cab from the airport to the board room. Give our love to the whole family.

Bill

St. Louis
May 23, 1968
Thursday

Dear Fisher:

I got home late from the office this evening and, with Jeanny at choir practice, decided to write you a short note. I really should go right to bed, but I am so keyed up with the tension of working two jobs I probably wouldn't sleep anyway. It is not the number of hours I'm physically active as much as it is the nervous tension of trying to do two full-time jobs at the same time. I can't allow myself the luxury of even a short repose.

I came in on the plane Monday night from Tampa just in time for a five-hour board meeting; on Tuesday morning I met with the administrative staff on campus for a briefing and problem-solving meeting. In the afternoon the college council met for two and a half hours in an attempt to finish up our year-end projects. On Wednesday I spent the day with Dr. Cosand in the president's council before dashing to the airport to spend three hours with Allen Brown, my new business manager from Kansas City.

I don't know when I'll get a chance to clean up the paper work; I have completely given up all thought of reading any of the professional literature that comes across my desk. It's unfortunate to have to work under such conditions. If I am to furnish any leadership or creative thrust at the college, I should have time just to sit and think or to have brainstorming sessions with the deans. I am paid too much money to spend my time putting out brush fires, but that's all I have time for these days.

After the council meeting on Tuesday, I met with a newly organized committee at the Forest Park Campus. It has been set up to give assistance to the dean of students who is responsible for student discipline. We are attempting to include faculty and students more and more in the administration of the college. The committee was made up half of students and half of faculty members. Their first objective was to define the function of the commitee. Because they had accomplished little in their first two meetings, they asked me to give them some of my ideas.

It was a rather interesting session because it revolved primarily around how autonomous a committee can be in a public-supported junior college with a locally based board which, by state statutes, has ultimate power. One of the faculty members felt that this committee would be "Mickey Mouse" if it were subject to any sort of veto, scrutiny, or second guessing by any member of the administrative staff. I assured him that if we used this rationale in any public-supported junior college, there would

137

never be any committees because the board delegates the responsibility to the administration but reserves all power for hiring and firing of personnel, for admitting and dismissing students, and for approving the basic functions of the college operation. Of necessity, all of these committees must be advisory to the president. Further, if an advisory committee is really going to work and not be a sham, there must be mutual respect among faculty, students, and administration.

I insisted that before calling it "quits" the group set up a structure that would assure that their recommendations were tantamount to a firm decision, and then find out how many of their decisions are overridden. This committee reports to our general policy group, the college council, which must review each committee at the end of each year. If at any time they feel that a committee is "Mickey ·Mouse," they can recommend the disbanding of the committee.

I further told the group I hoped they could work out a procedure whereby student discipline could be administered with firmness, yet compassion. Unfortunately, too often when student courts are given complete autonomy, they operate within very rigid guidelines and have little concern for unique problems of their peers.

I am still trying to get settled on my key administrative staff for Tampa. I suppose I really have a distaste for lonesome decisions. I am much more comfortable when I can receive recommendations from my staff and then play the devil's advocate to evaluate the soundness of these recommendations. Right now I am the only one who can make personnel recommendations for Hillsborough Junior College, and I have to make them all by myself.

I am considering very carefully the possibility of hiring Dr. Morton Shanberg from DuPage Community College near Chicago. His experience is excellent and most appropriate, since he worked with Dr. Charles Chapman in the formation of the community college in Cleveland and then went to DuPage as vice-president for program development when it opened in 1965. However, I understand there have been problems at the college. After calling several people who know the situation, I get a rather confused story—that DuPage is splintered into fifteen fragments requiring a 238 mile roundtrip to visit all of the locations where classes are held. It is small wonder that communications problems developed. In any case, Shanberg portrays the image that I am seeking, has the experience I need, and is young enough to have the energy required to accomplish the job.

I still haven't been able to find many strong candidates in the student personnel field. I have several that I want to interview, but I am not overwhelmed by their qualifications. I am considering hiring Tom Mastin, a young Ph.D. in counseling and guidance at Forest Park, as an assistant dean of admission and records. Although a third echelon job, it would be an opportunity for him to start on the ground floor and perhaps move into the dean of students position at one of our other campuses as they develop.

I hate to have anyone on the staff from St. Louis because it would most likely put Tom and my other administrators on unequal footing. Tom knows me and is aware of the type of program that I have implemented in St. Louis. I am sure that we could not refrain, however much we tried, from referring to the way it was done in St. Louis. There has been the same sort of problem between Cosand and me with regard to our continuing reference to the California situations. I am certain that many people on the staff think I was "Joe's boy" because we are both from California. However, you know I had never even met him before I came to St. Louis. I suppose it might be wise to avoid the problem altogether by not hiring anyone from St. Louis, but I'm beginning to get desperate in the face of all the things that need to be done with no staff to do them.

Jeanny and I are frantically trying to scrape enough money together for the down payment on the house in Tampa. I wrote to Jefferson City concerning the refund of my contributions into the retirement system, and when I got the answer I went right through the ceiling. I knew that because I had not stayed in Missouri five years, I would receive only my contribution, and not the interest that had been earned on my money. However, I discovered I cannot even apply for my refund until I have been

139

away from Missouri 120 days. Then I can expect the check any time within 60 days. In other words, they will keep my money up to six months after I have left the retirement system. Thus, I will lose well over $100 in interest which could be earned on the amount I have on deposit with them. I thought about writing a letter of protest beginning with "Dear Chislers," but what good would that do? You can't beat City Hall.

McGuffey called today to let me know he was progressing to the final stages of the master plan for HJC. He is now talking in terms of five campuses by 1985. I hope we can get the money to build one college about every three years for the next seventeen years. During our conversation he told me about some feedback that he had received from the Tampa area.

He got the impression that Frank Farmer would like to be more involved in our immediate problems. I told Mac that I had continually used Frank as my local sounding board. In fact, I pester him so much I am a little bit embarrassed to go to his office any more. In our conversation Mac and I considered the advisability of offering him a job with the junior college. Unfortunately, he does not have the specific skills that I need to fill one of the deanships nor does he have a doctor's degree. He might work out well as an assistant to the president where he could sit in on our policy discussions and help cover the many local assignments which I know will confront me over the next several years. He knows the community and would give us a tie-in with the school system.

I mentioned that the press of paper work is almost overwhelming. To alleviate the situation, I bought a portable dictating machine. By arranging my notes beforehand, I can get almost fifteen minutes of dictation on the machine while driving down the freeway in the morning. I even carry it around the campus with me and dictate memos as I think of them. The other day I was in a state of repose in the faculty men's room when several of the staff members came through the door. You can imagine their reaction when the dulcet tones of their leader came pouring from behind the stall.

The administrative staff invited us to Associate Dean Bob Richie's house for a steak dinner and an enjoyable period of socialization last Tuesday. The college staff is planning a reception for Jeanny and me on the 29th so that the entire staff will be able to bid us farewell. While I do enjoy talking with the people and getting better acquainted, I have to admit that I hate receptions where you stand around and talk with people for two solid hours. But I guess that's part of the game.

Steve called to tell us he will be coming home for a thirty day leave prior to embarking for Europe. He didn't say what his assignment would be but, as a parent, I much prefer his taking any assignment in Europe to his going to Vietnam. It's not that I'm unpatriotic: I just would rather not have him used for target practice.

I'll close for now. Jeanny is returning from choir practice and has just turned into the driveway. I will write again soon and keep you posted as to developments.

Bill

St. Louis
Sunday
May 26, 1968

Dear Fisher:

We just returned home from church, and Jeanny is preparing waffles for a late brunch. I'll start this letter now and finish it after we have eaten. Last Friday morning I drove to the office determined to make some decisions about my administrative staff. I decided to take a chance on Mort Shanberg from DuPage County Community College. When I called him, he accepted my offer with enthusiasm and agreed that he and his wife would come to Tampa over the Memorial Day weekend to look for housing and get acquainted with the city.

I then telephoned the two top candidates for the dean of students position to see if they were still interested. When each informed me that he had decided not to make a move at this time,

141

I talked with Tom Mastin, the assistant dean I told you about at Forest Park, and asked him if he would be interested in taking the associate dean of admissions and records job as a third level administrative position. I told him that if I did not find an experienced dean of students, I would promote him later on.

He wasn't too enthusiastic about accepting a position on this basis. In fact, when I told him the salary that I would be willing to offer, he told me he would not be interested. About ten minutes later, however, he came back into the office and said, "Don't count me out yet. I still want very much to go to Florida. Let me see what I can do to work it out."

That evening Jeanny and I were talking about the offer I had made to Mastin and it struck me as being a rather phony deal. If I don't have confidence enough in him to do the job, then I shouldn't offer it to him in the first place. In addition, I have received so many unsolicited compliments about him from members of my staff that he seems worth the risk. Further, when the college opens it will be very small and will provide him an opportunity to grow with the job. So I telephoned him and offered him the position of dean of students. He accepted immediately, and that was that.

After twisting my arm for a week, Jeanny finally succeeded in convincing me that she should spend the Memorial Day weekend in Tampa with me. Not that I don't want her, but they took the excursion rates off the airlines for this holiday weekend and I feel we might use the money better in other ways. After all, she is bugging me to get a boat as soon as we move. Anyway, her tenacity prevailed; she is going with me.

I didn't fly to Tampa last weekend because Dr. Cosand had asked Jeanny and me to reserve an evening so that the board and the officers of the district could entertain us before we left. We had a very nice evening at Joe's house last night mingling with all of the board members who have served during the time I have been in St. Louis and with the members of the central office staff with whom I have worked very closely.

When Joe arrived in St. Louis, he brought with him a gift from the Faculty at Santa Barbara City College where he had served

142

four years as president. The gift was a desk set with two fountain pens. From the moment we first saw it, we referred to it as Joe's status symbol and laughingly talked about the time that we would become presidents of multi-campus districts and get our own status symbols. So when any of the staff has left to accept a presidency, we have passed the hat and presented the out-going dean with a pen set. Hence I was not too surprised when a rather heavy box was presented to me by the members of the board of trustees.

After a sentimental presentation speech by one of the trustees who referred to my contribution to the district and my philosophy of community college education, I felt at a loss for words. Fortunately, I have always learned to be prepared for any emergency. Therefore, I was able to pull from my coat pocket a prepared poem which I entitled "A Eulogy to the Two Holer." The poetry was pretty bad, but the thought was there.

We're going to leave Ken and Dave at home alone over Memorial Day weekend. I suppose we really should not be concerned, but we left Steve at home alone several times when he was the age of the boys, and he didn't feel that he had to honor our requests. I suppose this shook our confidence in teenagers a bit. Each of them will have to stand on his own, however; so we're going to give Ken and Dave the opportunity to prove how responsible they are. Robin will stay with one of our friends so that the boys will not have to take care of her.

At last Monday's board meeting there was a rather interesting discussion of the potential candidates for the position I'm vacating at Forest Park. Our faculty screening committee met for an hour and a half with Dr. Cosand before coming up with the final list of candidates. The list includes four outside candidates and several local ones. Dr. Cosand said that he tried to get the committee to refrain from ranking them but that it was impossible for them to mask their feelings.

One of the candidates is an associate dean of instruction at Forest Park. While he has never had a line responsibility in a college, he is rapidly becoming an outstanding national figure in the area of the disadvantaged student. He is directing the Dan-

143

forth project which I told you about earlier. Before accepting the position with us, he spent a number of years as an elementary school principal but has little administrative experience at the college level. It is unfortunate in an institution as large as ours, that we are forced to specialize in our administrative positions. Therefore, he has no experience in student personnel work or in the areas of instruction other than that in which he is immediately involved. Although he is an extremely articulate Negro who is well-liked by the faculty, I question his ability to understand and cope with the day-to-day problems of college administration. At Forest Park I made dozens of decisions daily that demand a thorough understanding of the operations of the various departments. Much as I like Bill Moore, I don't really feel he is the best qualified person for the position. Yet, there is no question in my mind that he will soon become one of the outstanding junior college presidents in the country. It is indeed unfortunate that I have not provided him the breadth of experience necessary to qualify him for the job.

Another candidate from the local scene is my dean of instruction, Ray Pietak. Ray is thirty-four years of age and shows great promise and creativity as an administrator. He came to us from New York State, where he spent a couple of years an an admissions officer. Initially, he served as an associate dean of instruction and then as dean of instruction, in which capacity he has served for slightly more than a year. He is astute and perceptive, but because he is young and has been working in a job which has required him to veto various requests from the faculty, he is not the most popular administrator on campus. There is no question in my mind that, like Bill Moore, he will soon make a great contribution to education as the president of a college. In fact, he has been interviewed twice for the presidency of a small junior college in southern Michigan. He asked me whether he should seriously consider accepting the position or whether he should remain a while longer as dean of instruction at Forest Park to gain more experience. I am not sure that I gave him an objective answer. I went into the presidency at Palo Verde knowing virtually nothing about administering a college. I learned fast, but you will recall I took a few lumps in the process.

I know practically nothing about the outside candidates. One of them is from Florida and has reportedly had problems. It's even rumored that he resigned just before getting fired. Another is from New Orleans and, while he does not have extensive community college experience, made a very favorable impression on those who interviewed him. The third candidate is president of a college in Washington State. The final outside candidate is a University of Michigan post-doctoral student who has other practical experience and an extensive and recent theoretical knowledge of the community college movement but virtually no community college experience. He also impressed the committee. At this point it would appear to be a toss-up as to who will be my replacement. I really haven't the slightest idea who it will be, and the suspense is killing me.

On Friday night we had scheduled a dinner party with friends, but somehow I overlooked a commitment which I had made to attend the Student Awards Banquet at the college. So we attented two dinners with the intention of nibbling lightly at each of them. However, when my associate dean of student activities found that we had this conflict, he insisted that I say a few words to the group at the beginning of the dinner and then excuse myself.

I really think that college kids are great, and I get a tremendous thrill in watching them receive recognition for their efforts. In the course of my remarks I couldn't help mentioning the student demonstrations that are now plaguing the universities and colleges in the country. I don't know how I would feel if a group of students came into my office and ordered me to get out so that they could take over. We agreed in the president's council meeting the other day that if this were to occur, we would take the position that we were willing to talk with any student groups and allow them to demonstrate any place on the campus as long as they did not interfere with the civil rights of students attempting to gain an education. I told the group at the banquet that I certainly hoped that this would never be the case at Forest Park.

145

We have tried hard to set up a vehicle for communicating with students so that they will feel that their voices are heard without resorting to the demonstration route.

On the other hand, I basically agree with the students that much of the college program and curriculum is outmoded and inappropriate. I strongly feel that students should have the opportunity to challenge the curriculum and the materials offered in their courses. I am going to attempt to include students on our curriculum committees in Tampa, especially in the career courses where we do not have to worry about respectability and a favorable nod from the universities. If it weren't for the university domination of the transfer curricula, the junior colleges would have the opportunity to develop truly meaningful general education courses in many areas in which students plan to transfer to the universities to continue their education. Theoretically, this is the case in Florida because the universities have indicated that the associate degree will be accepted as the equivalent of junior standing. From what I can tell, however, there is little confidence that the universities really mean what they say. Anyway, most colleges are offering programs which parallel identically the programs offered in the university.

The papers have been full of Dr. Champion's resignation as president of the Florida State University at Tallahassee. You may have read that he resigned after students and faculty demonstrated against his alleged censorship of the school literary magazine because of four-letter words used in some of the articles.

Perhaps I was just lucky last winter when I censored two articles prepared for the Forest Park newspaper. I did have a visit from the editor of the newspaper, but I told him I was not opposed to four-letter words and even obscenity in an article if it made good journalistic sense. As a direct quotation attributable to a specific individual, swear words might be appropriate. As generalized adjectives in an article, however, I simply have to assume that the writer has a very meager vocabulary. I told him it was his job as a college newspaper editor to make sure that his reporters found descriptive adjectives that were respectable within an intellectual community. This response appeared to satisfy him and so far I have had no charges of censorship directed toward me. I have been endeavoring, however, to set up a publications board made up of students and faculty members who would establish the criteria for good journalism in our community college newspaper. I prefer not to have the faculty advisor assume the censorship role, nor am I particularly happy assuming it myself. I would prefer to have this board set standards of journalism and taste within which the newspaper would operate. Unfortunately, I have a feeling that the student newspaper staff would rather have me assume the position of censor so that they would have one individual upon whom they could focus their attention if censorship became an issue.

We are frantically trying to get our things ready at home so that the movers can pack. It's a miserable chore trying to decide just what should be discarded. I managed to get my airplane flaps inspected by the FAA and riveted together so that they can be packed in the van. I certainly hope they don't drop a piano on one of them or let something equally disastrous happen. When you're dealing with a homebuilt airplane, there is no use even thinking about insurance. If a part is destroyed, it's gone and you have to start all over again.

We're trying to get rid of as many things as we can so the furniture will fit in our three-bedroom house. Jeanny and I keep wondering what we're going to do with all our collective belongings. They have been much too easy for us to fit in our St. Louis home with its many rooms. We have sold our dryer, one refrigerator, one stove, and our camping trailer. We sold our trailer to newly-wed friends who happen to have ten children between them, ages four to ten. They are going to use the fifteen-foot house trailer as a central tent and buy pup tents for all of the kids. With that size family how else can you afford to take a vacation? I have just about decided to keep the LeSabre station wagon. The darn thing is running well and hasn't cost us any money for the last three months. Right now we think we would rather buy a boat with the money we have budgeted for a new car.

I think Ken is finally beginning to come around to my way of thinking. He now says that if his band does not have a major recording contract by September, he will come to Florida with us and attend college at the University of South Florida in Tampa. At least he wants to make application; so apparently he has seen the light.

Dave and Robin are just fine. As is to be expected, they are somewhat apprehensive about moving. Ken would like to go to California for a while before he begins the many jobs that his band has scheduled for the summer here in St. Louis. Dave is even talking about staying for a while with some of his friends.

I'd better close for now. I'll try to give you the details of our trip to Tampa over Memorial Day. Rember us to all of the family.

Bill

Tampa
Monday
June 3, 1968

Dear Fisher:

Jeanny and I are on the plane returning from five days in Tampa. We were lucky to get on the airplane because I forgot to reconfirm my plane tickets.. This is the windup of the Memorial Day holiday and the plane is jammed. Perhaps the fact that we are leaving just before a hurricane is scheduled to hit the area has something to do with the urgency of those departing. At any rate, we were able to get on standby and will make it back to St. Louis in time to retrieve Robin from our friends and resume supervision of the rest of the family. I hope that the hurricane dumps five or six inches of water in Lake Carroll so that the back yard of our new house will look more inviting than it did when we passed it yesterday.

We landed in Tampa Thursday night at approximately the same time that the Shanbergs arrived from Chicago with their two children. After a brief get-acquainted session, with the Mastins participating, we all decided that on Memorial Day the newcomers would take a whirlwind tour of the Tampa area while I would attempt to accomplish great things at the office.

As it was, McGuffey came in from Tallahassee and occupied most of my day telling me about his forthcoming master plan report for Hillsborough Junior College. He showed me the five areas where he thinks by 1985 we will have five campuses, the smallest of which will enroll 2500 students. Altogether he estimates that between 20,000 and 25,000 students will be enrolled. Right now, however, I am more concerned about the 750 that are due to arrive this September.

I got a shock when Mac casually mentioned that when a girl in his office stuffed the envelopes, supposedly sending student applications to the principals of the various high schools, a slight mistake had been made. Instead of sending student applications, she had mailed faculty applications! You can imagine the reception that this received at the high schools. There has been considerable concern on the part of the administration in the Hillsborough County Schools that we would be able, by offering a slightly higher salary, to skim off the cream of the faculty for the junior college. I suppose this is an example of how *not* to win friends and influence people you need on your side.

In the evening I was scheduled to make a speech for the Hillsborough County Student Personnel Association at the Embers Restaurant. As was my usual custom, I rented a small Chevy II for transportation. I didn't realize just how small it was until we tried to pile the Mastins, the Shanbergs and their two children, and Jeanny and me into the automobile. Fortunately, the restaurant was only a mile or so from our motel. I'm glad that the dignitaries who were expecting me as the guest of the evening were not standing in front of the restaurant when we arrived. After unfolding and disembarking from the Chevy II, Jeanny and I attended the dinner while the Mastins and Shanbergs proceeded to dine out in another local restaurant.

We were greeted at the door by Howard Sinsley, assistant registrar at the University of South Florida, who was master of ceremonies. Most groups of educators are pretty stuffy, but this group was more reserved than usual. Because they were interested in student personnel services, I devoted a major portion

149

of my remarks to some of the dreams that we have for Hillsborough Junior College in the future.

While discussing counseling services, I emphasized that our new counselors would soon need firsthand knowledge of the various local vocational opportunities. I think it extremely unfortunate when counselors are only able to point to a rack that holds printed vocational information. I have always insisted that our counselors make personal visits to industrial and business establishments. As a counselor, it's much easier to convince a student that you know what you're talking about if you can quote what some person closely associated with a given vocation has told you recently. Too often counselors are familiar only with what is included in the *Occupational Outlook Handbook*. I want them to be able to recognize the smell of cutting oil in a machine shop.

My thirty-five minute address seemed short when compared to the lengthy introduction. I'll have to admit I get uncomfortable when someone introduces me and drones on and on listing the various components of my pedigree. I am certain that most of the audience was completely uninterested in the fact that I have degrees in math and physics, in addition to graduate degrees in curriculum and higher education. Furthermore, they left out the startling fact that in 1946 I sang the "Poor Miriam" commercial on the Bob Hope Show. But what they don't know won't hurt them and probably won't destroy my image either.

On Friday I dashed madly around trying to prepare materials for the advisory committee meeting which was scheduled for four o'clock in the afternoon. I tried unsuccessfully all morning to contact Monsignor Scully, the head man at Tampa Catholic High School. I finally reached him about two o'clock and drove to the rectory. After much discussion, we agreed that $57,000 per year, including utilities and maintenance, would be a reasonable rental price for the school.

I got back to the courthouse, out of breath from running upstairs, at ten minutes to four. The meeting went off without a hitch and all the members appeared to be in good humor. Drs. Mastin and Shanberg were approved, but I had to laugh at Hardcastle's reaction. He started to point out to the board that Dr.

150

Shanberg was only thirty-seven years of age, which meant that I was not afraid to hire a young man for a key position, but before he had reached the end of his first sentence, he noticed that Tom was only thirty-two. He broke off with the remark, "My God, are you robbing the cradle?" I then explained that I wanted young administrators on my staff because the job ahead of us will require stamina and vitality. Mr. Thompson was concerned that hiring young, aggressive, and highly qualified people might mean that we would lose our good administrators after a short while. I pointed out that while his fears were probably valid, I thought we would be better off to hire young people who were promotable, who would do three years' work for every year they were with us, than to hire someone we knew would never leave the college because no one else would want him. I also told Thompson that one of the most critical issues in higher education today is the training of administrators for the junior college movement.

During the next decade more than 1,400 junior college presidents will be appointed. This figure is predicated on the assumption that there will be 150 new junior colleges per year during that period. If you project this figure to include an average of four new administrators per college, over 5,000 members of the teaching profession will have to try their hand at administrative duties. The Kellogg Foundation has sponsored a leadership training program in several centers throughout the country, but the number it is able to turn out each year hardly scratches the surface of the need for qualified people. Furthermore, because these administrative positions tend to be year-round assignments, faculty members promoted from the teaching ranks have little opportunity to take formal courses to prepare themselves for their administrative assignments.

I tried to set up a salary schedule for the non-certified personnel, such as janitors, clerks, secretaries, and the like, and ended up making my first real boo-boo. I worked very closely with the personnel office of the public schools and took their recommendations all the way. However, the superintendent's secretary has been a former teacher and is on a teaching salary schedule; so there was no way I could compare her salary with what the salary of my secretary should be.

Then I was advised that the civil service schedule used by the public schools is not competitive and is outmoded. Therefore, I tried to devise one that was in between. The result was a salary range for the secretaries to the deans that was more than a thousand dollars a year higher than the secretaries to the assistant superintendents. So even after the advisory committee approved it on Friday, I felt that I should change the schedule before it is submitted to the school board this coming Tuesday. Our clerical salaries have to be similar to those in other public agencies. I suppose if this is the biggest mistake I make, I'll be lucky.

I recommended the use of Tampa Catholic High School, and the advisory committee enthusiastically endorsed my choice. Now all I have to do is get it approved by the school board and we're home free. Keep your fingers crossed.

On Thursday and Friday I spent considerable time interviewing candidates for the position as my secretary. In April, when I first reported on the job, Betty Benson, Frank Farmer's secretary, let me know that she was interested in the job. I informed her that while she had been highly endorsed by Frank Farmer, I was not going to employ her without taking a look at what was available on the job market. Accordingly, I had the personnel department run an advertisement in the paper and set up appointments for me with the top five candidates.

I am afraid I was not too impressed by any of the applicants; one handled herself very well and perhaps would make a good secretary to one of the deans. I was somewhat surprised, however, when a woman who supposedly was employed in a $9,000-a-year position with an advertising agency simply fell to pieces in front of me when I asked her to take dictation. She told me that when given a test of any kind, she became completely rattled and could not control herself. I thus dispensed with any sort of a testing procedure. I must say that the same sort of thing happens quite frequently with students in school who freeze when under pressure of a test. However, as an executive secretary, it appears to me that she should be able to work under stress or in a difficult situation. In any case, I concluded that Betty Benson was the best secretarial choice I could make.

Betty is a gregarious red head who has had experience working for a newspaper and for the realty board. Her experience should qualify her to assist new staff members coming into the area and help out during the infancy of the junior college by preparing press releases and handling our relationships with the media. She has been secretary to the junior college advisory committee from its inception and has considerable background knowledge concerning the formation of the district.

I am still interested in hiring someone who is knowledgeable about the local scene and who has a feeling for legislative problems. I talked briefly with Frank Farmer about the possibility of his joining the staff. But because he is now assistant superintendent for instruction even without a doctorate, we concluded that it would not be feasible to hire him at a comparable salary since he knows absolutely nothing about junior college administration.

Ray Shelton cornered me this morning and suggested that perhaps Everett Prevatt, the chairman of the school board, might make a valuable staff member. He has a master's degree in administration and supervision and has taught in the public schools for approximately seven years. He will finish his term as chairman of the board in January, but because the state law prohibits a board member from being employed by the same school board for two years following his term of office, Prevatt is looking for a position.

I called Prevatt and asked him to drop by the office in order to discuss the possibilities of his joining the staff as assistant to the president. I certainly could use a "detail man" who could also shed some insight on local problems. He said he would let me know whether he is interested when I return to Tampa in a couple of weeks.

On Saturday morning Tom, Mort, and I went to Tampa Catholic High School to discuss with the principal the specific problems involved in our using the facilities for late afternoon and evening classes. Sister Ann Bernard is the principal but is leav-

153

ing this month for Puerto Rico. Another nun who will become the new principal was there to make the rounds with us. I must say that the atmosphere was rather frigid, even on a warm June day. Finally, I tactfully tried to remind the ladies that by having the junior college share the facilities, the Catholic church would profit to the tune of over $150,000 over the next three years. I asked them to consider how many personal donations it would require to raise that much money. Later, when I mentioned to Father Scully that the nuns had not been overjoyed at the prospect of having us as tenants, he replied "You know how women are." I told him I was fully aware of the difficult situation but reminded him that it was more appropriate for him to ease the situation than for me to have to argue to get a fair shake. We agreed that we would remain friends through it all. Let's hope!

In the afternoon I went by a new office building which is being constructed about a half a mile from the high school. I had previously talked to the owner about the possibility of renting some of the vacant space in the building. After considerable discussion he offered to build the junior college a facility of its own, provided that we would rent for ten years with an option to buy at the end of five years. The location would be ideal for permanent central office. It is centrally located in the county and will very likely be at the center of the various campuses.

At the Hardcastles,' where we were invited to meet the advisory committee members and their wives, I had an opportunity to discuss the offer briefly. Naturally, the board was reluctant to deal with a small, unknown contractor. However, they agreed to check him out and to consider hiring an architect to supervise the work. It would be nice to rent at a reasonable price a brand-new facility especially designed for us.

The entire evening with the board members and their wives was delightful. The Mastins, Shanbergs, Harrises, Grays, Hardcastles and Jeanny and I drove to Clearwater to have dinner at the Kapok Tree Inn which I previously told you about. We rode with Ken and Mia Hardcastle whom we found to be delightful company. Ken especially has an interesting background. In the process of getting his education and learning the engineering bus-

154

iness, he traveled to Europe, South America, and many parts of the United States. While he is extremely opinionated on certain topics and politically is an ultra-conservative, his faculty for picturesque speech and use of hyperbole to make a point keep the conversation lively.

Even though Ken was born and raised in Nashville his zeal for promoting Tampa can be illustrated by an incident he recounted during the evening. It seems he was sitting on the patio of his home which overlooks Tampa Bay one Sunday afternoon contemplating the lawn before him and the ripples on the bay beyond it. Turning to Mia he volunteered, "If by some quirk of destiny at death I'm elected to enter the Pearly Gates, God had better be up there cutting the grass, edging the lawns and trimming the shrubbery if He is to convince me I will have it any better in heaven than I now have it here in Tampa."

On Sunday morning Tom, Mort, Plano Valdes (the man I hired from the University of South Florida's Upward Bound Program) and I interviewed teaching candidates at the motel. I was surprised to run into Howard Sinsley on his way to talk to Tom Mastin about a job as registrar. While I think that we will hire him, I am first going to call John Allen, president of the University, to make sure that he does not get peeved about our hiring a member of his administrative staff.

In the afternoon we interviewed Yvonne Pierce, the attractive librarian I told you about earlier. This time I didn't blush when I talked with her because Jeanny was in the motel room with us. All of us were very much impressed by the depth of her knowledge of instructional aids. She was even conversant with the audio-tutorial technique of individualized instruction.

In the audio-tutorial method the student uses a study carrel as his lecture hall and laboratory combined. He receives instruction from written materials, tape recorders, 8-mm film loops, slide projectors, and any other lab equipment which the instructor has provided and is able to progress at his own rate, replaying the material as many times as he needs to understand the basic concepts. When he thinks he is ready to move to another section, he is given an oral quiz by the tutor who is stationed in the room. If

155

he successfully passes the oral quiz, he then takes a written exam. This arrangement works very well for the bright student, who progresses faster than the normal pace expected in a classroom, as well as for the slow student, who may repeat the material many times.

It's interesting how you learn to size up an instructor by asking a few very pointed questions. A woman I interviewed for a position as instructor of English let me know that she was not particularly up-to-date in her field when she did not know anything about transformational grammar. I'll have to admit I know very little about it myself, but at least I'm familiar with the term. I would expect an instructor in English to be highly conversant with the concept.

After finishing the interviews we took time for a mid-afternoon swim in the pool. As I relaxed at poolside with the sports page of the *Sunday Tribune* I was surprised to see my picture and an accompanying editorial. Then I remembered that last week I had answered a letter from the sports editor asking whether Hillsborough Junior College would have intercollegiate athletics this fall and just what kind of a program we would have in the future. I never dreamed he would print my response. Further, I was unaware that there had been a running battle between the sports editor and the University of South Florida over the university's failure to support intercollegiate football. So, in spite of my naiveté, I gave a straightforward answer.

I told him that at this time I am much more interested in getting a teaching staff and an academic program organized than in becoming involved with intercollegiate athletics. I also said I saw no reason why a junior college should maintain an intercollegiate sports program for the entertainment of the sports fans in the area. I would like to see a sports program developed which will serve the interests and the needs of the student body rather than spread the name of the college throughout the land.

The editorial implied it is the sports fans who give the financial support to colleges. Perhaps this is true at least in part in privately-endowed colleges that need to publicize their schools nation-wide in order to attract students and contributions. However, in a public-supported junior college, especially where there are more students than can be easily handled, I believe intercollegiate athletics should be an outgrowth of a strong intramural program. In other words, the sports activities should be developed around intramural teams, the best of which would represent the college in intercollegiate contests. While this is the goal of many college administrators, few have been successful in keeping excessive pressures from developing in the area of athletics.

I had better close now as we are letting down through the clouds near St. Louis. When Jeanny called the kids on Saturday, they said that it had been raining for several days. Steve is scheduled to be home tomorrow, so we are looking forward to a family reunion. We will keep you briefed as to the latest developments.

Regards to all.

Bill

St. Louis
Friday
June 7, 1968

Dear Fisher:

Well, it happened again. The school board failed to approve our use of Tampa Catholic High School. Apparently they thought it was improper to pay rent to a private school system. One of the board members said he saw no reason why the $150,000 rent shouldn't feed back into the public school system. Anyway, the topic was tabled until we could provide them with an exact cost estimate of what it would take to duplicate the Tampa Catholic facilities on the Hillsborough High School site. They gave us a week to do it, but with me in St. Louis, it's going to be difficult to get the information.

At this point I'm completely frustrated. I suppose we could wait until after July 1 and negotiate the contract with the Catholic school on our own, but that might be considered an affront to our sponsoring board. Besides, they might refuse to allow us to budget money to pay for the facility. I really don't think they would do it; on the other hand, I didn't think they would veto our use of Leto High School either.

Last week I was similarly disappointed when Dr. Shelton told me he thought it was out of the question to assume the school board would provide money to purchase a site for our initial campus. He said that he had been talking with the board, and they indicated they simply did not have the money to spare. And the new junior college law makes absolutely no provision for monies to purchase college sites. There is money authorized for buildings and equipment, but it is assumed the local county school board will provide at least the first site. Shelton said he would try to find a way the school board could get the money without hurting the local schools.

Therefore, to answer your question about construction of a campus, we are in a state of limbo. The legislature has authorized sale of bonds which will give us $1,600,000 for initial construction, but we cannot use any of the money to purchase a site. Stupid, isn't it? I don't know how we will solve the problem, but I wish I could devote more time even to thinking about it. It is a tremendous disadvantage to have to be engrossed in the immediate problems associated with opening classes in September when I should be spending my energy working on long-range problems. However, I will simply have to take first things first and do the best I can.

Ken graduated from high school last night along with 600 other Kirkwood seniors. Jeanny, Robin and I sat in the audience on the football field, Steve came late with Debbie (the girl next door), and Dave dropped by after his music lesson. The ceremony was typical of high school graduations all over the country, with three top students making the addresses.

Admittedly, I was more impressed with the students than I was with the parents in the audience. As a main theme the youngsters emphasized that today's generation has different values than their parents and that today's hippie might be tomorrow's President.

The parents appeared to be listening and applauded enthusiastically after the speeches. Then, as the graduates strolled across the stage to the monotonous droning of the principal reading all 600 names, the audience reaction was interesting. Whenever one of the star athletes was announced, there was scattered applause. However, when Ken with his long, curly locks brushing his shoulders arose to accept his diploma, you should have heard the cat calls from the adults.

As a parent, I suppose I was at first embarrassed; then I began to get hot under the collar. Finally, when a woman sitting directly behind me said in a quite audible tone, "I'll bet he wears lace on his undershorts!" I could stand it no longer. I turned around and informed her that he is really a pretty nice boy. I should have added that he lettered in basketball and in baseball at Kirkwood High School and with the money he earns from his band, he puts almost as much in the bank every week as I made for salary when he was born. It's too bad that those of us in the older generation cannot accept people for what they are rather than for what they appear to be. But I suppose that's the way it is and always will be.

Ken and one of the fellows in his band are leaving for California tomorrow for a week's vacation. I suppose you will have seen him before you receive this letter. He plans to return the middle of next week to take two courses this summer at Meramec Community College here in St. Louis. He is rather confused and doesn't know what to major in next fall, so he thought it might be interesting to take two courses this summer just to see what college is like.

I'm afraid he will be in for a disappointment because, unfortunately, most college instruction is not as stimulating as it could be. We do have some instructors who make their subjects exciting and pertinent for the students. In fact, this is the type of instructor we attempt to recruit. However, many of the teachers we get are so enamored by the university image of the professor that they gear the level of instruction to be respectably dull.

I spend a great deal of my time trying to challenge our instructors and get them to make their courses functional and relevant to the student's needs. However, after a year and a half of attempting to accomplish this in my subject field, music, I finally

159

gave up in despair this last week. I was asked to approve a course outline for an advanced music theory course which contained such exciting topic headings as the German Sixth, the Neopolitan Sixth, the Enharmonic Chord and so forth. I had hoped that this material could be included in a course in such a manner that a student could immediately see the practical use and application of these techniques. For example, a church organist who must modulate smoothly from a hymn into an anthem to be sung by the choir could make very good use of enharmonic chords. However, most college students sitting down to study enharmonic chords are hard-pressed to see this very practical application.

Steve got home last Tuesday morning after driving straight through from Ft. Bliss, Texas. He doesn't have much to say about where he is going (other than to Europe) or what he is going to be doing when he gets there (other than something in the field of ordnance). I must say that I do see small signs of his growing up. He is much less defensive and appears to be trying less eagerly to prove himself to be an adult. Kids should realize that they prove they are adults much more by their everyday actions than by their overt attempts to be "adult-like." He has had several dates with Debbie, whom he used to date when he was living at home. They seem to enjoy each other's company, and I have a feeling they may be more serious than Debbie's mother would like to believe. He has worked several days for the moving company for which he used to work. Since we are employing this firm to move us to Florida, we hope that Steve will be able to make the trip at no cost to him. He is trying to save money so that when he gets to Europe he will be able to buy a car and have transportation to see the sights.

After Ken Hardcastle called to tell me that the school board had postponed its decision on the approval of Tampa Catholic High School, I called McGuffey to see what suggestions he had. During our discussion, he agreed to go down next Monday and make a detailed analysis of the cost requirements for putting Hillsborough High School in satisfactory condition for our use. Actually, if they were to remodel all of the science labs and allow us to build approximately 6,000 square feet of prefabricated buildings on the faculty parking lot, we could make very good use of the school. After all, antiquated classrooms have little to do with the quality of instruction which goes on inside. To be sure, visual aids are important in today's pedagogy, but portable equipment can be used if the teacher wants to make instruction stimulating.

I had better close now because there are a hundred and one things yet to do before I phase out here in St. Louis and get the family moved to Florida. I'll try to keep you posted as to our activities when I get the opportunity. Give our regards to all the family.

Bill

Saturday
June 15, 1968

Dear Fisher:

I am writing this letter in a motel in Granada, Mississippi. We arrived about 6:30 last night after the usual frantic time one has in transit during a move. I will report for work day after tomorrow on the 17th. While my contract in St. Louis runs through June 30, technically I will be on vacation the last two weeks of the month.

For the past two weeks Jeanny has tried frantically to sell all the surplus furniture and appliances we accumulated while living in our six-bedroom home. She managed to sell everything except the washing machine.

The packers arrived Wednesday morning and spent two days putting our belongings in boxes. They reminded me of a huge vacuum cleaner scooping up everything in sight. Fortunately, Jeanny was able to salvage a couple of pairs of shorts and a pair of socks for me to wear until our belongings arrive in Florida. But we had to go out and buy some casual clothes for me because all of mine were packed, and I hated the thought of spending five days in one suit.

Jeanny casually mentioned to the woman who was packing the dishes that we also had an airplane that needed to be packed.

161

The woman calmly replied that they had some fairly good size boxes and that she could pack paper around it as long as the wing span was not more than eighteen to twenty inches. You should have seen the look on her face when Jeanny informed her that the wing span was twenty feet, not twenty inches. She refused to believe that we had a real airplane until she saw it for herself. She did a fine job of crating it by using boxes designed for large portraits which she slipped over the wing panels. If I'm lucky, it will arrive in Florida without a scratch. If not, an insurance adjustment won't be much help in replacing it.

The van was supposed to arrive at eight o'clock on Friday morning so the loading process could begin. Of course, it did not show until 1 p.m., which meant Jeanny could not supervise the last portion of loading because we had to go to the college graduation ceremony in the evening. On the way home (or perhaps I should say on the way home back to the Wagners', our friends who offered us lodging our last two nights in St. Louis), we went by the house to see how the loading had progressed. There were the usual foul-ups. Several boxes had not been loaded and many of the things we had anticipated leaving had been packed in the van.

I had sold Robin's swing set to the man who purchased the house. Of course, the swing set was in the backyard half disassembled with nuts and bolts lying all over the ground. Apparently an eager employee of the moving company had gotten it half ready for shipment before he received word that it was to stay. This morning we were up bright and early so we could get a good start and drive at least 500 miles. Of course, Steve informed us a belt that turns the generator on the Buick station wagon had broken while he was driving the car the night before. So I took the car to a filling station. Before I was through, we had replaced two engine mounts and the water pump. I had a tremendous urge just to walk away and leave it. I really should have sold it while I was in the mood. Anyway, about 11:30 we got on the road and drove 400 miles today.

Only Steve, Jeanny, Robin, Boots and I made the trip. At the last minute Dave had the chance to spend a month with one of his friends in St. Louis. He will fly down some time in July. We

162

managed to pack all of our belongings in the trunk of the small Buick so the five of us have two automobiles completely cleared for passenger comfort. Steve, Robin and Boots rode in the big station wagon while Jeanny and I brought up the rear in the coupe. All day long we watched the three heads bobbing in the car in front of us. Boots decided he liked the seat right in front of the air-conditioner so that he could stick his nose into the cold air stream. These modern dogs! When I was a kid, my dog used to like to stick his nose out of the window. Not Boots though; he's a swinger all the way.

My last two weeks as a lame duck were extremely frustrating. Under the circumstances, I was not in a position to implement new ideas, only to bring to fruition some of the projects which had been previously started.

The rumors concerning the appointment of my successor have run rampant. I told you that Ray Pietak, our dean of instruction, had applied for several presidencies around the country. Yet, because he is young and relatively inexperienced, none of us gave it much thought. Last Monday, however, he got a firm offer from a junior college in southern Michigan and has asked to be released immediately from his contract. Now the troops are really shaken! Dr. Cosand has assured him that he will try to release him early in July, when a suitable replacement has been found. It may be difficult to justify to the board the release of two key administrators from a campus at the same time. Someone may get the idea that we are dispensable.

During the last few days of school, the faculty were busy suggesting theme songs for the administrators. One suggestion for Pietak was "Let Me Go, Let Me Go, Let Me Go." Because my replacement has not yet been announced, his song was "You'll Never Know." My tune was to be "Please Don't Talk About Me When I'm Gone."

Dr. Snead's appointment as my replacement was to have been announced this past Monday. However, because it is common knowledge that the faculty's choice for the position was Bill Moore, a Negro, there was concern that sections of the community might be aroused because of the selection of a Caucasian for the position. During the past few weeks there have been pressures from the NAACP and other community organizations to promote a Negro to the position.

Incidentally, I am trying to get used to using the term "black" instead of "Negro." I have always been taught that the terms "black" and "nigger" are derogatory, while "Negro" is acceptable. Now, however, much of the dark-skin segment of the community prefers the term "black" to "Negro." They claim that "Negro" is a misnomer. It has its roots in the Spanish language and they feel that we should use the English translation "black."

Nationwide pressures from the black community are becoming quite strong. John Dunn, president of the Peralta District in Oakland, California, hopes to select a black president at Merritt College. Ed Ruddy, dean of students on our campus, visited the Peralta District for three days this past week where he talked with the administrators, faculty and students at Merritt College, which now has a majority of black students. In his opinion, the black activities are in complete control of the student government and the student newspaper. One of the student leaders felt very strongly that there should be a separate student union building for black students. It is interesting that this philosophy is diametrically opposed to what we have been planning at Forest Park. We favor an integrated campus, yet apparently many of the black students would like to return to segregated status.

At Merritt the students have demanded and received special courses designed around their interests and their backgrounds. Merritt's black curriculum goes beyond the usual course in black literature to include structured English composition courses which are restricted to black students. These students do not wish any penalty grades to be issued. They maintain that, because of their weak academic backgrounds for which the white community is responsible, they should not be forced to compete on an equal basis with white students. The student who cannot earn at least a "C," they argue, should have the option of withdrawing from the course with no penalty. By repeating the course several times, the student would gradually bring his background up to the level of the white students.

164

To illustrate what can be done under the extreme pressure from black activists, in California, where the credentialing laws are very rigid and cumbersome, teachers were certified to teach Swahili as a foreign language in four days time.

Last week Percy Green, a black activist leader in St. Louis, was a guest speaker in one of the seminars arranged for our teaching staff. He claims a person from black stock is superior to those of us who are white. As he explained it, most of the Caucasians who came to this country were from persecuted minority groups and were running away from trouble in Europe or were criminals attempting to escape punishment. The African slaves, on the other hand, were from selected stock. The fact that only the hardiest were able to survive the trip means that the black man, who descended from this select stock, is superior to today's Caucasian.

Another problem in establishing courses which are satisfactory to the black students is proper selection of instructors. Just because an instructor's face is black is no reason to believe that he is best qualified to teach a course in the black curriculum. Ironically, many Negro instructors who have themselves escaped from the ghetto very often have little empathy for the students who are still entrapped. They take the position that hard work and dedication will enable any person to pull himself up by his own boot straps. Some black students identify this type of individual as being physically black but constitutionally white.

By comparison it is much more difficult to locate highly qualified Negro instructors than white instructors. Further, I have refused to compromise quality of preparation just to have another Negro on the staff. Even though only fifteen percent of the population of Hillsborough County is black, I certainly hope to be able to find capable Negro instructors so that we will have a balanced faculty.

Last Sunday afternoon, Mort Shanberg flew to St. Louis from Chicago so we could spend the day working on the calendar and preliminary curriculum details for the new college. Not knowing where our physical facilities will be located, we spent less time

165

on the curriculum and class schedule than on devising an academic calendar which would allow easy articulation with the senior institutions in the state. Since all of the universities have slightly different calendar patterns, Mort and I felt it most logical for us to coordinate closely with the University of South Florida. After all, it is the largest public university in the area, and we can assume that most of our students will transfer there.

Unfortunately, because they prefer that junior college students transfer at the beginning of their junior year, most universities feel it inconsequential whether or not their calendar coordinates with that of the junior college. My experience has shown, however, that large numbers of our students, especially those who work at full or part-time jobs while attending college, complete all of their requirements for graduation in the middle of an academic year. I would like for these students to be able to transfer immediately to the university. I'm not particularly interested in encouraging students to attend our college for one or two terms and then go on to the university, but those who have spent more than two years with the junior college certainly should be able to transfer in the middle of the year.

My last official act with the Junior College District in St. Louis was to present diplomas to the graduates from Forest Park Community College. The ceremony took place in Kiel Auditorium jointly with the other two colleges in the district.

The featured speaker was Dr. Sharvy Umbeck, president of Knox College in Illinois since 1949 and current chairman of the American Council on Education. A delightful speaker with a fine sense of humor, Dr. Umbeck commented that there were hundreds of commencement exercises in process that same evening and that if each one of the commencement speakers were laid end to end, it probably would be a good idea! He further commented that, as a student, he had participated in five commencement exercises and had to confess that he couldn't remember the contents of any of the speeches that he had heard. As a parent, he said he had heard three other addresses which had little impact on his view of the world. He said he preferred to talk about a topic which interested him, even though it might

166

not interest the students. I'll have to admit that his remarks were very interesting to me as an educator and as a fellow college president, but I did not think that they were too relevant to the graduating class or the parents in the audience.

He believes that the university is out of touch with reality and has undergone little change during the past 100 years. Since 1862 when the Morrill Act brought a radical change in the curriculum, there has been little change in the techniques of teaching students. He recalled the old cliché that "a lecture is the method whereby the information on the notebook of the professor reaches the notebook of the student without going through the minds of either." He called for more efficiency in the classroom and more overall production from the teaching profession. (Referring to faculty salaries, he stated that production nationally had increased 4½ percent per year compounded in industry, yet we are still handling college classes in much the same manner that was done 50 to 100 years ago.)

Defining a small class as mediocrity passed on in an intimate setting, he challenged higher education to involve itself in product research in order to determine what the optimum size of a class should be and the optimum number of subjects that could be taken by a student. I'm afraid I have to agree wholeheartedly that we in higher education have spent a great deal of time on the psychology of learning but have made little effort to apply it to classroom situations. Dr. Umbeck feels that we are now in a period of folk education and must begin to utilize scientific data to increase our productivity

On the question of unionism in the teaching profession Dr. Umbeck had some interesting comments. He said he felt it was a mistake for teachers to forego their professional status by tying so closely with the union movement, as they had done in southern Michigan, New York and California. (Although it was not directly associated with the American Federation of Teachers, the Florida teacher walkout this spring utilized the union technique of a strike.) Under unionism, recognition based on merit is not supported. Dr. Umbeck believes it is a mistake for the teaching profession to reject quality of workmanship as a criterion for finan-

167

cial reward. He laments that professional educators place loyalty to their academic disciplines above loyalty to individual colleges. He closed his address with a plea to educators to reconsider their basic objectives rather than attempt to do more and more of the same a little better.

It is interesting that with over 10,000 students, we had fewer than 400 graduates. There are several reasons why junior colleges do not graduate the same proportion of students that the four-year universities do. In the first place, an associate degree is rather meaningless to those students who plan on two more years to obtain bachelor's degrees. Therefore, many students who are certain that they will be able to complete the four-year degree do not even bother to meet the requirements for the associate degree. Some junior colleges cope with the problem by asserting that the student qualifies for the associate degree if he has met the standards for junior standing at a four-year college.

On the other hand, those students who have completed career programs value their associate degrees very highly. For them this marks a real milestone in their careers because it specifically qualifies them for employment at a higher level than they would be able to obtain otherwise. So among our 350 graduates were a large number of dental assistants and clerk-typists who completed a one-year program.

I'm sorry to admit that I know personally very few of the graduates. I was feeling rather bad that I had been remiss in not getting acquainted with more of the young people when Glynn Clark, president of the Meramec Campus, confessed that several of the students had called him Dr. Graham or Dr. Carson. It seems that the majority of the graduates don't know him either.

During the ceremony I suddenly realized that I have never sat with the faculty at a graduation exercise. When I was a professor at East Stroudsburg State College, I directed the choir and thus had a place on the stage where, as an administrator, I have sat ever since.

Jim Kneebone did an excellent job with the Forest Park chorus. I sympathize with him because I know the problems he must have

168

faced. Of the fifty students in the chorus only three or four graduated. The rest Jim had to ask to perform a full week after the term was over. As a choir director, I always had my fingers crossed when it came time for us to perform for the graduation exercises because I never knew how many tenors or basses would show up. It usually is personal loyalty to the conductor that makes a student take off from a summer job to sing for an audience of rather unenthusiastic parents, faculty, administrators, and graduates.

While our chorus did an excellent job, I have a feeling that because of Kneebone's enthusiasm some of students may have been exploited this past year. You will recall that when I was an instructor at Pasadena City College some fifteen years ago, I objected vehemently to the exploitation of students in the music department there. Too often, in order to satisfy the expectation of "the establishment," little regard was given to the welfare of the students who participated in the musical organizations. During that period the Bulldog Band had cut its outside performance schedule to thirty-five during the year, and we were severely criticized by the administration because we were not giving the nity what they had come to expect. I don't believe that athletic teams should be fostered for the entertainment of the sports fans in the community, and I'm going to continue to resist community pressures to exploit students in any field.

I must close now because we have a hard day's drive ahead of us, and I know the next week will be frantic trying to get settled in our new home. But this should be the start of a new chapter in our lives.

Love to all the family,
Bill

CHAPTER IV

Full Time — South Campus

Tampa
June 24, 1968

Dear Fisher:

Well, we have been permanent Tampa residents for one full week. Although the weather has been warm and humid, I admit I don't find it as objectionable as the hot "dogdays" we used to have in St. Louis.

Our trip from St. Louis to Tampa took us through Mississippi, Mobile and down through the Panhandle of Florida. Somehow we took the wrong turn and drove quite a bit out of our way along the Gulf and through Panama City. It was a delightful drive. At least we enjoyed looking at the emerald water and snow-white beaches even if we did not delight in crawling along at twenty miles per hour in the Sunday afternoon traffic.

We arrived in Tampa about 3:30 Monday morning. Even though I managed to get to work about 8:30, I'm afraid my first day as a full-time employee of Hillsborough Junior College found me a little bleary-eyed. The vast number of visitors who dropped by to pay their respects didn't alleviate my condition, either. This is the beginning of the vacation for classroom teachers, as you are probably aware, and many of them have used the opportunity to visit Florida. While they are in the area they seize the opportunity to drop by and see if there are any positions open for which they qualify. At this point I cannot afford to turn away qualified, experienced people, even those who are in town only temporarily. So I usually take the time to talk with them.

Betty Benson, my new secretary, made my first day complete by showing me two newspaper articles which had appeared over the weekend. Somehow the press obtained the portion of the McGuffey report concerning the master plan and site location for the various campuses. I knew that the Plant City people would

170

be extremely unhappy to find that, in McGuffey's opinion, theirs should be the fifth campus started. I didn't think, however, that this information would reach the general public before the final report was submitted to the advisory committee.

Upon checking the source of the leak, I found that Ken Hardcastle had in a way been tricked into giving the information to a reporter. Apparently the reporter called him to check on some rumors about the proposed site locations. Ken felt that because the rumors were close enough to the truth to be misleading if printed inaccurately, it would be better to have the truth printed in the paper. As I subsequently pointed out to him, however, had he simply refrained from making any comment at all, the unconfirmed rumor probably would never have been printed.

Right after lunch Ray Shelton dropped by to tell me he had just met with a group from Mayor Greco's office who wanted a commitment from the school board to purchase a site in Ybor City for a junior college campus. Ybor City, the former Latin community which is rapidly becoming a ghetto, is the focal point of a Model Cities planning grant administered by the Mayor's office. Apparently Mayor Greco did not know I was in town, so I was not invited to the presentation. In any case, the *Times* stated that a formal presentation would be made to the school board requesting that it purchase a thirty-three acre site for almost a half-million dollars. I decided I had better go to the board meeting and find out what was happening.

At the meeting Everett Prevatt, chairman of the board, invited me to sit on the platform. The first item was not even on the agenda but was announced as a presentation from the Mayor's office. I then listened for twenty minutes to reasons why the school board should purchase the site in Ybor City. It was argued that the college would qualify for extensive construction monies and special programs could be funded as part of the Model Cities operation. It was also implied that unless the college were placed in a redevelopment area, it would not qualify for Work-Study Program or National Defense Educational Act Funds. I could be wrong, but I assume as an urban junior college we will qualify for any of these funds, whether we're in a Model City demonstration

171

area or not. And we'll have use I'm sure for Economic Opportunity Act money which will enable us to create jobs for students and pay a very small amount of their wages out of local funds. In St. Louis our students found these loans, scholarships and jobs to be very helpful.

After the presentation Dick Elston, Mayor of Plant City and member of the junior college advisory committee, formally offered on behalf of the Plant City Chamber of Commerce either of two Plant City sites to the school board. One site would be financed by a city bond election while the other would be provided by the city.

After both presentations had been made, one of the members of the school board moved that both sites be tentatively accepted, pending approval by the junior college advisory committee. In the discussion which ensued, other members of the board went on record saying that they favored the Ybor City site.

Dr. Shelton then asked me to give my reaction to the proposal. I tried in as affable a way as I could to indicate that I would prefer not to ignore the forthcoming ACE report by committing ourselves to a site which we know is not located in any of the areas recommended by McGuffey. While it is possible to masterplan an educational program around any site, we should if possible look toward the future by projecting as far as a hundred years ahead. I therefore told them that before I recommended to the advisory committee that the site be accepted, I would like to consult with the county planning commission. Immediately chairman Prevatt asked what the reaction of the planning commission had been. The Model Cities group indicated they really had not discussed it in detail with the commission. Then, without further debate, the board voted unanimously to secure a loan for $430,000 to purchase the thirty-three acre site (and only that site) for the junior college if the advisory committee decides it wants it.

I appreciate the school board's desire to furnish a site for the junior college before July 1st, but I hope we aren't pressured into a hasty decision. I'm beginning to realize why the newsmen

172

smirked when I said I was looking forward to a challenge in Hillsborough County.

On Wednesday, with Mort Shanberg and Al Brown putting in a few days' work at the office before reporting full-time on July 1, I dropped by to get acquainted with Mayor Greco. He was very cordial and apologized for not including me in the preliminary planning before breaking the story on the Ybor City site offer. He explained that this was a last-minute attempt to develop the Model Cities application.

While I agree that the junior college in the Model City certainly would contribute greatly to the educational development of the area, I do not feel we should build a college anywhere just to help rebuild one segment of the City. The educational programs offered to a community should benefit all the people; if, coincidentally, the location of the bricks and mortar helps the overall development economically and culturally, so much the better.

By the time I could return to the office Al had unravelled the intricacies of the state financial regulations and Mort had put the finishing touches on our academic calendar and had proceeded with interviews of candidates for teaching positions. Both agreed to accompany the advisory committee, the school board chairman (Prevatt) and me on a tour of the facilities at Tampa Catholic and Hillsborough High Schools.

I received McGuffey's report from his one-day visit to Tampa last Monday just in time to estimate renovation costs necessary to make Hillsborough a viable interim facility for the junior college. Just before the scheduled advisory committee meeting following the tour we attempted to make an objective analysis of the relative merits and weaknesses of the two installations. Finally, we concluded it was not worth spending an extra $135,000 over a three-year period to use Tampa Catholic High School.

As you know, I have been apprehensive about our using Hillsborough High School. However, Shelton's staff offered to rebuild one chemistry, one physics, and two biology laboratories, to repaint the interior of the building, to give us forty parking spaces, and to allow us to locate temporary pre-fabricated administrative offices on the north side of the building. Under these circumstances we agreed to request Hillsborough High School for our temporary home.

I'm worried about the inadequate parking for our students, but perhaps the neighborhood residents will be understanding. At any rate, after this long delay I'm certainly relieved to have the interim facility problem settled.

On Friday morning we had our first official administrative staff meeting. I'm pleased with the staff of administrators we've been able to attract. Even the diversity in age of the deans seems quite logical. Al Brown is an old man like me, 46, while Shanberg at 37 is a balance between us and Tom Mastin, who at 32 I'm sure will be very popular with the students.

We agreed that it would be impossible to put out a printed class schedule before the first of August. Even though we now are reasonably sure the college will operate in Hillsborough High School, Mort thinks it will take till the middle of July to work out the details.

We're going through the agonizing process of getting located in our new home. None of the furniture seems to be the right color or the right dimension to fit the places we'd intended them to go. Jeanny would like to throw most of the things away and start over, but our budget won't allow it.

The moving van arrived with the furniture in reasonably good condition. The string bass had come unglued near the peg, but we think it was the heat rather than rough handling that caused the defect. The airplane had been stacked on top and appears to be no worse for the wear. I missed an opportunity to have some fun with the movers though. The fuselage was in pieces with the skins rolled up in packing boxes. I thought it would be fun to insist the fuselage was in one piece when I left St. Louis and that it was the moving company's responsibility to put it back in the same condition that they found it. I was going to show them my compressor, rivets and plans, and tell them not to leave until they had riveted it back together.

Yesterday the president of the local Experimental Aircraft Association chapter offered temporary storage for the airplane in a shop downtown. It took four trips in the station wagon to get all the pieces moved, but at least they're all safe from damage.

All in all we really like the house, and Robin is delighted with the neighborhood. There are at least half-a-dozen little girls her age to play with. Already she has been invited to swimming parties and has been taken on boat rides around the lake. While this is a lovely area in which to live I'm not certain it's the most ideal place to raise children. Even the dogs are strictly middle class. I am afraid I will be raising my daughter in snob-urbia.

Boots prefers Carrollwood many times over to St. Louis. Because the leash law is very loosely enforced he can come and go as he pleases. He also likes the ducks that frequent our back yard and lagoon area, and we all like to sit in the family room and eat breakfast while looking out across the lake.

Steve left Sunday morning for New Jersey on his way to Europe. He had a rather dull time here in Tampa. There are few young people in our immediate neighborhood, and we're not yet well enough acquainted to find a compatible companion for him during his brief stay. It's not very exciting to help Mom unload boxes of books and put up can openers. He and I did watch the local Class A baseball team play a double-header on Thursday evening, but he spent most of his time soaking up Florida sunshine.

On Sunday we went to the airport to see him off. Robin was quite upset, not so much that he was going away, but that she would have no brothers at home to love. During her entire lifetime she has always had at least one brother to tease and in return to be teased. Also, she has been able to pick up a little extra candy money by scratching the back of one of the boys. I believe her current rate is five cents for fifteen minutes.

It's Sunday night and right now I am exhausted. Jeanny and I thought we would do a little yard work this afternoon. We have an extremely thick St. Augustine grass lawn, which, fortified with a can of beer, I set about to mow with our old rotary mower. One trip around the front lawn and I was ready for another can of beer. Instead I talked Jeanny into taking a turn. She managed to get half way around before I took pity on her and tied a rope

175

to the front of the mower. While I pulled; she guided. Suddenly we became aware the neighbors were watching and having a hilarious time at our expense. I suppose it did paint a rather ludicrous picture of the president of the new junior college playing volga boatman while trying to bring his lawn up to Carrollwood standards. Well, at least I proved a college president is not afraid to pull his share of the load.

I'll close for now while I still have the energy to sign my name. Remember us to the rest of the family. We'll keep you posted as the Hillsborough Junior College story develops.

Bill

P.S. I just learned that Dr. Robert Harris from Michigan State University has been appointed President of Johnson County Community College. It may sound like sour grapes, but I think I made the right decision when I decided to come to Florida.

Sunday
June 30

Dear Fisher:

Summer is here, and we are thoroughly enjoying it. Each morning begins with clear blue sky and bright sunshine but by 11 streaks of clouds form which gradually thicken into late afternoon thunder showers and squalls. It's strange to see the lake in back of the house filling up inch by inch after each downburst. While the weather has been warm and humid there seems always to be a breeze to make it comfortable out of doors.

Now that Jeanny has things pretty well straightened in the house we've begun to enjoy our new ski boat. Robin is excited about learning to ski but is a bit apprehensive. Once she gains confidence I'm sure she'll have fun.

Progress this past week with the new college has been almost nil. Talk about frustration! On Monday the school board approved our use of Hillsborough High School and approved construction of prefab buildings on the campus. Then after spending three days drawing detailed floor plans for our offices and library,

176

we stumbled across a state regulation limiting the size of a pre-fabricated building to 1,000 square feet (the size of a classroom). If we comply with the law, rather than one large building we must build at least nine small "rabbit hutches!" In an elementary school separate buildings are functional, but why must we build our library as two or three separate buildings? It's expensive e-nough to staff for maximum student use when the books are all under one roof, but you can imagine the inefficiency in staffing three separate buildings.

I tried to call Lee Henderson in Tallahassee, but he was at a conference in Denver. I'm chafing at the delay. There are so many details to complete before we can occupy our buildings. First we must sketch floor plans and compute the square footage, then write specifications for competitive bidding. After we se-cure the approval of the state department we must advertise in the newspaper for three weeks, open the bids and get the approval of our trustees, then allow sixty to ninety days for construction. And we're trying to accomplish all of this in less than sixty days! There'd be no problem had we been able to settle on temporary facilities when McGuffey first made his study. Last April we had plenty of time to do the job right.

Everett Prevatt, chairman of the school board, came by the of-fice this morning to talk about the job as my assistant. We agreed on terms and he is to report for work on July 8. It will be great to have a person familiar with the community to assist with the details that keep me running morning, noon and night.

We're still trying to estimate our income for next year. We're supposed to submit a budget to the state department in July, but we don't know how much money to ask the local school board to contribute. They are supposed to match state funds using a for-mula which requires an accurate estimate of enrollment. If our projected figure is high, they will levy too much taxes (for which they could be subject to a taxpayers' suit). On the other hand, if we underestimate our enrollment, insufficient taxes will be col-lected and we won't be able to balance our budget. You can im-agine our confusion as we try to plan an educational program on an income which varies as much as 30% from to day while we

177

gaze into our crystal ball in search of next fall's enrollment figures.

This past week has confirmed my theory that in states with rigid regulations successful college officials tend to be cook-book administrators and creative connivers. If all decisions at Hillsborough Junior College were to be made according to the most rigid interpretation of Florida law, I have a feeling we would not be able to open the college on schedule.

Next week we plan to move into our new administrative offices in the unrenovated section of the Hillsboro Hotel. We eagerly accepted the offer of a suite of rooms at no cost to the college. While the owners have been very considerate, the lady manager has made it clear that as non-paying tenants we don't improve her profit-loss statement. I won't say her attitude is hostile, but Tom Mastin suggested we nominate her for "Miss Nasty, 1968."

We got a letter from Ken saying he successfully enrolled in Meramec Community College in St. Louis, taking courses in music theory and political science. He said he enjoyed his trip to California but was sorry he didn't get to Southern California to see the relatives. He and his buddy spent their time in San Francisco and Monterey listening to pop music groups.

Steve called us from New Jersey just prior to leaving for Europe. We'll send you his address as soon as we hear from him. As for Dave, we haven't heard from him since we left St. Louis two weeks ago. I suppose no news is good news, though.

Love to all,
Bill

Tampa
July 7, 1968

Dear Fisher:

The past week has been frantic. Mort Shanberg and Allen Brown reported for full-time duty Monday morning just as three members of Lee Henderson's staff arrived from Tallahassee to orrient us to the Florida way of doing things. In junior college circles we talk about the "enabling legislation" that gives us the right to operate a college. In Florida it should be called "disabling legislation!" I never knew there were so many things you can't do, but Tom Baker, Jim Strawbridge and Jerry Leonard enumerated them one by one. I realize the state department personnel serve a watch dog function, and I suppose this is proper. If the legislature directs through the statutes the way a college may be administered, somebody has to make sure the law is not circumvented intentionally or through ignorance. I must say, however, at times freedom to act independently would certainly make it easier to do the job well. And as an example, we've already lost ten percent of our lead time waiting for approval by the state department of plans for our pre-fab buildings. I hope we hear from them soon.

Tuesday was devoted to unravelling the complicated state accounting system. I sometimes wonder why we have local trustees when most of our transactions require the approval of the state department. For example, all budget transfers must be approved by Superintendent Christian's office. Technically, we can spend no money prior to the approval in August of next year's budget unless Mr. Christian concurs. However, Tom Baker suggested our board pass a resolution empowering me to make expenditures until the official budget is approved. Even so, I'm afraid we may have to hire a clerk just to handle the correspondence between the college and state department.

We are now settled in our administrative offices downtown in the Hillsboro Hotel. I have always looked forward to having a restroom adjoining my office. Because we're using hotel rooms every office has its own "executive john." I won't say that the plumbing is antiquated, but when I absentmindedly pull the chain to turn on the light, the toilet flushes. And as you would expect in hotel rooms the lighting is atrocious. We are trying to borrow floor lamps because I hate to buy desk lamps we won't need once we have our own facilities. It's frustrating to waste time on these inconsequential problems when there are so many things that need to be done before the college opens this fall.

179

The board meeting Wednesday afternoon was a fiasco. It dawned on us in the morning that the first official meeting of the board of trustees was an historic occasion. While I hastily tried to locate a circuit judge to administer the oath, my secretary, Betty Benson, called the media to make sure the news photographers were on hand. Naturally, there was no time to brief the board members as to what to expect. Sure enough, midst the grinding of the TV cameras and explosion of flash bulbs, the judge and Hardcastle mixed up the name of the college. It took three tries before they agreed Ken was to be a member of the board ,of trustees of Hillsborough Junior College. Finally, the entire board was sworn in, Hardcastle elected chairman and Jim Gray my vice-chairman. I'm sorry if any of the trustees were embarrassed; I can only blame it on our poor planning.

My recommendation of Everett Prevatt as assistant to the president created a tension which was obvious from the beginning of the meeting. I knew his appointment would cause comment in the community, but I thought I had taken the necessary precautions when I had asked Hardcastle to check on community reaction to Prevatt. But I neglected one small detail. I assumed Ken would also check with the other board members. However, he did just what I asked to do and no more. Therefore, Prevatt's name on the agenda came as a complete surprise to the other trustees.

On Wednesday morning I had given the editors of the two newspapers and the news director of WTVT the complete story including my reasons for recommending Prevatt. I assumed stories would be forthcoming after the board meeting. But wouldn't you know, the *Times* carried the story in the two o'clock edition. As a result, by the time the board met to discuss his appointment the story was already in the paper. I don't blame the board for resenting being asked to rubber stamp my recommendation; however, if they refused the appointment, Prevatt would be placed in a very awkward position. Therefore, I agreed in the future to send the agenda with background materials to the board on Monday before the meeting. If there are questions about personnel or other items which might need further study, the trustees can contact Hardcastle or me and, if necessary, the agenda can be revised before it becomes public.

The board suggested that Prevatt's title be changed from the assistant to the president to executive assistant. It never occurred to me that they, as well as the press, would assume that he was to be the number two man in the college. However, in higher education administrative assistants to presidents usually fall into one of two categories: the young, inexperienced educator who wants to learn college administration in a practical laboratory or the heir to the throne being groomed for the position. I carefully pointed out to the press and to the board that Prevatt's position is really an assistant to the whole administrative team where he will help with the detail work which has inundated us.

All in all, the media treated us well. They followed my suggestion and emphasized that the appointment was not politically oriented. The first telecast confirming the appointment included a taped interview on Channel 13. I'm enclosing a verbatim account of my conversation with Hugh Smith which Jeanny recorded for me.

July 3rd TV News Cast—Channel 13, 5:30 p.m.
RE: Everett Prevatt

Hugh Smith: The Board of Trustees of Hillsborough Junior College voted unanimously within the past hour and with only a minimum of discussion to hire Prevatt as the Executive Assistant to the college president, Dr. R. William Graham. Following Graham's recommendation, Prevatt, who will be paid $13,500 a year, is expected to submit his resignation soon to the County School Board. One of the reasons for hiring Prevatt is to give the college some identity with the community it serves since most of its top administrators now are from outside of Florida. President Graham also told me there was no pressure or power politics applied in his decision to hire Prevatt.

Dr. Graham: I was interested in a person with wide local contacts, local acquaintances, and a feeling of the pulse of the community. And you will have to admit that people in political cir-

181

cles certainly do acquire these skills. However, there was absolutely no pressure; I was approached by no one. This was simply a case of my looking for a key staff member who was knowledgeable about the local community. I think this is necessary if Hillsborough Junior College is going to be a college of the community and one that will reflect community needs. It's unfortunate in many respects that we have felt it necessary to go outside to fill the other administrative positions we have, and I felt it was very important that we find a qualified educator who could furnish this local contact for my staff.

Hugh Smith: Did Mr. Prevatt at any time approach you about this position?

Dr. Graham: No, not at all; I approached him.

Hugh Smith: The junior college has run into several obstacles in getting into operation, Dr. Graham. Would you say that one of Prevatt's first assignments will be to see that the college opens this fall?

Dr. Graham: I have had to spend a great deal of time on details because we've had no staff. I'm in hopes that his appointment will free me to spend time in the community getting acquainted with key persons during the summer.

Hugh Smith: But he would also be sort of a liaison between you and the state legislators?

Dr. Graham: Well, certainly he will help me get acquainted. I'm sure he will be able to speak for my office.

Hugh Smith: So he will possibly be representing you in legislative committees and this sort of thing.

Dr. Graham: Yes.

Hugh Smith: Dr. Graham added that Prevatt's teaching experience and the fact that he holds a master's degree in administration qualified him for the job. Also, at the college board of trustees meeting, a previously set ceiling of 750 students for the college was raised to at least 1,000.

We're still being needled by the press for holding closed meetings. I get a little irritated when the newspaper account includes a blow-by-blow description of how the press was asked to remain

182

outside of the meeting until we finished our private business. I don't see how I can work with the board if every discussion is open to the news media. Contrary to what the reporter implied, no decision was made in private. We discussed the ramifications of Prevatt's appointment, but frankly, I didn't know what the outcome would be until after the vote was taken in the public meeting. I believe we're on solid ground so long as we only discuss the pros and cons in private, then in the regular meeting each member votes according to his conscience. Our attorney also believes we can meet privately if no official action is taken. However, I have a feeling we will continue to wage a running battle with the press on the subject of open and closed meetings.

The day the newspaper announced we would hold classes at Hillsborough High School, Betty Benson got a phone call from an irate woman whose daughter now attends the school. She was upset that her little darling might have to share a locker with a college student. And under no circumstances did she want her daughter to have contact with one of those! I suppose she is afraid the student might keep dope or "pot" (which supposedly is available on college campuses) in the locker. At any rate, we assured her that our students would not use lockers.

The tropical rains we've had have raised the water level in the lagoon a foot or so since we moved in. And how the grass does grow! I bought a frontwheel drive mower which swings its two-bladed machete through the St. Augustine jungle. Boy, could I use one of your grandsons now.

Two workmen began yesterday to enclose the carport making it a garage. I'll be glad when they finish so I can move my airplane into it and start working again. While many garages in Carrollwood have boats inside, as yet I haven't seen any with an airplane.

I had better close now; give our love to the family.   Bill

Tampa
July 13, 1968
Dear Fisher:
We just got a letter from Steve telling us he landed safely in

Germany. He will be stationed in Wiesbaden to be trained as a cryptographer. As a father who is proud he's never been intoxicated, I was a little disappointed to learn his first act upon arriving in Germany was to get drunk on dark German beer. He says it really knocks you for a loop. I suppose we each must develop our own standards of conduct.

The college melodrama continues. On Monday, I interviewed several builders who claim they can construct relocatable metal buildings suitable for use as administrative offices. While talking with one of the salesmen, he asked if the high school were still in the class-one fire district. He said he has never been allowed to erect metal buildings in this area because even though the metal will not burn under intense heat, it loses its structural integrity and will collapse even sooner than a wooden building. Consequently, where there are older frame buildings, metal structures are prohibited.

Rather than ask the city building department for an answer, I went directly to the mayor's office. Greco didn't have the answer but told me he would find out whether the problem could be licked. I had my answer early Tuesday morning. Hillsborough High School is not in a fire district at all, but is an island surrounded by the class-one fire district. Therefore, our offices can be either wood or metal. How about that!

The telephone began to buzz late Wednesday evening after it was announced the school board's request for permission to purchase the Ybor City site for the junior college had been approved by the state department. The reporters were anxious to get my reaction. I told them I wasn't going to recommend acceptance of any site until we at least have had an opportunity to study the McGuffey report. Incidentally, McGuffey told me yesterday it will be another three weeks before the printer can finish the report. Gee, I wish we could get it sooner. I'd like to settle the site problem before it becomes an emotional issue.

Already the press appears to be stirring up a controversy. On Wednesday WTVT broadcast an editorial recommending that the college accept the Ybor City site. Then the first thing Thursday morning Hugh Smith called Hardcastle to see if he were interested in taping a rebuttal. Hardcastle advised him that when we have facts upon which to base an opinion, he will be happy to debate the issue with anyone. Until then, he said, he saw no reason to pit fantasy against fantasy. I concur wholeheartedly.

This afternoon's *Times* carried a lengthy article about the politicking supposedly taking place over the junior college site selection. I am enclosing the clipping; I'm sure you'll find it interesting reading at your leisure. Contrary to the newspaper's accusation I'm not aware of any political commitments made by the school board. Various other groups, however, have made concerted efforts to pressure the college trustees to build the campuses in Ybor City and Plant City. Somehow, I must convince both boards that we should have the best sites available rather than the most expedient.

Ken called from St. Louis to tell us he was doing very well with his studies. His music theory class is not exactly what he had anticipated but he's making an A. He made a C and an A on his first two tests in his government course.

One of the guitar players in the Belaeraphon Expedition has quit and Ken wanted Dave to take his place for the rest of the summer. Dave agreed with his mom and me, however, that he should probably come to Tampa right away. So we sent him a ticket, and Jeanny plans to meet him at the airport on Wednesday. It will be nice to have him with us again. Ken plans definitely now to attend the University of South Florida and will drive to Tampa after he has finished his band commitment.

Speaking of USF, I had lunch with president John Allen and his administrative staff last Tuesday. Tom Mastin went with me to discuss coordinating of our two calendars and establishing a continuing flow of students between the two colleges. In our informal chat before lunch, Allen certainly appeared anxious for the junior college to assume its appropriate place in the community.

After lunch Dr. Allen suggested I talk about HJC and the problems we face. When one of the deans asked where we were going to find our faculty, I suggested they might loan us a few of

Junior College Site Mired in Politics

Despite some rather clumsy attempts at concealing the fact, the new Hillsborough Junior College is knee-deep in politics. This could easily result in the institution's acquiring a black eye before it ever gets a foothold in the community.

The threat is being posed by the unorthodox manner in which the county school administration is offering the college its initial campus site.

The school board has negotiated a $430,200 loan with the Exchange National Bank of Tampa to purchase a 33-acre tract of land within the Urban Renewal section of Ybor City.

THIS TRACT is being actively promoted by Tampa Mayor Dick Greco. Several representatives he sent before the board last month easily got a commitment to buy the land for the college's first campus. A site for a second campus also is to be selected.

It's an "all or nothing" type of proposition.

If the site isn't acceptable to the college board of trustees, the loan will be voided. The school administration is proceeding as if the offer will fulfill its obligation to provide a site.

There have been no expressions by board members to the effect that an alternate site will be provided, if the Ybor site is ruled undesirable by the trustees.

IN FACT, just the opposite has taken place. The board has explicitly declared the loan can be used only in buying the Ybor tract.

The college trustees have not openly expressed an opinion on the proposition, since a formal offer has not been received.

The college president, Dr. R. William Graham, has refused to make a firm yes or no decision on the matter.

He's hinging it on the college's master plan, now being prepared by the Associated Consultants in Education Inc. of Tallahassee. The final report is to be delivered in about three weeks.

A preliminary report released by the consultants detailed five general areas where the college should be located, to best serve the community.

THE YBOR tract did not fall within any of the five areas.

The tract is bounded by Interstate 4 on the north, 21st and 22nd Streets on the east, Palm Avenue (to be built in the present area of Eighth Avenue) on the south and 18th Street on the west.

Graham said he wants to study the report in depth, and possibly make extensive revisions, before he starts worrying about where the first campus is to be located.

The college will open in September in temporary quarters, at Hillsborough High.

Observers of school board proceedings blinked with astonishment at the June 18 meeting over the haste in which the board used in providing the college a site.

Four or five representatives of Greco appeared before the board, armed with bulky reports and elaborate presentations. They voiced about 25 minutes of platitudes over how beneficial the Ybor site would be to the college, and vice versa.

(Continued

186

(Continued from Page 1)

THEN THE board promptly ordered School Supt. Raymond Shelton to start proceedings for a loan to buy the site.

The entire proceeding took place so smoothly, it almost appeared to have been rehearsed.

The matter undoubtedly was discussed at one, or more, of the board's frequent closed door meetings, at which the public is barred.

The ostensible reason expressed for the board deciding to buy the Ybor tract was because of a so-called July 1 deadline it was facing at the time.

On that date, the junior college became an independent entity, taken out of the school system's jurisdiction by a legislative act passed during the special session.

THIS WAS true for all of Florida's other 26 junior colleges now in operation. The Legislature apparently felt school boards had enough to worry about with the elementary and secondary schools without having to fret over higher education problems.

For this reason, the board quickly moved to provide the site.

It was possibly the first time ever that the Hillsborough school board has decided to acquire a site without detailed pre-planning.

The normal course of action is to obtain a recommendation from the State Department of Education school survey team on where an educational facility should be located.

Another routine step is to have the City-County Planning Commission study the entire county area to rule on where a multi-million dollar plant should be situated.

NEITHER WAS presented to the board at the open meeting. Possibly, either or both might have been offered at an earlier executive session.

The action further totally ignored the Tallahassee consultants' preliminary report and the obvious exclusion of Ybor City as a likely place for the college. The consultants, incidentally, were hired to plan the college's founding at a cost of $30,000. The contract has since been extended at an extra charge of several thousand dollars.

THE SCHOOL SYSTEM normally advertises it is interested in acquiring a school site within a particular area, and then invites offers from landowners. No such advertisement was published prior to the Ybor tract action.

At the same meeting, the school board assured a Plant City delegation that a second campus would be constructed in or near that East Hillsborough municipality. Plant City is to get a branch of the junior college, in temporary quarters, starting in the fall of 1969.

FOR A WHILE, Brandon waged an active campaign to get the second campus located within its area. The drive sputtered to a stop after Board Member Carl Carpenter of Plant City succeeded in nominating Plant City Mayor Dick Elston to the college advisory committee (which became the trustees on July 1) and the subsequent designation of Plant City for the second campus.

Another political overtone in the junior college picture is Graham's selection of Everett Prevatt as his executive assistant. Prevatt resigned as District 5 school board member and as board chairman to take the position.

Some quarters question Graham's choice. Although Prevatt is an experienced school teacher and holds a master's degree in administration, he is best known as a politician.

He waged an unsuccessful race for county tax collector in last spring's Democratic primary, and made numerous overtures toward running for school superintendent several years ago when the office was elective. It since has become an appointive post.

187

their professors on a part-time basis. I was promptly advised that their policy prohibited moonlighting. I then pointed out that of necessity two-thirds of our staff will teach on a part-time basis. If we hire only secondary school teachers, we'll soon be known as a "high school with ash trays." Upon reconsideration Dr. Allen and his staff agreed to "bend" the regulation enough to help us get the college underway.

On Wednesday Allen Brown took a tentative draft of our budget to Tallahassee and returned with the state department's solution to our temporary buildings problem. We may construct one large building if it's used only for faculty and administrative offices. But we will have to build two structures of less than one thousand square feet each for the library. Now we'll need two librarians instead of one. It just doesn't make sense, but that's the way the game is played.

Speaking of unrealistic regulations, I understand some of the Florida junior college presidents are upset at the number of square feet required for restroom facilities. In a public secondary school, since most of the students dash madly to the restroom between classes, many commodes and urinals are needed. State regulations for junior colleges are based on the same assumptions. However, in college most students are not confined to rigid schedules. Consequently, the restrooms tend to receive continued use throughout the day rather than maximum use at peak periods. As a result, Florida junior colleges are equipped to handle severe epidemics of dysentery without anyone having to stand in line. We've been trying to figure out how we can legally get around these regulations. Perhaps we should stack the urinals in order to get more of them in less space. We could even label them according to height; midget, normal, and basketball player.

Jeanny and I spent most of this week-end fighting the battle of the St. Augustine grass. Boy, how that stuff grows during the rainy season! It even covers up the sprinkler heads. Before I knew it I had decapitated two of them—one a full-blown, upright rain-bird!

I must buzz off now because the battery in my portable tape recorder is running out of juice. Give our love to the entire family.   Bill

188

Tampa
July 20, 1968

Dear Fisher:

I just got home and found that Jeanny and the kids have gone shopping, so I'll drop you a line. This morning Ken Hardcastle, Ben Higgins, director of buildings for county schools, and I flew in a twin-engine Apache to Boca Raton and North Miami to look at pre-fabricated buildings. The weather was beautiful and I certainly enjoyed flying over the east coast of Florida. It doesn't take long to discover that Florida is developed mainly along its coastlines.

We chartered an air taxi, but wouldn't you know, we can't pay the bill directly with college funds. Of course, we could have traveled by commercial airliner at far greater cost to the college and taken two days instead of one. I just don't understand this concept of efficiency. (I also don't know how we'll pay the bill!)

We're still trying to cut through the red tape delaying our pre-fabricated buildings. After looking at a number of products we decided the buildings manufactured under the trade name Panel-fab best suit our purpose. Now we have ten days to prepare specifications and advertise for bids. Then it will still take ninety days to construct the buildings. At best they won't be finished until November. In the meantime we plan to make do with additional house trailers on the parking lot. Because the library won't be operable for at least a month after school starts, we're trying to get a branch of the public library located across the street from the high school. While it is not the ideal solution, it would work for a while.

Last Wednesday the college trustees met for the second time this month. The meeting went much smoother than the previous one. There's no substitute for preparation, and all of us had done our homework this time. Al Brown conducted an hour-long work session on our proposed budget for next year. We plan to present the budget in a public meeting next week, then submit it to the school board for review prior to August 1. I'm not at all con-

189

cerned about the approval of our trustees, but I have no way to anticipate the reaction of the school board.

We're projecting a million-dollar budget for our first year of operation based on an anticipated enrollment of 1,000 FTE students (approximately 1,500 different bodies). To recruit that many students will require a Herculean effort, but we're going to try. It's unfortunate that the only way we can generate income is by enrolling students. It would make more sense to limit our enrollment to 500 students and use this year planning a five-year program, but if we do we won't be able to cover our fixed expenses.

I suggested to our board that we employ a public relations firm to assist us with the recruiting campaign. I think it will be money well spent because our overhead and administrative costs are the same regardless of the size of the student body; our only additional expense is the cost of part-time teachers at two-thirds of the normal rate. Therefore, for each additional full-time student we enroll we will net $750. It's not that we're greedy, but nothing helps to make a program successful like money.

While I suggested we hire a public relations consultant, I didn't want to recommend a specific firm. Therefore, the board appointed Ken Hardcastle, Jimmy Gray, and me as a subcommittee to make the decision. After considerable deliberation we selected a small advertising agency run by Bob Ensslin. He has only been in business for eighteen months, but on the basis of his first job he won top prizes in the Florida Advertising Association. He is an enthusiastic, talented young man who, I am sure, will be able to plan a campaign to attract students to the college this fall. While the newspapers have covered most of our activities, the emphasis has been on site selection rather than on fall opening. In the future I know we'll need a full-time employee to prepare news releases and lay out our brochures telling the HJC story. However, I have more confidence in Ensslin than in someone we could hire off the street. And we can't afford to make a mistake; the stakes are too high.

Mort Shanberg did a fine job at the board meeting explaining the educational advantages in our shortened term using semester

190

credits. (The *Tribune* article covering this part of the board meeting was the most positive reaction I've read since I have been in Tampa.) As soon as possible I want to establish procedures for year-round registration and open-ended instructional programs. Unfortunately, in an urban area many students attend college only if they have the money for fees at the time of registration. I don't see why we shouldn't accept money at any time for a course to be taken in the future. After all, what's wrong with a youngster walking in the office, announcing he won $21 in a crap game the night before, and asking to reserve an English course for next March?

Moreover, we know students have varying abilities and work at different rates. Yet, we insist that they all progress through a course at the same pace. I want to devise a system of individualized instruction where a student may work at his own rate and take all the time necessary to complete the course. We'll have problems with the administrative details, but I have some ideas. What would you think of a lease-purchase plan? That is, rather than registering to purchase credit for a course (as is the case in all colleges today), a student would lease the services of the college as they pertain to his course. He could make use of the facilities and library as well as an instructor. He would proceed at his own rate until at the end of the term he would elect either to accept credit and a grade or renew his lease and continue to work until he and his instructor have agreed he is ready to receive credit. After all, what is sacred about the twelve-week quarter or the eighteen-week semester? It should be the amount of learning or the skills acquired that qualify a student for credit in a course.

Last week I got a call from the Tampa Chamber of Commerce asking if I wanted an endorsement of the Ybor City site. Apparently, the Ybor Chamber is soliciting support. When the man wanted me to discuss the pros and cons of the site with the education committee, I politely declined to evaluate any specific site, but volunteered instead to discuss the criteria for site selection for junior colleges. (He in turn declined my offer.)

On the same day the Brandon Chamber agreed not to pressure the junior college to consider any sites until after the McGuffey report has been studied. Then on Thursday Jim Strawbridge called from the state department to tell me he had just talked with a *Tribune* reporter concerning our insistence on waiting to study the report before reacting to the Ybor City site. He is confident they'll print a favorable editorial in the near future.

We could certainly use some positive support. I still can't get used to sensational news reporting, even though we had a negative press in Ventura. We were fortunate in St. Louis to have the *Post*, which was more interested in objective reporting than in sensationalizing the news. Every few days the news account of HJC's activities includes a mention of the "political" appointment of Everett Prevatt. I guess I wasn't convincing when I talked to the editors.

Incidentally, Everett is doing an excellent job on the detail work I assign him. It is too early, however, to evaluate his overall effectiveness. At least he works hard and gets along well with the staff. I wish people would evaluate him on his ability rather than as an unsuccessful candidate for political office. His appointment will either be the best or the worst move I have made.

In his quiet manner Tom Mastin has gained the respect of the staff and the board. He'll have a new office next week when we move a forty-foot house trailer onto the parking lot at Hillsborough High School. It will be easier for students to locate the junior college there than on the second floor of the courthouse.

Tom bought a 21-foot sailing sloop the other day which is badly in need of repair. He has it docked in his back yard where he will begin renovation. I hope his six-month venture doesn't turn into the ten-year project my airplane has. The plane is still in storage downtown until the garage is completed. Hopefully it will soon move into its Samara Drive hangar.

Mort Shanberg moved into his house across the lake from us yesterday, and Allen Brown's wife flew down from Kansas City to spend the weekend selecting a home for their family. While Mort sold his home in Chicago almost immediately, Al has still not been able to make a deal on his.

Dave arrived in all his glory yesterday after two unsuccessful attempts at getting on the plane from St. Louis. Who says summer isn't the tourist season in Florida? We bought him a standby ticket and for two days in a row he was unable to get a seat. Finally, we procured a regular ticket so he wouldn't have to continue to sponge off his friends in St. Louis. It's nice to have him home, but he seems more interested in water-skiing than mowing the lawn.

We live about four houses from Allen Kempton who was last year's international water-ski champion and Carrollwood's local sports hero. He's Ken's age and I understand will attend St. Petersburg Junior College this fall. Last week he defended his title at Calloway Gardens in Pine Mountain, Georgia, but I haven't heard how he made out. We have enjoyed watching him practice on the lake.

Robin still hasn't mastered her new water skis. She doesn't like the splash of the water in her face as the boat pulls her up. But she is still working at it and one of these days she'll make it.

Jeanny enjoys the lake and her new Carrollwood friends. She and Frank Farmer's wife, Janis, swim daily before joining friends to play bridge. Jeanny visits most of her friends by boat rather than drive the car. She says it saves wear on the tires, but I think it's an excuse to use the new boat.

I'd better close for now. We enjoy getting your postcards, but would rather have a little more extensive news of the family. How are Al, Betty and the kids getting along?

Love to all,
Bill

P.S. I just got a letter and a news clipping from St. Louis. A Dr. Baxter has been appointed to replace Ray Pietak as Dean of Instruction at the Forest Park Campus. Dr. Snead must have decided he would be more comfortable with a dean selected from outside the college. The appointment will be a bitter pill for the ambitious junior administrators in St. Louis to swallow because they've been led to believe they've been trained in one of the outstanding junior college systems in the country. I understand the staff is quite upset—reactions ranging from bewilderment to anger.

193

Tampa
Saturday, July 29

Dear Fisher:

Will wonders never cease! The school board approved our budget the first time they saw it. In view of their reaction to our request to use Leto and Tampa Catholic High Schools, I was prepared to have it rejected at least once. So after receiving a favorable nod from our trustees on Wednesday, Al Brown and I went with temerity to beard the lion's den, the school board. For an hour and a half we answered questions. Interestingly enough, the junior college board had few comments because they don't have the experience to question the administration; but, more important, they hired us to run the college and are confident we can do it. On the other hand, the school board tried to evaluate our budget in terms of high school requirements. You'll recall I had the same problem in Blythe. At any rate, we were honest and admitted our estimated needs were based only on prior experience in other junior colleges.

At best, a budget is only an educated guess as to what the expenditures will be for the next year. And it's extremely difficult to be accurate when there is no history of past performance. Further, by state regulation we are restricted to two percent for contingencies. Even in an established college you can't guess with that accuracy. What actually happens is a small cushion is added to each category so the overall budget has sufficient surplus to cope with unforeseen requirements. I prefer a five to ten percent contingency so that I can insist that the staff plan realistically.

All in all, I was pleased with the general attitude of the school board. In most of the articles commenting on their hasty decision on the Ybor City site, the newspapers have depicted them as villians. I had the feeling the board members were trying to prove they wanted the college to succeed and were really good guys after all.

Well, my airplane is finally stored in our garage, packed in twelve boxes which I plan to leave intact until I have time to work on it again. I'm concerned about the excessive humidity

194

down here. It would be a shame if it were to corrode before it's finished.

As usual, Saturday morning was reserved to pay homage to our St. Augustine lawn. I didn't cut it this morning, but instead suggested Dave give it the treatment next Tuesday. I did, however, borrow an edger from Ray Shelton to trim around the fringes.

Oh yes, as I had hoped, the *Tribune* ran an editorial on Monday supporting our trustees and their position on the Ybor City site. I hope editor Clendenon's agreeing that it makes sense to study the problem thoroughly before taking action will take some of the pressure off our trustees. Also, on Tuesday a *Times* article quoted Mayor Greco as not being interested in applying political pressure to get acceptance of the site. And he certainly hasn't tried to badger me. Over a month ago he promised to take me on an inspection tour, but, as yet, has not contacted me. However, Don Taylor (model cities) and Tom Fox (urban renewal) let me know they were upset at the editorial's insinuation that there were political motivations behind the site offer. (I have a feeling one of our problems has been the newspapers' desire to sell copies.)

I reaffirmed to Fox and Taylor that I had an open mind and assured them that our board would consider all sites objectively. If I keep repeating this statement long enough, perhaps someone will begin to believe me. However, when Jeanny and Robin were at the pool at the country club this week, one of the women casually mentioned to Jeanny that she hoped the college would be located in a nice section of the county. Then Robin volunteered, "Well it won't be in Ybor City, because my daddy doesn't like it down there." I really don't know where she got that idea. Even ·at home I have emphasized that we must take an objective look at any site before it's accepted or rejected.

Because Friday was Betty Benson's (my secretary) birthday, our whole staff went to a restaurant for an extended lunch hour celebration. It was a nice gathering which served to ease the tension. She has quite a demanding job when you realize she must prepare the board agendas and take the minutes in addition to making detailed notes of all our staff meetings and keep the entire office organized. It bothers me that she sometimes has to work week-ends to stay on top of the job, but then we all put in long hours. I know eventually we'll have to hire an additional secretary to take care of the demands of my office, but I really hate to do it while we're so small.

The Wednesday board meeting went just as smoothly as the preceding one. We had a small group of visitors, mostly from Plant City. Horace Hancock, Alex Hull, and Frank Moody hardly ever miss a meeting.

As the weeks go by, I am more and more pleased with our trustees. I really don't believe that we could ask for a more devoted group of men. While Thompson, Harris and Elston are intensely interested, the leadership on the board comes from Hardcastle and Gray. I was apprehensive a few months back about the problems Hardcastle's conservative political background might cause. However, his educational views and business procedures are anything but conservative. And he wants to do the job right; last week he spent eighteen hours on junior college business for absolutely no remuneration and very little glory.

We are still trying to cut the number of architectural applicants down to a workable size before we start the final interviews. At our informal board meeting on Wednesday we asked each trustee to nominate his top choice from the list of eight previously selected. Gibbs Harris was on vacation so there were only four members present. And wouldn't you know, each one recommended a different architect. So we're going to ask each of the four to make second presentations to the board and administrative staff.

Later, in the informal session, I asked Crosby Few, our attorney, to discuss the "conflict of interest" clause in our policy statement. Last week, when I asked Hardcastle as board chairman to authorize deposit of our funds in the First National Bank, he wanted to know why we didn't open an account with the Marine Bank where Jimmy Gray is Executive Vice-President. "After all," as he put it, "the Marine Bank allows us free use of their board room; the least we can do is use their bank." It never occurred to him that there could be a conflict of interest. Crosby Few explained that while in this instance it would not be an illegal conflict of interest, it is generally considered unethical for public boards to do any sort of business with a board member or allow any member to profit through his membership on the board. Therefore, as much as we would like to reciprocate for the Marine Bank's generosity, we decided to use another bank.

Bob Ensslin, who will handle our student recruiting campaign, was at the meeting to report on our progress. It's too bad he couldn't have reported the reaction of eighteen representatives of the media at a meeting yesterday morning. There I explained the necessity for our attracting a maximum number of students and was pleased with the apparent desire to help. Ensslin offered to develop the radio scripts, TV film loops, copy for the outdoor board advertising, etc. if the media will use them as public service materials to promote the college. We will meet again next Friday to determine how far the media will go to assist us. I'll keep you posted.

Our offices in the Hillsboro Hotel are working out reasonably well. However, the rooms directly over our offices are being renovated. All day long pieces of lumber are thrown down a huge metal pipe made from steel culvert sections hung outside our window. When the wood drops from the upper floors it bangs back and forth on the trip to the ground. Sometimes the noise gets so loud you can't even hear the telephone ring. But, as I said before, the price is right—free.

On Wednesday morning Jeanny held a coffee for the administrators' wives and the wives of the board members. Al Brown's wife, Sally, was here from Kansas City, and Jeanny wanted the other wives to meet her. According to all accounts the affair was a success, even though Jeanny said the bakery cookies she bought were awful.

Dave is bored with life, but hasn't yet made an effort to get acquainted with the young people in the neighborhood. He seems to enjoy the boat but spends most of his time at the piano or with his guitar. I shouldn't get annoyed; it's difficult for a teenager to make new friends in the middle of the summer.

197

We haven't heard from Ken since Dave arrived. However, these were to be his busy weeks. He is taking finals in addition to working at the Lake of the Ozarks about 150 miles from St. Louis. We understand why he hasn't taken time to write.

My letter writing time has elapsed, so I must close now. Give our love to all the family.

Bill

P.S. I'm flattered by your suggestion that I use my letters to you to compile a book on junior colleges. Do you really think I have the talent? Perhaps if it were entitled *Sex and the Community College* with a book jacket featuring nude women posing in the library I'd have a best seller.

Tampa
August 3, 1968

Dear Fisher:

The pace I keep is wearing me out. Last night after dinner I lay down on the couch for a short nap; three hours later I got up, put on my pajamas and went to bed to sleep the clock around. When I awoke this morning Jeanny, Robin and I decided to explore the Gulf Coast and soak up some sun in the process. Right now we're sitting on the beach at Dunedin watching the seagulls between dips in the gulf. The sand is like granulated sugar, and you can see numerous varieties of fish in the surf. The sky is clear but on the horizon cumulus clouds forecast the usual afternoon showers. Before they arrive I want to relax and reflect on some of the happenings of the past week.

Because the oak trees around Hillsborough High School are covered with Spanish moss, we're concerned about the safety of our students returning to their parked cars late in the evening. I visit the Mayor on Monday to see if the city would provide additional street lighting for several blocks around the high school. He was cordial and said he would do whatever was necessary. Soon our conversation turned to the offer of the Ybor City site. He told me he had just explained to each of our trustees that

198

there were no political motives behind the offer. (Apparently the *Times* article upset quite a number of people.) At any rate, as we discussed the characteristics of a desirable college site, I casually mentioned it would be a shame if none of our campuses were located within the Tampa city limits. (McGuffey, in his preliminary report, recommended the first two campuses be built outside the city.) I want the Mayor to get so hungry for a junior college campus in Tampa that he will help us obtain an even more desirable site than the one now offered in Ybor City.

In the afternoon Bob Bondi, the new chairman of the school board, dropped by the office to sign our budget before it goes to Tallahassee. He claimed he's anxious to see good relations develop between the school board and the junior college trustees. He further contends the school board wants to provide a good site for the college. However, the newspaper account of the Tuesday night school board meeting quoted Bondi as saying the school board no longer has any responsibility whatsoever for the junior college. I certainly hope the news report wasn't accurate.

Yesterday afternoon I taped the *Insight* show for WTVT (the same telecast I did with Hugh and Cy Smith last spring). When we discussed the pros and cons of the Ybor City site, I was pressured into giving an unofficial opinion of its merits. Cy asked if I thought the site too small for a junior college. I explained that while smaller sites have been utilized in New York City, the cost to build on minimal space goes up markedly because of the increased expense of high rise construction. Further, because New York has good subway service, the parking problem is minimized. We could provide high rise parking facilities at a cost of $2,000 per car, but with cheaper land available, I wonder if it's a wise expenditure of public funds.

Insight is supposed to be broadcast tomorrow afternoon, but when I got home yesterday evening, there I was as big as life on the 5:30 news. At least five minutes of the interview was shown as part of the newcast. I suppose the double exposure won't hurt anything.

Our campaign to recruit students is underway. At our second meeting with the media Bob Ensslin reported that we have been

199

offered fifty-five free billboards, eight radio stations are willing to feature our public service announcements, personnel directors in several large businesses will post materials on their bulletin boards and will distribute information to their employees, every bank in the county will include a brochure with the September statements, and the three TV stations will air HJC film clips. We were disappointed the newspapers declined to donate any services. They assume their news coverage has given us all the publicity we need. However, if they had not devoted so many inches to our site problems, people wouldn't assume, as many do, that we won't offer classes until we have our own campus. At any rate, if we don't generate interest in the college, it won't be because we haven't tried.

Ensslin's association with the junior college made the news when a man from south Hillsborough county blasted the school board for spending $27,000 to hire a public relations firm. Personally, I thought it humorous. Not only was the dollar amount ridiculous, he even complained to the wrong board. Apparently our communications have been so poor he didn't even know there is a separate board of trustees for the junior college.

I suppose when you say public relations many people think of the professional speech writer and Madison Avenue image builder. Actually, every job we contract through Ensslin would have cost us money or staff time even if he had not been engaged. Few people would object to our publishing a catalog, printing stationery, and preparing public service announcements to be broadcast by the radio and TV stations, but the idea of a public institution hiring professionals to do the job sends some people into orbit.

We've been trying, with little success, to develop a workable floor plan for the temporary buildings at the high school. I have a hunch whatever is built we'll outgrow at twice the rate we anticipate. Even now we need two trailers on the parking lot to accommodate our student personnel services staff. There never seems to be enough room.

On Wednesday we interviewed two architectural firms interested in building the first campus. It was intriguing to compare

200

the two presentations. Because the architects had previously talked with our trustees while I was in St. Louis, I arranged for a special presentation to our staff prior to the board meeting. After about forty minutes the trustees joined us as the questioning continued.

The first architectural firm is a large organization with headquarters elsewhere but a rather large office in Tampa. While the architects admitted they had never built a junior college, they were confident it would be duck soup. When asked if they planned to employ a consultant with junior college construction experience, they said they didn't see why one was needed. I then explained that our trustees had deliberately hired an experienced president and administrative staff who had been involved in over fifty million dollars worth of junior college construction. Certainly we will provide educational leadership, but we also have a college to open in a few weeks. Therefore, we simply do not have the time to conduct a course for the architects in the philosophy of the junior college. We were all taken aback when the spokesman for the firm exclaimed how wonderful it was that the trustees had been able to select a president so soon; he further wondered when he'd have the opportunity to meet him. Hardcastle was rather embarrassed but informed him he was *now* talking to the president.

I really should have mentioned my title when I introduced myself to the architects. However, I thought they took a rather poor approach to a new client. If I were a partner in a firm being considered for a twelve-to fifteen-million dollar contract, I would certainly know who I was talking to. And the senior partner kept emphasizing that while their headquarters aren't located here, he lives in Tampa. It's hard to believe he could read the local papers and not know the junior college indeed has a president.

Speaking of Tampa residents not in touch with the local scene, last week when Jeanny attended a neighborhood coffee she was amused at the varying reactions of the ladies she met. Some fawned *ad nauseum* over the wife of the new junior college president while others had never heard of a junior college in Hills-

201

borough County. Jeanny really didn't mind because it gave her a chance to extol the merits of junior college education. As you know she gets just as enthusiastic as our professional staff.

When we interviewed the second group of architects we discovered they had a total staff of seven persons. If they get the job not only would they make extensive use of consultants, they would have to increase their staff appreciably. In St. Louis one of the campuses was designed by a very small firm which had difficulty meeting deadlines because the staff was overextended.

The spokesman for this firm proposed as a first step they travel across the country visiting junior colleges and taking prolific notes. No doubt it would be a worthwhile trip, but I wonder if this orientation to junior college construction problems will do the job. Knowledge gained by first-hand experience is of more value than that absorbed vicariously.

A large cumulus cloud just floated over the beach, and I can count nine birds soaring in the thermal under the cloud. Their graceful maneuvers remind me that I should be home working on my airplane. But what the heck, this is "living" of a different sort.

Our staff has concluded that putting a college together overnight isn't easy. It would be great if we brought only creative recommendations to the board, but often it's more practical to borrow from other junior colleges. In fact, Mort, in writing course descriptions for our fall offering, plagiarized half-a-dozen college catalogs. But why should we write original descriptions when we don't even have a faculty to help us decide what should be covered? Moreover, how many instructors include all the topics in an official course description anyway?

Dave appears to be happier now that 17-year-old Steve Erickson moved in down the street. Dave took it upon himself to greet the newcomer on behalf of the neighborhood. That's a laugh, isn't it; Dave's only lived here two weeks. Perhaps he knows what it's like to be lonely.

Last Sunday afternoon, Milton Jones from St. Petersburg Junior College (former St. Louis intern) and his wife, Barbara, drove over from Clearwater to barbecue steaks with us. It was pouring rain when they arrived, but in true Florida style it cleared up

202

completely in half an hour. We sat on the patio to watch the s.
boats on the lake, but Robin stole the show when she invited ht
new friends, Gertrude, Greta, Frank and Ingrid, four domestic-
type ducks, for a bread crust dinner.

Eventually Milt and I wound up talking shop. He said he was
concerned about their faculty's insistence upon extremely high
grading standards in all academic courses. I've heard from several professors at the University of South Florida that the St. Pete
J.C. graduates are excellent students. While I agree that our students should be well prepared for transfer to the university, I
don't believe excellence has to be insured at the expense of the
marginal student who, given a chance, might earn his bachelor's
degree.

Ken telephoned last weekend to tell us his job fell through at
the Lake of the Ozarks. Apparently after the first night, the manager decided he really wanted a "soul" band rather than the Brit-
ish rock style. Naturally Ken was disappointed because he was
counting on the money to get him through the rest of the summer. Also their band had turned down all job offers during this
three-week period. (The same thing happened to me several
times when I was Ken's age.)

Ken says he thinks he did well on his final exams. I hope he
decides to come to Florida soon; I know he'll enjoy it here.

I'd better close now as it is past lunch time and Jeanny wants to
get back to the house to see what Dave's plans are for the afternoon. We all send our love.

Bill

Tampa
Saturday
August 10, 1968

Dear Fisher:

Only thirty-four more work days until school opens, and there
is still so much to do. To date, we've received over 400 applica-

tions and actually registered almost a hundred. I'd feel much more confident if we had 700 applications, but considering we started our student recruiting so late and could tell the students so little about the college, it's truly remarkable to have the number we have. While applications are coming in from all over the county, the greatest concentration is from around Hillsborough High School. (It's interesting we have had no applications at all from Ybor City.) I'm curious to see just what kind of a student body we'll have when school opens. So far, the average age of our applicants is 23, with the range from 17 to 61.

Tom Mastin remarked the other day that among our Negro applicants he had noticed few from men. I'm not at all surprised, because it appears to be a national phenomenon. I recently read a study which claimed the Negro woman is more aggressive and has more ambition than the Negro male.

We spent the early part of last week putting the finishing touches on the plans for our prefab buildings. To make sure they are aesthetically pleasing we contacted Sam Malone, an interior decorator, who has a reputation for effective use of inexpensive materials to plan the appointments and select the colors. If we ask the faculty to teach full-time in the evening in an old high school building, we should at least provide offices which are as modern as the teaching methods we insist they use.

The word is getting around that we are about to embark on a building program. I've had several calls from architects in Chicago and New York asking if they could still be considered. Even though I have told each of them our board decided not to interview any additional architects, on Monday Bruce Dunsmore of Daniel, Mann, Johnson & Mendenhall called from California to let me know he had been talking with Watson & Company, a large engineering firm here in Tampa and one of our finalists, about proposing a joint venture for the college project. I met Bruce in Boston last winter at the AAJC convention where we discussed the Moorpark campus in Ventura, of which he had been project director, and the various other junior colleges DMJM designed.

Bruce wanted to know how I felt about a local architect associating with a national firm as master planners. With the many things we have to accomplish in a short time, it would lighten my load to work with an architect who has had experience designing junior colleges. The Harry Weese firm did a fine job on the Forest Park campus in St. Louis; however, the staff and I spent a great deal of time educating the architects as to the special needs of a junior college. There are many well-known firms such as Perkins & Will from Chicago or Caudell, Rowlette & Scott from Texas who have had this experience. While the campus should not be a carbon copy of another junior college, it's easier to teach a person who has a driver's license how to drive a semi-truck than to start from scratch with someone who has never driven a car on the highway.

I spent all day Wednesday in meetings with the staff and board. (In this business a callous on the derriere is an occupational hazard). We discussed Tom Mastin's proposed academic probation policy. Hopefully, our second-chance institution won't penalize a student who enrolls in a curriculum, does poorly, then wants to change. An engineering major who discovers he can't handle the math and physics courses should be allowed to complete a law enforcement curriculum without having to make straight A's to compensate for his poor engineering record. Therefore, we're proposing that the best 64 credits (C grade average) be counted toward graduation. After all, if the student makes respectable grades in a complete course of study, I see no reason to penalize him for previous mistakes.

While philosophically our position makes sense, no doubt devising a computerized system acceptable to the colleges to which our students will transfer may cause problems. However, I strongly believe the system must benefit the student rather than the student serving the system.

We adjourned our staff meeting at 3 o'clock to attend the board meeting across the street at the Marine Bank. When the meeting opened there must have been twenty-five visitors in the room, including photographers and TV cameramen. Obviously someone told the news media there was going to be a discussion of the Ybor City site. When we came to the section of the agenda entitled, "Petition From Citizens," Tom Fox from the Urban Renewal Agency and five others made brief presentations. A city engineer offered a written plan and sketch proposing two-story buildings which covered all but six of the thirty-three acre site. The remaining space was to be used for parking. He assumed 1600 parking spaces would be adequate for a college of 5,000 full-time students, whereas, nationally, architects are recommending one space for each full-time equivalent student. He didn't say where we should stack the remaining cars; perhaps he assumed a high rise parking structure, but if he did he forgot to mention it.

At any rate, Hardcastle assured the group the board would seriously consider Ybor City when we're ready to study sites. He further suggested they return with a more detailed proposal at some time in the future. Don Taylor, educational director for the Model Cities Program, asked if we planned to make a final decision within two months. I reminded the board that sixty days from now classes will begin. With all we have to accomplish in the interim I think it's unrealistic to assume we will have selected an architect and a site by then.

Thursday's *Tribune* reported the action of the board with the headline, "Ybor City Confab Fizzles." It's too bad we impressed our guests as being lukewarm, but until we study the other available sites with an architect's assistance I can't get excited about any site offer.

Well, the college finally has a logo. After considering many sketches, we finally returned to the one which Leon Anderson of the Forest Park art department and I designed early last May. It's not particularly unique, but we had to make a decision in order to use it in our advertising campaign. Mary Ann Corpin wrote a rather clever article for the *Tribune* describing our discussion at the board meeting. I hope you find it amusing.

On Friday Al Brown and I drove over to Polk Junior College at Winter Haven, about fifty miles east of Tampa. Several weeks ago President Fred Lenfesty invited me to visit him, but I couldn't get away. Their new campus, master-planned to handle 5,000 FTE students, only cost $15 a square foot compared to $25 to $30

'Lamp of Learning' Points Right

In the middle ages when it mattered, you could tell if someone was illegitimate by looking at his coat of arms. The insignia faced left.

So guess what happened when the Hillsborough Junior College board of directors saw the new HJC insignia — a lamp of learning — was designed to face left.

At the board meeting last week, chairman Kendrick Hardcastle took one look at the lamp and asked, "Can you flop it the other way?"

"It's a bar sinister."

"A what?" asked board member Ray Thompson, who was becoming perplexed by the whole tempest-about-a-teapot.

"Bar sinister," said Hardcastle. "It's either a bar sinister or a bar dexter."

He went on to explain the bar sinister, pointing left on the coat of arms, indicated illegitimacy. Legitimate? It faced right. (The terminology all comes from the Latin. Sinister evolved from the word meaning 'left,' dexter from 'right.')

The board members wanted to see what the mirror image would look like. Mrs. Betty Benson, secretary to HJC president Dr. R. William Graham, produced a compact.

Ensslin reflected the lamp in the mirror. Hardcastle peered over his shoulder, said all he could see was Ensslin's face, and moved the compact for a better look, Tom Mastin, dean of student personnel, tried it.

Hardcastle, known for his conservative leanings, came up with another reason for reversing the lamp: it could be interpreted that the college is looking to the left.

207

a square foot we spent in St. Louis. Before long, as we talked, I concluded that the problems in Florida junior colleges are not much different than the problems elsewhere.

I was interested in Lenfesty's reaction when I asked about teaching hardware such as responder units in the lecture halls. I don't think I told you about the ones we installed at Forest Park. There a student can press a button (a, b, c or d) on his desk in response to a multiple choice question projected on the screen. The results appear on the console in front of the instructor where lights or counters indicate the number of students answering the question correctly. Further, when the system is connected to a computer, the instructor can get a print-out showing the grade distribution, an item analysis of each question, etc.

Lenfesty said when he visited installations around the country where responders were installed he hadn't found the faculty making extensive use of them. He doesn't think it makes sense to install the equipment if the faculty won't use it. I agree wholeheartedly. However, I believe it's the responsibility of the president and his administrators to make sure faculty use new and effective teaching techniques.

Tuesday was Jeanny's birthday, so I took off work early for a celebration. I know she was relieved when I didn't suggest we fly to Rockford, Illinois, to the "fly-in" of the Experimental Aircraft Association. As you know, we usually celebrate her birthday by my ogling the home-built airplanes. This time we drove down the coast to Sarasota. We had intended to have dinner along the way but instead returned to Tampa to dine At Bern's Steak House. Bern's is not a two-bit steak joint, but a quality restaurant which compares favorably with Tony's in St. Louis. At any rate we enjoyed celebrating Jeanny's 39th for the ? time.

Sunday noon
August 11

I didn't get a chance to finish this letter yesterday, so I'll give it another try this afternoon. At 1:30 I want to watch a TV interview I taped Friday evening for WFLA (NBC). As on other panel shows, the interrogators on *News Conference* asked the usual questions to which I gave stock answers. The questions and comments covered our projected enrollment, my reaction toward student agitation, and even made reference to my "political" appointment of Everett Prevatt. I don't know what to do except to deny political maneuvering and assure people that Everett is not being groomed as the next president at HJC.

Gordon Alderman was particularly interested in the public's impression of Ybor City and expressed concern for the safety of our students if a campus is built there. I suppose he hit a sensitive nerve because I believe it's essential for us to create a respectable image of the college if we are going to serve a maximum number of persons. If students are afraid to attend a campus because the crime rate is excessive, the image of the college will be impaired. While Ybor City has deteriorated, hopefully through urban renewal it will not long retain the stigma it has today. In the meantime I think the college should build a reputation as an institution suitable for all qualified students before a thrust is directed toward a depressed area. If, however, our trustees decide to build the campus on the thirty-three acre site, I will do my best to make it the greatest college in the state.

We're going to have to turn on both TV sets because Tom and Mort recorded a program on WTVT (CBS) which will be aired at exactly the same time. At least we're getting maximum coverage for a half hour in the middle of Sunday afternoon. Mort and Tom said they emphasized the breadth of the college offering, including education for leisure as one of the functions of our continuing education program. With the shortened work week and extended vacations projected for the future, its important that people learn to adjust to the additional free time. I realize you may find this hard to comprehend because you enjoy retirement. But not everyone is so fortunate.

Robin and Jeanny accompanied me to the television station on Friday evening. When Sam Latimer gave the three of us a guided tour, Robin met Bill Henry, Ted Arnold and the various TV personalities we watch every evening. It's amazing how glamorous a person becomes when his visage is reflected on a vacuum tube. But that's show biz.

209

I just finished watching the two programs. I had hardly switched off the sets when HJC trustee, Ray Thompson, called to congratulate me on having handled myself well. As we chatted I became aware of some of the pressures he faces living in a rural section where people are particularly susceptible to rumors. One of his neighbors insists that our waiting for the McGuffey report is just political blarney. The man contends Hardcastle has had a copy of the report for three weeks. Ray says it does no good to deny it. Further, the gentleman contends he checked throughout the country and found that most junior colleges are built on ten to fifteen-acre sites; he says our contention that it's desirable to have more land is just a political smokescreen to keep us from accepting the Ybor City Site.

It's difficult for most lay board members to challenge their constituents until they gain confidence through familiarity with the facts. Perhaps I can arrange to go to Ruskin and talk to some of the local civic groups and get the facts before the citizens.

I still haven't found a way to handle the problem of your grandson's grooming. Last Sunday Dave and I went 'round and 'round before going to church. Finally, I got him to shave off the most moth-eaten moustache you've ever seen and trim the hair over his eyebrows so you can tell he has eyes. Honestly, he looked like a sheepdog. Further, I insisted he put some dressing on his hair to make it look clean. He washes it every day, but doesn't replace the natural oil. (He thinks the dressing makes him look like a "greaser.") Consequently, it looks dull and dirty. Can you suggest a compromise which will please him, yet not embarrass me? This generation gap is miserable.

I'd better close now. The rain has almost stopped, and it looks as though the afternoon will be clear and pleasant. Remember us to all our loved ones in California.

Bill

P.S. Somehow we missed Phyllis' birthday last week. Many happy returns; we'll get a remembrance on the way before the next one comes around.

210

Tampa
August 17, 1968

Dear Fisher:

Jeanny and I are completing a day of relaxation sitting on the back patio admiring the reflection of a pink sunset on the lake. It gives her a beautiful copper suntan. A cool breeze puts the crowning touch to a lovely southern summer afternoon.

Right after breakfast this morning Mort called seeking my advice as to which kind of spinet piano to buy for his daughter. Before we had finished talking we had agreed to take our families to Dunedin Beach to bask in the sunshine and let the kids swim for a while. Later we drove north to Tarpon Springs and spent a couple of hours frequenting the tourist traps in the little Greek community there. After researching the Florida sponge industry (tourist style), we arrived back home about 4:00 after a pleasantly useless day.

My week's activities at the college kept me leaping from one brush fire to the other with my little can of boron. As long as we continue to extinguish the flames I suppose we can call it progress. Having fifteen instructors under contract means we've almost completed recruitment of our full-time staff. We would, however, hire a few more if we could find good ones at this late date.

Last Monday, I interviewed a man who has master's degrees in history and philosophy. After discussing his qualifications with Mort I decided not to offer him a contract, but a small and rather insignificant observation contributed to the decision. As you are well aware, I'm not particularly good at spelling. But, so help me, on the application form in his own handwriting was the notation, "I have served the past four years as a *principle* of a parochial high school." How in the world can you be a principal for four years and not learn how to spell your title?

Later in the week I met a young man recommended to us by Charlie Hampton of WTVT. We've been considering offering a few courses in music and Al Heller's extensive professional experience in New York, including coaching Jan Pierce, prompted

211

us to talk with him. While scanning his scrapbook of clippings of his professional productions, I remembered he was the musical director of *Oklahoma* which we attended with the Mastins early in July. We discussed some of the show's production problems; then I asked his reaction to working with amateurs rather than professionals. Professional experience can be excellent training for work with amateurs, especially when it comes to efficient use of talent. In fact, I always assumed, even in amateur productions, that rehearsal time cost at least $1000 per hour. Consequently, I seldom found it necessary to overextend the amateur performers. However, some professionals get too interested in perfection. I remember a rehearsal at Pasadena City College when the symphony director coached the second flutist for twenty minutes while sixty of us waited impatiently for our chance to play. I would like to hire a music instructor who can hit a happy medium.

Heller was obviously apprehensive about disclosing his thoughts on possible music curricula because his (and my) philosophy is not usually endorsed in higher education. After awhile, however, he even suggested a two-year career program for rock 'n' roll musicians. (I wonder if long hair would be a course prerequisite.) Basically, he wants to develop courses which will cater to the musical tastes of the entire community. Even when I taught music appreciation in college, we studied the entire gamut rather than snobbishly restricting ourselves to classical music.

I heard via the grapevine that both Lee Henderson and commissioner Christian are disturbed about a possible site controversy, and last night's paper insinuated a conflict is brewing between our trustees and the school board over the acquisition of the first site. I called chairman Bondi to assure him the last thing we want is a litigation between the two boards. Let's just hope the school board volunteers to let us use the $430,000 to purchase without restriction the best available site. In the end the Ybor City site may be the most logical and suitable site in the county. But until we have studied our master plan and surveyed all available land, who can say which one is best?

212

The Plant City site backers are still pushing their sites. Both are free to the college, but they're a long way from the center of population. If the city were to deed us a free site and $500,000 for buildings, we probably could justify matching their contribution and build part of a small campus right away. Later we could move the prefab buildings from Hillsborough High School to complete a facility which would serve the eastern part of the county for a long time.

I suggested this plan to the Plant City civic leaders and last week the Rotary Club pledged $5,000 as a start on the $500,000 fund-raising program. However, one of the city commissioners resigned in a huff because someone suggested taking $250,000 earmarked for city improvements to donate to the college fund. I won't even speculate on the outcome.

On Wednesday we interviewed two more architects: the first a small firm proposing an association with a large architectural firm in the Midwest. Because I am still apprehensive that a small local architect might not be capable of doing a job the size of our first campus, I probed to get a direct answer as to exactly how many people were in the local firm. But I kept getting generalized statements such as, "Both firms combined have approximately 600 employees." Finally, it was admitted the local staff consisted of three architects, two draftsmen and an office manager; the rest of the 600 are employees of the larger firm. While they pointed out the desirability of being able to utilize the services of different civil, electrical, and mechanical engineers to handle special problems, I would be more comfortable working with a more comprehensive organization.

We then talked with representatives of Watson & Company, accociated with D.M.J.M., the architects from California I told you about in my last letter. We discovered Watson & Company has an impressive record for accurate cost estimation. Estimating an overall budget figure is one of the first steps when planning a building. Then, as working drawings are completed, the architect hopes his design will not produce a building out of line with the original estimates. The proof of the pudding, however, comes when a contract is to be awarded. Two years ago in St. Louis we awarded almost $5,000,000 worth of contracts based on drawings from three architectural firms in two different cities. When the bids were opened, the lowest were 24%, 25% and 26% higher than the architects' estimates. You can imagine what this did to our budget. Watson & Company claimed during the past two years all their estimates have been within 1% of the low bids. That's a pretty fair record when working with contracts of several million dollars each.

I just got a letter from McGuffey promising delivery of the belated master plan by August 26. However, the board agrees we must begin discussing the report even before we receive the final copy. Therefore, because we anticipate few changes in the first five chapters, we'll begin our public discussions at the board meeting next Wednesday. Then if we're lucky and get the final report on the 26th as promised, the trustees will have a week to study the later chapters before the September 4th meeting.

On Thursday evening I was on *Meet the Expert* on WFLA radio. It really should be called *Bait the Expert* because the format encourages telephone calls from the listening audience. After about fifteen minutes moderator Ralph Baum and I were interrupted by a call from a woman hostile to an open-door college. (From her comments I'll bet she's an English teacher.) She couldn't understand how a student can get a true "college experience" if he's inadequately prepared in the traditional disciplines. And as the questioning continued she became quite nasty. Through it all Baum sat rigid, eyes a-bug, waiting for me to blow my stack. I refused, however, to take the bait, informing her that even our two-year career students devote at least one-fourth time to general education subjects. And a data processing programmer need not prepare critiques of great literature to profit from higher education. We would rather he get a thorough grounding in the art of communication. We know he'll have to write reports, and we certainly hope he'll take an interest in civic affairs. Thus, he should also be able to interpret newspaper editorials and evaluate radio and television news commentaries. Even though our approach to teaching communication skills may not include

214

instruction on preparing a college research paper, it's post-high school education in every sense.

Yesterday afternoon Ted Rohr, assistant librarian (audio-visual) at Forest Park, and his wife, dropped by to say hello while vacationing in Florida. I enjoyed reminiscing about old times but was really curious to know how things have worked out since my departure. Ted said he's had difficulty getting answers to some critical questions, but I understand why Snead is hesitant to react hastily before he gets familiar with the situation.

Last week we decided to employ a consulting firm to set up a personnel office. Mort and I will still interview and hire the full-time instructional staff, but we need help screening the non-professional applicants. Further, right now our organizational structure is based more upon expediency than upon good business administration practices. We must plan for expansion several years into the future if we are to have orderly growth and avoid disaster.

Ken called yesterday morning from St. Louis to let us know he and his friend Bill Entenman are coming to Tampa after Labor Day. The band has broken up, so they will finish the engagements they already have booked. Because Bill plans to stay with us for awhile, we'll make a bunk room out of the tool shed in the garage; Ken and Bill will sleep there.

I'm sure Jeanny will be happier having young people around once more. We've become used to an extra boy or two in the house, because several of Steve's buddies lived with us when he was home. While Ken attends USF, Bill will work for a printer (if I can get him a job with his long hair). But more important (to the boys at least), Ken, Bill and Dave intend to form a band. I hope I can stand the noisy rehearsals.

Other than his first letter from Germany, we've heard nothing from Steve. (And he promised to write often now that he can't telephone every weekend.) We'll let you know when we hear from him. Robin, Dave, Jeanny and I are all doing well; I suppose you could say we're as happy as mudlarks. At least we like Florida.

Love to all,
Bill

Tampa
Sunday
August 25, 1968

Dear Fisher:

I only have time to start this letter to you because we're leaving soon for a hamburger and beer party at the Shanbergs in honor of Ross Moreton, our new associate dean of instruction, and his wife who have arrived from the University of Mississippi, where Ross just completed his doctor's degree. We want very much to make them feel welcome.

Occasionally, I make a snide remark about Jeanny spending too much time playing cards with the neighbors, but I'm really glad she likes to make new friends. A family across the lagoon from us is moving back to Chicago. Evidently, the wife, who made little effort to get acquainted, has been unhappy in Tampa. We've learned through experience you can't decline invitations when you're a newcomer and expect people to include you in their activities. After you become a part of the group you can become choosy, but not when you're new.

Early last week I met with the education committee of the Tampa Chamber of Commerce, told them about the junior college, then asked their assistance. We're still trying to locate part-time instructors, but it's not easy to find qualified "moonlighters" to teach three nights a week. The committee volunteered to query the chamber membership in search of potential staff members. Perhaps a nudge from the boss will induce an employee to teach a course for the junior college.

On Tuesday morning I was supposed to attend a meeting with the HJC and Hillsborough High School administrative staffs to discuss our joint operation this fall. However, a goofed-up appointment calendar which suggested I attend two meetings at the same time precluded my attendance. I was sorry I could not participate; there are so many problems when two institutions share the same facilities. For example, coordination of athletic events, custodial services, auditorium facilities, PTA and open

216

house programs in the evening, parking, and security after 4:00 in the afternoon are just a few of the headaches which will plague us. Articulation won't be easy but, fortunately, the high school administrators aren't hostile to the college. Perhaps they will be before we're out of their hair.

We're still having problems with our prefab buildings. Just when I thought we had found a way to cut red tape in the bidding procedure, we got shot down at home. Last month we devised a complicated procedure to screen manufacturers before selecting Panel-fab from Miami. The state department even agreed that we had adequately complied with state bidding procedures. However, at the last minute our attorney, Crosby Few, got cold feet. He now insists we advertise ten days for bids before letting a contract. Meanwhile, we'll have lost more time. We've tried so hard to expedite the schedule, but here we are handcuffed. Perhaps the delay is really to avoid the handcuffs. Anyway, we've resigned ourselves to the fact that our buildings will not be ready until long after school is open. We will have to rent additional forty-foot trailers for faculty offices. Trailer City, here we come!

I'll sign off for now, but will finish this letter later when I'm full of beer and hamburgers.

8:30 p.m.

Sunday evening

We just returned from the Shanberg's patio party. We're certainly putting together a young, dynamic staff. The Moretons are swingers like the rest. I have a feeling it's going to be fun this year.

Let's see, where was I? Oh yes, last Wednesday trustee Gibbs Harris introduced me as the featured speaker at the Downtown Kiwanis Club. The proceedings were covered by Channels 8 and 13 and both newspapers. The printing and contraction of rumors in the newspapers seems to be a major activity here in Tampa. That morning the *Tribune* had quoted a member of the Urban Renewal Agency Board as having heard we were looking at sites near Highways 60 and 301. His pure speculation became the

217

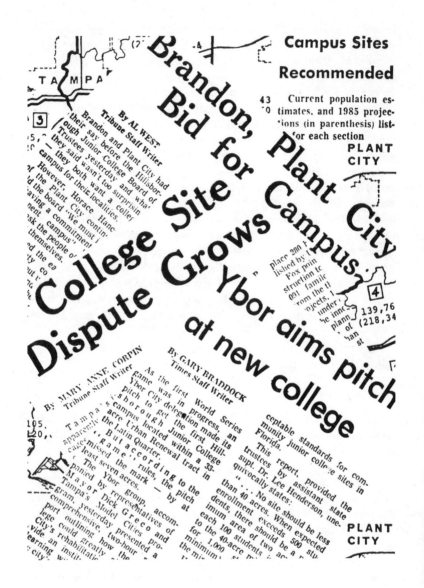

main part of the story. And when, during my remarks, I denied looking at *any* sites, the *Trib* was set for an article in Thursday's paper. What a way to fill up space!

At Wednesday's board meeting we began our discussion of the long-awaited McGuffey report. I distributed a list of basic decisions to be made by the board before we seriously consider a site for the college. More and more pressure is mounting for us either or accept or reject the Ybor City site. The other day a man suggested we just accept it and then decide whether we can use it. According to him, we can always get rid of it. This approach, however, could end up as a waste of tax monies. Now that we have a chance to do the job right, I hope the pressures don't force the trustees into an irrational decision.

Some of the items included on the list to be discussed in Mcguffey's final report relate to the maximum size of a campus, the nature of the instructional offerings, and the open-door admissions policy. In his first chapter, McGuffey reported the average educational achievement in the country as 10.1 grades of school. Further, of the adults over 25 years of age only one in three has completed high school. These figures, which place the county far below the national and state averages, certainly show the need for adult education. However, is it our task to duplicate the adult education program now offered in the public schools? Our trustees must decide whether to open the door to all adults 18 years or older or continue to restrict admission to *bona fide* high school graduates.

In determining the character of the initial campus, the trustees will have to decide how large it will be allowed to grow, the types of instructional programs to be offered, and the nature of the instructional techniques to be emphasized, e.g., lecture, seminar, audio-tutorial, etc. If we have several campuses we must decide how much autonomy to extend to each, because a strong centrally-controlled system will provide services from a central office rather than requiring space on each campus. I hope to get answers to these and other questions over the next few weeks so we can evaluate the various site offers.

When, later in the meeting, we discussed my recommendation to contract with a national firm to provide library services for the college, the board became intrigued when I mentioned we would no longer have card catalogs. Offhand, Dick Elston couldn't see how a library could operate without one. I explained we would substitute printed books for the cards. In fact, every six months we'll print three different books: one each for author, title and subject. At least fifty copies will allow placement in many locations, not just in the library. Because each faculty member can have his own copies, he can compile bibliographies in his office. And even in the library a student will not have to elbow his way to the card catalog.

I'm convinced over the long-run it's cheaper to buy library books already processed than to hire a staff of catalogers. Further, because books are only one source of information, libraries are becoming depositories for all sorts of learning materials. In the near future we will keep inventories of all sorts of learning materials on the computer. Students at Hillsborough Junior College will check out as many audio-tapes, visual materials, etc., as they will books. And to make it simple to administer all materials will be checked in and out by computer.

As a matter of information for the board, the agenda materials included the course descriptions for our catalog. It became evident Hardcastle had done his homework when he began asking probing questions. He wasn't hostile or antagonistic, just trying to unravel the mysteries of higher education. He couldn't understand why course descriptions use broad generalities which tell little about the content. I told him we purposely avoid reference to specific content so our credits will transfer without question to almost any other college or university.

My explanation seemed to satisfy him, but, in passing, he mentioned that our staff must be highly competent to be able to offer as a course, "An inter-disciplinary approach designed to enable the student to place the problems of man and his society in perspective. Selected readings in the areas of anthropology, sociology, psychology and biology will be required. Five 75-minute sessions per week. Prerequisite: None." While Hardcastle's caus-

220

tic comment, "Einstein would have had difficulty covering this course even if he had used reference materials from three college libraries. Yet we purport to do it at Hillsborough Junior College for three credits!" appeared to make us look foolish, the course is actually designed for a remedial student studying arithmetic, reading and English grammar. Because we want him exposed to college-level instruction even before his skills are adequate, the breadth of the course description gives the instructor the necessary latitude to make the content relevant to the students' interests here and now. I believe the offering is educationally justifiable, but when you look at it from Hardcastle's perspective you have to admit it's a pretty large order for a lowly junior college instructor to fill in one three-credit course.

The meeting produced a little bit of levity when Hardcastle got his tongue caught on the tachistoscope. He loves to use large words and, as I mentioned before, he has an extensive vocabulary. But somehow he simply couldn't pronounce tachistoscope, even though he and the board agreed to let us purchase one. (It's a remedial reading machine.) One of our perennial visitors from Plant City summed up the feeling of the group when he said, "This meeting has been worth the 17-mile trip just to find there's one word in the English language new to Ken Hardcastle."

We got a letter from Steve asking us why we hadn't written to him. That's a switch, isn't it? He's enjoying his stay in Wiesbaden, but apparently the army is up to its usual tricks. They sent him to school to learn crypto, then promptly assigned him as a switchboard operator. At any rate, he says the duty is easy, and he has lots of time for sightseeing. I hope the Czechoslovakian situation doesn't turn into a hot war. Perhaps he really would be safer in Viet Nam. Let's keep our fingers crossed.

Dave has made quite a few friends but spends most of his time practising the piano. He and Robin are looking forward to school next week with different emotions. Robin says she doesn't like school, but we all think differently; Dave, on the other hand, really believes he accomplishes more with his piano while he has time to concentrate. I hope he'll change his mind when he starts his classes.

Jeanny is out back getting the boat ready for a three-day trip next weekend. Several families in the neighborhood are planning an excursion from Sarasota to Ft. Myers Beach. I'm sure it'll be fun—tell you all about it when we get back. Love to all.

Bill

August 29, 1968

Dear Fisher:

I'll dictate this letter while driving south on Highway 19 on my way home from Tallahassee. I've just finished a two-day session with Lee Henderson and the Council of Presidents. All the junior college presidents get together once a month to discuss common problems and to help Henderson coordinate the state-wide activities.

I'm beginning to appreciate Lee's frustrations. While he wants desperately to help the junior colleges get the job done, because of the restrictions of the statutes and the state department regulations, he spends much of his time telling us what we can't do. But I suppose that's the nature of a bureaucratic control of tax money.

Along the same line, Wayne Betts, from the department's school planning section, addressed the group and offered his assistance. Again, however, his main concern is to keep the president out of trouble. While I'll have to admit I welcome his help, I don't think it's necessary to send every set of plans to Tallahassee for extensive perusal by a state department architect. Betts even suggested every time a new building is proposed for a campus, a modification of the master plan be included with the proposal. I've always thought a master plan thoroughly developed would necessitate few changes when the individual buildings are designed.

I have a feeling before we get very far into our building program we'll have to organize a chapter of the AAAC (American Association of Active Connivers) to find legal ways to expedite our projects and keep them from bogging down in our Tallahassee bureaucracy.

222

The council discussed a very complex space utilization formula in an attempt to estimate the capital funds required over the next seven years to keep ahead of junior college enrollment projections. To devise a formula which will anticipate the construction requirements of twenty-seven extremely diverse institutions is a difficult task. The needs are different because the colleges with partially completed campuses will most likely build vocational laboratories and support facilities while those of us who are just getting under way will emphasize academic classrooms. Of course, it is much cheaper to build classrooms than technology labs, so the formula must channel the money where it is needed most. As I see it, we should come out with a good slice of the pie because of our large urban population. We'll need at least $20,000,000 by 1975. Even though this amount will not be sufficient for our purposes, I'm not sure we can plan wisely and expedite a building program of any greater magnitude.

I enjoyed meeting the other junior college presidents. Last night I ate dinner with Mike Bennett, President of St. Petersburg Junior College; we enjoyed comparing notes. Mike was upset that the state department had projected no increase in enrollment over the next five years for St. Pete J.C. While HJC will cut into their student enrollment, with the population growth anticipated in Florida, it is inconceivable that any urban junior college will not grow. I should add, however, that only 6400 students were projected for HJC in 1975, whereas McGuffey's projection was 9500. While the rural junior colleges may remain relatively stable over the next seven years, Mike and I contend the urban junior colleges will grow much faster than the state department anticipates.

We need our new buildings at Hillsborough High School by the 16th of September when the faculty arrives, but I'm betting they won't be ready until at least the first of December. And the latest word I got from Shelton's office is the science labs in the high school won't be usable until the term is well along. Fortunately, we were pretty sure the renovation would not proceed on schedule so we scheduled no science labs for the first term.

223

I got a letter this week from the Southern Association of Colleges and Schools advising that because we have neither a library nor laboratories to begin the school term, we cannot be recognized for correspondence status in the accreditation association. If our original proposal for temporary facilities had been implemented, we could have secured accreditation six months sooner. But that's water over the dam.

Dave had quite a time yesterday trying to get registered at his new high school. Because he had been water skiing when he and his mother arrived at school he was barefoot. Jeanny said she thought nothing about it since most of the young people in the neighborhood don't wear shoes. Naturally, Jeanny took him home to dress properly. When they got back to school, however, he was told he couldn't register until he got a haircut.

I'm afraid Dave has developed a negative attitude toward the school even before classes begin. He claims all he has to do to get along well is play the role of a typical suburban snob—get a conventional haircut, peel rubber from a hot rod, plan to be an insurance salesman after college, and claim to hate niggers. If he will only give the school a chance, I'm sure he'll find the educational experience rewarding.

Driving home has been miserable—one thundershower after another. I'll sure be glad to get home and see the family again. Wish you were here to go to Ft. Myers Beach with us next Saturday. We hope to have fun. Bye for now.

Bill

P.S. Wouldn't you know, this letter sat on my desk all week under a stack of papers. Before I drop it in the mail let me tell you about our Labor Day weekend outing on the inland waterway south of Tampa.

We had a wonderful time, but the trip was destined to be a fiasco from the outset. We were supposed to leave at 6:45 a.m. Saturday, but one of the boats was late arriving at the assembly point and we got under way forty-five minutes behind schedule. Then McNultys took off on their own while the rest of us waited at an intersection for another twenty-five minutes before we re-

224

alized they had gone ahead of us. We finally launched the boats in Sarasota about fifty miles south of Tampa at 10:30 a.m.

Things went very well for about a mile when the Elozorys' boat began to act up. It stopped at least six times before we finally decided to leave it at a marina and transfer the Elozory family to the other boats. Can you imagine our little 16-footer plowing along with four adults, two kids and half a ton of food, beer, and luggage.

At any rate the scenery along the waterway was interesting with palm trees and semi-tropical growth lining the shore. Then, for no apparent reason, about thirty miles further the Sletcolens' boat stopped dead in the water. After a forty-five minute struggle to get the motor started, I went to find a mechanic at a marina. But just as I located one, Sletcolen managed to get his boat started again. So with apologies to the mechanic, we took off to the south once more.

Well, to make a long trip even longer, we turned left instead of right near Ft. Myers and went ten miles in the wrong direction before we discovered our error. At last at 10:30 p.m., twelve hours after beginning a leisurely five-hour trip, we arrived at Ft. Myers Beach. As we pulled into the motel dock it occurred to us that our reservations were good only until 6:00 p.m. Fortunately, our anxiety was short-lived because the manager had saved our rooms for us.

On Sunday we lounged around the pool, swam in the Gulf, and fished from the pier. The six-inch catfish Jeanny caught caused great excitement, but I enjoyed most my afternoon repose. It has been years since I allowed myself the luxury of a Sunday afternoon nap. I even forgot about the Ybor City site for a few minutes.

Our trip home was uneventful until about two hours out we stopped to refuel and I couldn't get our boat started again. The alternator had quit working and the battery was dead. It usually isn't too much trouble to start an outboard motor by hand, but when you have to do it while straddling gas cans, fruit baskets, water skiis, and suitcases, it can be frustrating. At any rate, we managed to get to Sarasota in slightly over seven hours.

225

We docked the boat and I started to back the trailer into the water when Jeanny discovered a bubble on the left trailer tire the size of a cantaloupe. We had no spare, but were fortunate to find a marina where I bought a new tire and wheel. That little episode cost us another hour. We got home about 6 p.m. to finish the maiden voyage of the Carrollwood Cruise Club. I hope our next venture is better organized; for sure the Grahams will have a well-operating boat.

Once again, take care.

Bill

CHAPTER V

Stretch Run

September 8, 1968

Dear Fisher:

It's Sunday afternoon and the rain is coming down in buckets. I'll bet the lake has risen two inches in the last half hour, bringing it up to the top of the seawall.

Well, we still haven't resolved the hair problem. Even after Jeanny had taken Dave to the barber before getting him enrolled, Dave's last period teacher did not feel that his haircut was neat enough. I called the principal and we talked for half an hour. When I mentioned Dave's hair had been cut according to the written directions in the handbook, I was told they are not interested in a by-the-letter interpretation of the regulations. What they really want is neat, short hair. I find it awkward to question the standards of the public schools. Even though I personally may not agree with them, in my position I really must support the school officials.

Ken is due to arrive from St. Louis this week. Because of his shoulder-length hair, moth-eaten sideburns and a moldy moustache, I have mixed emotions about his living with us. We're having a group of administrators and board members to our home in a couple of weeks, and I really could use his help at the party. However, with his present appearance, I'm ashamed to be seen in public with him. On the other hand, it's a rather insignificant issue to break up a father and son relationship. Ken is adamant, but I'm going to try to get him to cut his hair, then buy a wig. You should see the mangy one Jeanny bought for Dave. It looks as though it were snatched off of Gravel Gertie. He wears it around home, but so far not in front of his friends.

It's unfortunate the hair issue has become so emotional. There have been several articles in the paper about students who have

227

been expelled because of their long hair. Tampa is about three years behind the rest of the country, where the issue has been faced and resolved in one way or the other. Superintendent Shelton says it's the responsibility of each school to establish its own standards; he just hopes the parents will cooperate. If they choose not to force their youngsters to conform they, not the school system, will deny the students the education they deserve. I suppose this problem is symptomatic of the larger issue confronting our country: law and order *vs.* individual rights. Yes, these are interesting times in which to live, and they are made more so when you have teenage sons.

I've been by Hillsborough High School several times this week to check on the facilities. I'm glad we didn't plan on using the remodeled laboratories, because they haven't even begun to install the equipment; they're still working on the rough plumbing. One by one we're adding trailers to the parking lot as the staff continues to grow. We now have a trailer for the library and Tom has expanded the Admissions Office. Three counselors are frantically trying to register students. Goodness knows, we'll have panic a-plenty before the college opens.

We have also had to expand at the Hillsboro Hotel. Fortunately, the law firm which owns the hotel has generously helped us solve our temporary office problems. However, we continue to have trouble with the lights. The floor lamps we rented use 500 to 600 watts in each office, and the recently added Xerox machine and large coffee maker pull juice from the one antiquated circuit that serves our wing. I was aware we were blowing fuses right and left, but no one has been able to suggest a solution. Then yesterday Miss Nasty dropped by my office with blood in her eye. Fortunately, just then I received a call from Tom Fox of the Urban Renewal Agency, who wanted to discuss the Ybor City site. I asked my visitor to be seated until I finished the telephone conversation, then talked with Fox at length about our problems in getting the college open and about the many philosophical questions which must be answered before the board can reach a decision. As Miss Nasty listened to the one-sided conversation, she apparently realized her problem was insignificant when compared to the ones she overheard. By the time I had finished she was as sweet as pie and even offered to help us find better lamps. Who was it that said, "Every cloud has a silver lining?"

We are making progress toward putting together a qualified part-time teaching staff. For two weeks Plano Valdes and Ross Moreton, our HJC "Kelley Girls," have labored on the telephone talking with prospective instructors. To tell the truth I could panic easily if I didn't have confidence in our administrators. But as long as Mort puts together the instructional program, Tom gets the students counseled and registered, and Allen keeps our business activities in the black, we'll open on schedule. It's a case of team work and I'm optimistic; I firmly believe we'll have a fine college from the day school opens.

Our campaign to recruit 1,500 students (1,000 FTE) by September 30 is really picking up. The sixteen banks in the county are mailing 100,000 HJC brochures with the September bank statements. It's difficult to tell how effective our efforts will be, but last Wednesday we received 285 requests for applications. Today's newspaper included a separate 16-page TV guide size insert describing the college and listing the course schedule. There were 117,000 of these distributed throughout the country. The advertising should make people aware of HJC; everywhere you drive around town you see billboards touting the college.

Last Wednesday's board meeting went off without a hitch. Each meeting goes smoother than the last; I'm extremely pleased with the rapport which is developing between the staff and trustees. The board enthusiastically approved my recommendation to waiver all fees for full-time college staff members. I've gone around the community asking businessmen to pay the fees for their employees to attend the college. It's logical that we practice what we preach and offer the same benefits to our staff. Some of our clerks will surely want to upgrade their skills; free instruction will make it easy for them.

Last February, when I was interviewed by the board, Hardcastle asked my thoughts on handling controversial topics on campus. However, neither he nor the trustees reacted to my comments. Therefore, knowing Hardcastle's conservative philosophy,

229

I was not sure how he or the board would react to a liberal position on academic freedom. Nonetheless, I stuck out my neck and drew up a statement which made sense to me and one which I felt I could defend. I was pleasantly surprised when the board wholeheartedly endorsed the policy and Hardcastle even pointed out what he thought were the key statements. He concurs it's the board's responsibility 1) to develop broadly informed citizens, 2) to develop the respect of students for differing points of view, 3) to encourage expression of diverse points of view, and 4) to insure that opportunity be provided to challenge these views. I'm still of the opinion that our board chairman is one of the most liberal ultra-conservatives I've ever met.

We took a long time to study the recommendations in McGuffey's final report. Finally, the board decided to postpone acceptance or rejection of the overall report until they can question Martin Smith (County Planning Commission) who gave McGuffey his basic figures. Unless the data are proven to be completely inaccurate, I'll recommend the board accept the report as sound and proceed as he suggests to develop five campuses in Hillsborough County. The thought of our having 17,000 students in ten years and 25,000 by 1985 is staggering, especially when you consider we have our hands full getting ready for a measly 1,500 students in three weeks. This must be the challenge I was looking for.

I was irritated when the final report took so long to reach us. In retrospect, it may have been the best thing that could have happened. The pressure from the Ybor City and the Plant City groups has given our board opportunity to react under fire. As a consequence, I believe they have demonstrated that regardless of pressures and vested interests they intend to proceed on a sound basis, avoiding hasty decisions they might regret in the future.

On Thursday I spoke to the Brandon Chamber of Commerce. My remarks, when covered that afternoon on Channel 13, included an appeal for sites anyplace in Hillsborough County. I believe the board should consider all available sites, even though they may not be in areas recommended in the McGuffey report.

The telecast also included my answer to a question about our

230

proposed athletic program. It's unfortunate but the community appears to be more concerned with inter-collegiate athletics than with education or culture. However, from the comments I heard, many in the audience approved my conservative position. I was surprised when Don Garlits, newly crowned world dragster champion (who lives in Brandon), shook my hand after the meeting and said he agreed wholeheartedly with me. I expected him to suggest we include drag racing as one of our varsity sports. I'll have to admit I've never seen a drag race, but I respect anyone who excels in a legitimate activity, especially when he is the best in the world.

Speaking of excelling in athletics, last night we watched Allen Kempton perform on the Johnny Carson TV Special about Cypress Gardens. Perhaps you saw him do his back flip off the ski jump ramp. Every morning at breakfast we watch him practice on Lake Carroll. He's amazingly consistent; in all the time we have been watching him, I've only seen him fall once. What the heck, I make more mistakes than that every day!

After the luncheon, I was given a tour of Brandon by Paul Dinnis of the Chamber of Commerce and some leading citizens. We visited several sites near McGuffey's recommended second campus location. As with the Plant City group, I was impressed with the sincerity of those promoting a campus in Brandon. These admitted Florida crackers claim they and their fellow conservatives may have interfered with progress through their unwillingness to develop the rural areas of Hillsborough County. However, they now see the handwriting on the wall and are anxious to help the county reach its potential.

Thursday night on the way downtown to the Tampa Bay Art Museum Jeanny and I tuned the radio to WFLA to hear Mort and Tom on *Ask the Expert*. They did very well in fielding the usual run of questions, but I had to laugh when Tom was asked about our probation and exclusion policy. Of course, this is one of the little items which we have not yet gotten around to discussing; so Tom invented one on the spot. Fortunately, the policy he formulated is compatible with my philosophy.

Essentially, he stated that a student will be given two chances

231

to make a C average if he attends HJC as his first college. One who does poorly in his first semester, however, must under the guidance of a counselor plan a program which would be more meaningful to him. If he fails in his second attempt he will be asked to leave the school unless his counselor can make a logical case for his continuing in remedial courses.

Most junior colleges make an excluded student lay out one semester as a punitive measure to force him to reassess his objectives. I have never felt this made sense, however. When you ask a student to leave school, he seldom finds his way back on his own. But if he remains in college taking one or two specifically prescribed courses which will strengthen his background, the counselor does not lose contact with him.

As for the transfer student entering after having made a poor showing at another college, we will treat him as though he has had one semester of unacceptable work at HJC. While we call ourselves a "second chance" institution, if it is in the best interest of a student, I see nothing wrong with giving him a third chance.

Ken and his buddy, Bill, arrived from St. Louis Thursday. Ken will begin his classes at USF about October 1. I certainly wish his appearance were more conventional. With his long hair, sideburns and moustache, he looks like a teen-age version of the Messiah. When he and Dave come into the lagoon after water skiing I'm reminded of St. Peter on his fishing boat. I'm sure the neighbors have had some comments about the hippie living in the neighborhood. At any rate it's nice to have him home as part of the family again.

After one week Robin appears to like her new school. Of course, she thinks she already knows it all because they're reviewing second grade work, but I'm certain this will change shortly. She enjoys riding her banana bike to and from school, and believe me it's a relief that Jeanny and I don't have to drive the kids to school as we did in St. Louis.

Boots has become a real southern dog. In fact, he's getting lazier each day. He used to lap water from the edge of the lagoon, but he now has decided it's easier to walk into the water until it's

232

up to his chin. Thus, he doesn't even have to bend down to get a drink. I suppose that's living, dog style.

What do you hear from Al and Betty? We haven't received any word from them since we got to Florida. Tell them to drop us a note once in a while.

Love,
Bill

September 14, 1968

Dear Fisher:

We're headed down the stretch; our full-time faculty reports for duty on Monday to begin an intensive two-week orientation program. It won't be long until classes will begin ready or not. While some of our preparations have gone well, others have hit one roadblock after another; I really can't tell if we're in good shape or not.

We now have six 40-foot house trailers at the high school to use until the pre-fab buildings are ready. Ray Shelton told me this morning he has had complaints from people in the neighborhood who think the trailers will remain there for at least three years. And the other day a woman tried to convince Jeanny we'd have sewage problems. Even when assured the restrooms wouldn't be hooked up, she was sure it was too far for the staff to walk to the high school every time they wanted to use the washroom. When Jeanny left, the woman suggested we caution the staff not to wait until the last minute to go potty. I'll put out a directive.

It looks as though we'll have only a minimal library when classes open. We'd hoped to use a branch library across the street from the high school, but it's so crowded with books that there simply isn't room to add a college collection. Now we plan to make our own bookmobile out of one of the trailer shells. When we tried to borrow 2,000 books from the city library until ours arrive, the head librarian objected to our using "his" books. I asked Mayor Greco to intercede, and we finally secured the loan upon our guarantee to pay for lost or damaged books.

233

I was surprised to learn the USF library charges fifty cents a day for overdue books. (Knowing how Ken loses his glasses three times a week, I'm not sure he'll be able to afford to check out books.) I always thought the object was to *encourage* students to read.

While we have our problems, things could be much worse. Sixteen full-time faculty are under contract and another eighty persons have agreed to teach part-time if we need them. Further, we only have thirteen classes for which to find staff. So far we've been fortunate to find well-qualified part-time teachers. A circuit judge will teach our business law course, and a well-known building contractor will teach accounting. We even have two bank vice-presidents on the roster.

Our student recruiting campaign has taken off like wildfire. Last week we got 1,300 phone calls in response to our Sunday newspaper supplement. As of last Wednesday, we had registered 850 students and had received over 1,100 applications. With two full weeks yet to go, we may even balance our budget.

The entire staff is infected with the excitement of the pending opening. The pandemonium caused by the parade of young people tramping through and the jingling telephones give a political campaign headquarters atmosphere to the trailers. We laughingly say we wish things would slow down, but we really wouldn't want it any other way.

In the midst of all of the activity, Mort, Al, Tom and I took time off yesterday to do some long-range planning. With the faculty coming on board in a few days and the many time-consuming activities facing us in the weeks ahead, we're afraid we'll lose sight of the big picture—HJC in 1975, 1980, 1985. It may seem ludicrous to plan far into the future when the college isn't even open, but in the ninety days the administration has been together expediency has reigned. We'd like to do things right from here on.

As I see it, we'll need two campuses of 2,500 students each by 1972. Further, to avoid chaos we must provide for controlled growth. In this vein we agreed to recommend opening another major center like the one at Hillsborough High School and three

234

or four smaller branches to handle 3,000 students next fall. It's frightening to think of doubling or even tripling our student body the second year of operation. However, this price we must pay when a college is started ten years too late.

We've received offers of potential sites from all over the county. One woman even offered to sell us five acres east of Brandon. How about that! We're planning a joint meeting with the school board and our trustees early in October to express our appreciation for their assistance in giving birth to the college. At that time we hope to present a pictorial display of the available sites. I've told you about the $13,000 per acre site in Ybor City and the free one in Plant City but I don't think I mentioned the ones in Brandon at $1,500 an acre and those in northwest Tampa at $3,500 an acre (prime McGuffey areas). To me it's logical to purchase two inexpensive sites rather than one costly one. We could certainly use the Plant City site for future development as a third campus location, but I understand the offer is good only if we begin construction immediately.

I'm sitting in the back yard on this beautiful Saturday afternoon. The heat has dissipated after two days of rain and a soft breeze is blowing. Ken, Dave and Robin are romping on the back lawn with several neighborhood dogs, Clyde, Arthur, Charcoal and Boots—the fearless foursome. Arthur, a little black mongrel, just slipped off the seawall and fell into the lagoon. Lucky dog, Dave fished him out. Charcoal, a black retriever, is swimming around the lagoon chasing the ducks, Frank, Mildred and Gertrude. Let me tell you, the dogs and the ducks really enjoy Carrollwood.

Last Tuesday night I taped a half hour TV show as a member of a panel honoring Dr. David Delo, president of the University of Tampa, who is celebrating his tenth year in the position. I wonder if I'll be around to see HJC complete its first decade in higher education. If I am, what will have been my personal contribution to the educational system, the community, and our society as a whole? At times I may have to settle for less than ideal solutions to problems, but if I'm still president in 1978, you'll know I've never been asked to compromise my integrity or ethics.

235

While watching the program on TV I concluded it was very dull. However, I was impressed by the contribution a liberal arts college can make to a community. While the University of Tampa enrolls very few students from this county, for years it was Tampa's only institution of higher learning and brought status, prestige and culture to the community.

It is unfortunate the university has financial problems. Not being church-supported, it is completely dependent upon private donations and tuition from its 2,000 students. The campus includes the formerly plush Tampa Bay Hotel built around the turn of the century. Its towering minarets, a visible landmark on the Tampa skyline, are an example of Moorish architecture. When the college was founded in 1931, the first classes were held in Hillsborough High School. At that time they counted seventy-two students and six full-time instructors. Quite a contrast with our projected charter year, isn't it?

After the taping session Delo mentioned his Chiselers. At first I thought he was talking about his administrators (remember our organized connivers), but Delo explained the Chiselers are socialites who work for the improvement of the university. They got the name while scraping mortar off the fireplace tiles used in renovating the main building. When asked what they were doing, one woman replied, "We're just a bunch of Chiselers." And the name stuck.

I appreciate your sending the newspaper clipping about the Needles students who prefer to travel 300 miles to San Bernardino Valley College rather than 200 miles to Barstow to attend a smaller college. It would be unfortunate if students were to shun a campus in Plant City because of the limited curricular offering of a small campus. And we certainly don't want to force a student to attend his home campus by restricted admissions.

I'd better close for now. Jeanny and I are going to the neighborhood drug store to replenish my tobacco supply. The day has been so delightful we thought we might enjoy a short walk before the afternoon wanes. Remember us all to the family.

Bill

236

September 21, 1968

Dear Fisher:

Oh what a frantic week—hectic but gratifying. On Monday morning Ken Hardcastle launched our faculty orientation session by reminding us it was less than a year ago the junior college advisory committee was appointed by the school board. From there he read a well-organized, but rather stuffy, "let's present the image" address. During the question-answer period, however, his informal, relaxed manner completely captured the faculty. It was amusing when one of the staff asked him to describe the other trustees. Who but Hardcastle would refer to Jimmy Gray as the flint-eyed banker keeping watch over the public funds and Ray Thompson as the poor dirt farmer who drives the biggest Cadillac he's ever seen? While Gibbs Harris was described as a dedicated and solid citizen, Dick Elston was depicted as the *bon vivant* of the junior college trustees, the bachelor mayor of Plant City, and east Hillsborough county's gift to the Playboy Club.

I may have embarrassed history instructor Glen Westfall when he asked about the role of the faculty in planning the classrooms for the new buildings. Without thinking I broke in and asked, "Who said we're going to have classrooms?" I believe it's essential that we face all of our problems with an open mind. While we probably will build conventional instructional spaces, I want the staff also to think in terms other than traditional classrooms.

On Tuesday morning Lee Henderson flew in from Tallahassee to focus our attention on the Florida picture and the problems we'll face during the coming decade. Again, the faculty proved they aren't timid when it comes to asking questions. After hearing Lee I'm convinced the state-level financial support must be increased if the junior colleges are to approach their potential. For too long college officials have quoted costs ratios of one dollar for lower division (freshman-sophomore), two dollars for upper division (junior-senior), and four dollars for post-graduate education. Consequently, everyone assumes a comprehensive community college should operate at one-fourth the cost of a university graduate school. However, if we are to offer mean-

237

ingful programs to all students on an effective, individualized basis, the cost will be higher than the lower division university model. Our problem is to convince the public as well as our legislators that the additional funds will produce positive results. Once again it's the product that must be evaluated.

In the evening Maas Brothers department store graciously hosted a banquet for the trustees, staff and their wives in recognition of the opening of the college. Shortly before 3 p.m. I dashed to the airport to meet our featured speaker, Dr. Charles Chapman, president of Cuyahoga Community College in Cleveland and drive him to our home for a hospitality hour with the college administrators, trustees and their wives before the banquet. You may have hear me mention Chuck when he was president of Barstow College in California. In fact, back in 1960 I interviewed for the charter presidency, but Chuck got the job.

I often attend a banquet in a ballroom, a terrace room, or a gold room, but this is the first time I ever had dinner in a stock room. That's right, the banquet was held in a large room occasionally used for special events but most of the time as a stock room. You can imagine my reaction when on Monday I checked on the table arrangement and found the room full of toys and boxes. I will admit, however, that the transformation was startling. Early American decor turned it into a charming banquet room that evening.

The dinner began in a congenial atmosphere, Hardcastle setting the tone with his subtle humor. While chattering with Chuck during dinner I discovered he was married on the same day and at the same time as Jeanny and I in 1944. When introducing him as our speaker, I casually mentioned this coincidence and observed that after almost twenty-five years we still had the same spouses. I asked Chuck to explain this phenomenon; "No guts!" he quipped.

By the end of the meeting Chapman had sobered us with the realization the faculty are the key to the quality of the institution. "While students are transitory," he emphasized, "the faculty provides the stability which allows the college to develop." Their recognition of their roles and acceptance of responsibility will determine the success or failure of Hillsborough Junior College. The faculty must change with the time just as the students change over the years. He suggested they treat students with respect and dignity, recognizing that basically the junior college is not a state but a community institution. When pointing out that the student body will be extremely heterogenous, he cautioned the faculty not to "teach the best and shoot the rest." Yes sir, he made us truly grateful for the opportunity to participate in the founding of Hillsborough Junior College.

I wasn't able to attend the faculty briefing sessions on Wednesday because of the board meeting. There always seem to be last-minute details that require attention. Martin Smith from the County Planning Commission came to the meeting to discuss the validity of the data and projections used in the McGuffey report. Also, Lee Henderson was still in town and I asked him to give his reaction. Both Smith and Henderson said they could not fault McGuffey's techniques or conclusions. So, after a brief discussion the trustees agreed to accept the report and use it as a basis for planning the college.

I again asked the board to ratify the basic concepts discussed during the summer. It was agreed that Hillsborough Junior College would develop as a multi-campus district with the campuses varying from 1,500 to 5,000 FTE students who will be allowed to attend any campus they wish. Also, each campus will offer a wide variety of programs designed to serve the students who reside in the immediate locality. Moreover, the college will allow as much campus autonomy as is possible within limits of the state regulations. That is, each campus will develop its own programs and courses where philosophically and economically justifiable.

Once again we antagonized the news media by calling a closed executive session. Having completed the interviews with the architects, the board wanted to discuss the relative merits of each in private. When the public meeting was reconvened the trustees asked me to negotiate a contract with Watson and Company in conjunction with Daniel, Mann, Johnson and Mendenhall to prepare the master plan and architectural drawings for a campus.

239

I'm pleased with the choice. Both firms are large and DMJM has had extensive experience in the junior college field.

While we were in our closed session, I asked for guidance with a personal problem. Last Monday Jeanny came home quite disturbed after having lunch with a *Tribune* reporter who is preparing a feature story on the wife of the junior college president. She became upset when the reporter insisted on including a family portrait. My first reaction when she told me was to find a place to hide Ken and his long hair. I can see the headlines now, "Wife of College President—Mother of Hippie Son." I suppose we could insist he play golf while the photographer is taking pictures, but I don't want, even symbolically, to reject him as part of the family. On the other hand, our trustees are businessmen in a conservative community where the public has a preconceived notion of the image to be projected by a college president and his family. So I took the problem to the board. After considerable discussion they concluded I, not my family, was hired to run the college; how I resolved my family problems was my own business. They did say they thought Jeanny's image in the community was important, but reminded me they did not interview the entire family. As an aside, Hardcastle confided he personally could see nothing immoral nor fattening about long hair on 18-year-old males.

I realize it is *my* ego that's hurt. I've always been anxious to put my family on display, but even though I love Ken I find his grubby appearance repugnant. Yet, if he were to get in trouble with the authorities, I wouldn't hesitate to stand by him with all the support he needs. Consequently, I don't want to issue an ultimatum over the length of his hair. In every respect other than his physical appearance, I'm proud of him. He has high moral values, is honest, and some day will accept a responsible position in our society. I suppose I'll just have to swallow hard and say, "The subjects in the photograph are the Grahams. Take them as they are and judge them by their accomplishments."

In the same vein, the next morning a group of future students met with our faculty to discuss, among other things, a campus dress code. Right away the faculty and students agreed there are

240

neither moral nor hygenic grounds for requiring that dresses rather than slacks or neckties rather than tee shirts be worn. However, when someone asked, "What will people think?" I couldn't help noticing the similarity between this problem and my concern for Ken's appearance as it reflects on my image.

It occurred to me that role identification in the family and the college present similar problems also. Traditionally, the father has been the head of the family with the rest subservient. Likewise, the teacher has been master in the classroom with students playing secondary roles. I see movement away from this authoritarian concept toward equal rights and similar role identification by all members of the family and all participants in learning activities. But just as the family needs a leader, so must there be instructional leadership in college. Therefore, our faculty must become managers of learning to direct the activities of their charges.

The young people were enthusiastic and excited about the opening of the college. Tom Mastin had selected from what he thought might be a representative sample of our student body to help organize a student government association. The diversity in their backgrounds was striking. While one girl graduated last spring from Hillsborough High School, another completed her high school equivalency through taking the G.E.D. test five years ago. She is now working as a clerk and hopes to upgrade her secretarial skills and eventually get a degree in secretarial science. One of the young men graduated from high school in 1952, studied part time at USF, and now plans to continue his work in political science. A young man who graduated last year from Leto High School referred to himself as one of the "surfer group." He let us know in no uncertain terms he thinks student government should provide for widespread student participation and, above all, should not be dominated by faculty through imposed regulations.

A charming young black girl said she plans to become an English teacher, while a more mature student who graduated from Jefferson High School in 1958 before entering the Coast Guard is now employed as an air conditioning repairman. He hopes even-

241

tually to graduate with a degree in physical education. One of the more vocal students also graduated from Jefferson High School, but in 1967. He had planned to attend the University of Tampa but changed to HJC because it is so much less expensive. All in all, the students were poised and mature; I was proud of them.

Dr. John Allen, president of the University of South Florida, met with the faculty just before lunch on Thursday to discuss the roles of our two institutions. While the university grew from 1,700 to 13,000 students in eight years, when Allen was appointed in 1957, he started with a 1,700 acre site and three years to prepare for the charter student body. Our staff has had ninety days to get ready, and it appears we'll open next week with almost as many students but no site.

Dr. Allen was cordial and very supportive of junior colleges in the scheme of higher education in Florida. He mentioned the Florida twelfth grade tests which our counselors use only for guidance but which the universities use for screening students. He said he had opposed selective admission of university students until the junior college system was begun. The university accepts only the top forty percent of the high school graduates based upon class rank and the twelfth grade tests. While Allen doesn't believe his institution should become more selective it's obvious in a few years when HJC prepares three to four thousand students annually to enter the university as juniors, admission of freshman will have to be limited.

I'd better close this rather lengthy letter and take some time to enjoy the lake. I've pretty much ignored the family. Sorry I got so carried away describing our college activities.

Love to all,
Bill

P.S. I was startled a few minutes ago to see an odd-looking airplane flying low across the lake. Then I recognized it as Breezy, one of the simplest home-built airplanes. (I haven't had a chance even to think about my T-18, much less work on it.) A tubular steel fuselage with no covering and a pusher engine gives Breezy an appearance similar to the old-fashioned Curtis pushers. It was the hit of the show at the fly-in at Rockford a couple of years ago. Sitting in front dressed in a bright red vest, goggles and cap turned backwards, the pilot with his passenger in back would roar down the runway at full speed, then take off like a Boeing 707. Can you imagine flitting around in the open at ninety miles an hour with the bugs bouncing off your goggles?

September 29, 1968

Dear Fisher:

I have simply fallen apart at the seams. Apparently the emotional tension building over the past months has finally caught up with me. All I've done this weekend is sleep. We went to a Beta Sigma Phi dinner and dance last night because Jeanny had already made arrangements, but frankly I would rather have stayed home. Even so, we came home early and I slept the clock a-round. I really miss not having had a vacation this year.

Perhaps I'm beginning to relax now that it looks as though we'll make our projected enrollment. Preliminary estimates project more than 1,500 students, just double the goal set last April.

I was delighted this week when we had one of the smoothest college registrations I've ever seen. Few students spent more than thirty minutes in line. As a contrast, it took Ken three hours to get registered at USF. You must bear in mind, however, the university accommodated 13,000 students-almost ten times our enrollment. Still I'm pleased Mastin and Sinsley organized a system that works efficiently.

The enthusiasm of the students and staff is infectious. Over a thousand new freshmen attended orientation last Friday afternoon. (In St. Louis the best attendance we had for a similar program was 400 out of a potential 2,000.) And do we have a good looking student body—especially the coeds in their mini-skirts! (When I was a student the only way you could tell a girl was knockkneed was to listen.) For the most part they were a mature

243

group; I'd estimate the average age at 25. The men were conservatively dressed and I saw none with hair as long as Ken's. Offhand, I anticipate few discipline problems during the coming year.

Our final faculty meeting was scheduled for Friday morning, but when on Thursday we found we had no meeting room, we decided to invite the faculty and administration to our house for lunch. Thus, Jeanny got a day's notice to arrange a meal for thirty people. She, Kenna Mastin and Marty Shanberg made enough hamburgers, potato salad and cake to serve the whole crew. Perhaps the informal discussion in the living room and the lunch served on the patio set the stage for the promulgation of high faculty morale at the college. We'll wait and see.

The first part of the week Dr. Don Stewart from California conducted an interesting workshop for the faculty. We thought it might be effective for an outsider to help the staff begin developing their courses of study. Stewart's educational philosophy is similar to mine in that he thinks before learning can really occur there must be a change in the learner's behavior or attitude. Further, these changes are measurable A thru F, but not by the traditional bell shaped grading curve where we assume competition among the students will determine the most skillful or knowledgeable. A normal curve will allot 10% A's, 20% B's, 40% C's, 20% D's and 10% F's, regardless of the amount of learning that has occurred. Of course, most instructors vary the distribution to fit their subjective evaluation of the quality of the performances. But, frankly, most profs can't really tell the difference between a B minus and a C plus.

Stewart contends it won't be long before educators who can't make this differentiation will be sued for malpractice. In most colleges you have to have a B average to be accepted into graduate school. Thus, the lives of many students are influenced by instructors' differentiation of the performance of their charges. Therefore, Stewart contends parents, taxpayers, and students have a right to challenge the validity of the discrimination process.

244

He also suggested that as an open-door college we could be vulnerable unless at least 90% of our students are successful. As you well know, the diverse backgrounds of our student body will necessitate our helping students develop many skills before they can be assured of success in our society. While it's a large order, the community-junior college has accepted this task as a major objective.

You might find Stewart's approach to testing interesting also. He pointed out that in industry quality control makes certain that the C, D and F level products are rejected so they don't reach the market. Also, many rejected parts are reworked until they reach an acceptable standard. In education, however, when a student repeats a course he usually does little better the second time because we employ the same methods that have already been unsuccessful once. In addition, we insist the entire course be repeated rather than letting the student devote his efforts to topics he doesn't understand. Stewart believes the main function of tests should be to diagnose weaknesses so the student can concentrate on correcting his faults.

In passing, Stewart mentioned a West Coast university where students take a test on Monday after getting the week's assignment the previous Friday. Those who pass with B or better are not required to attend classes during the week. Thus, the instructor is freed to work with those who need the additional help.

While the reactions of our staff varied from extreme enthusiasm to open hostility, I think the seminar will influence the future development of the college.

On Monday evening the photographer came to the house to take pictures for the *Tribune* article. Keep your fingers crossed.

After the picture-taking session, I spoke at the dinner meeting of the Phi Delta Kappa education fraternity. During the question-and-answer session a friendly argument developed with one of the young professors (Joe Bondi, a cousin of the chairman of the school board) from the University of South Florida who works with the Model Cities Program. During our discussion it suddenly occurred to me why we've had difficulty communicating with the promoters of the Ybor City site.

245

If we assume, as has our board, the objective of the college is to provide education for a *maximum number* of students at a *minimal cost,* it's difficult to justify paying $13,000 an acre for a site which might also require expensive high-rise construction. On the other hand, if we assume our goal is to bring educational opportunity to those *least likely* to secure a higher education *regardless of cost* to the taxpayers, a case can be made both for the Ybor City and Plant City sites. Because Plant City is a long way from USF, many students have transportation problems which preclude their attending college. And around Ybor City many residents can't qualify for admission to the university nor can they afford to travel outside their immediate neighborhoods to get an education. As a consequence, unless concerted efforts are made, these two groups are the least likely to take advantage of post high school education.

Lee Henderson reminded me last week that inasmuch as his office must approve all sites we should evaluate our site offers according to state department criteria. I still don't agree with the stipulation requiring at least 140 acres for a campus of 5,000 students. Lee admitted it wasn't justifiable in an urban area, but said it would be difficult to approve a 33-acre site. Let's wait and see.

Dave seems to be getting along all right in school, although I expect we haven't heard the end of the hair bit. As long as he tries to lead the pack with the longest hair of any boy in school, he's asking for trouble. He, Ken and Bill spend every free hour rehearsing their new band. And the garage fairly explodes with sound.

Robin is adjusting to her school, but did have a problem last week, however. She's just like her mother and can't keep from talking when she's supposed to be quiet. I couldn't help feeling sorry for her; she is absolutely crushed when she is disciplined.

Jeanny and I went with the Shanbergs to the University of Florida-Air Force football game this afternoon. We sat there and cheered along with the other 50,000 roaring spectators. But I wonder how we justify a collegiate institution entering the entertainment field to this degree. Naturally, there are many Gator

246

alumni in Tampa, but most of the people attend because they enjoy the sport. And the revenue at $6.00 a head must have made the college administrators cheer also. The parallel between our modern football games and the coliseum in ancient Rome has been drawn many times. Even so, I couldn't help wondering when the Christians would be led onto the field to be destroyed by the lions for the pleasure of the crowd.

I'll have to close now and go bring Boots back home. He (and all of the dogs in the neighborhood) is currently in love with a poodle down the street. We try to keep him in the house, but he sneaks out at every opportunity.

Love to all,
Bill

Tampa
October 6, 1968

Dear Fisher:

Ready or not, Hillsborough Junior College began classes with 1,625 students last Monday afternoon. By the end of late registration we had collected fees for 1,065 FTE students. Our budget is balanced!

But most amazing, opening day was not chaotic. We had assumed there would be confusion when our faculty and freshman students tried to find their classrooms. Fortunately, the staff's detailed planning paid off.

I have mixed emotions when I try to evaluate our accomplishments over the past few months. I'm delighted when I observe our competent teaching and administrative staff, but I'm embarrassed when I visit our library. Lining the walls of a house trailer are the 800 borrowed books from the Tampa Public Library plus 150 volumes loaned by St. Petersburg Junior College. I know the situation will improve when our books arrive and the pre-fabs are finished, but right now we don't have much to offer our student body. And we have even less for the faculty. With no office space available, all sixteen instructors make their headquarters in one trailer. While we have desks on order, they now sit at tables and use cardboard files to store their materials. Yet when you observe their enthusiasm, you realize physical facilities aren't the most important ingredient for high staff morale. At this point you might say Hillsborough Junior College is little more than an attitude. We have dreams and enthusiasm. And, what's more, it's infectious—even Miss Nasty is smiling these days.

The Monday morning *Tribune* article featuring Jeanny and the family showed Ken's shoulder-length hair but it's not the stand-out feature. The family pose included musical instruments as props—Ken and Dave with guitars, Jeanny holding her string bass, while I sat at the organ with Robin at my side. The photographer suggested we start a combo called the Generation Gap; unfortunately, we don't all play in the same decibel range.

At Wednesday's board meeting we heard another presentation by the promoters of the Ybor City site. Tom Fox had asked for forty minutes, but the discussion lasted over two hours. Little new data was brought to light, but interestingly it was inferred several times that urban renewal land is inexpensive property be-cause the federal government picks up the tab. To be sure, the tax base is broad at the federal level, but I believe all tax funds should be spent wisely regardless of the source.

At the joint meeting between our trustees and the school board next Tuesday night, we plan to discuss all the various sites and their educational and financial ramifications. Perhaps we only have two choices, but if that's the case I'd like to know so we can get on with the business of education. I can't help hoping we'll be allowed to use the $430,000 to secure the sites best located to serve our students.

On Thursday I drove to Plant City to have lunch with a group of civic leaders. They feel slighted by our trustees because months ago they offered to provide temporary facilities and a $250,000 site free if the college were built in Plant City. So far, neither offer has been accepted. However, only twenty-seven stu-dents from Plant City registered for classes last week. If we had accepted their offer and opened the college in East Hillsborough county, I doubt if we would have attracted 1,600 students. I again

248

told the group I would be willing to recommend a small campus there after we have facilities in the metropolitan area.

It's almost midnight and I should get some sleep. Tomorrow Jeanny and I are driving to Gainesville to attend the inauguration of Stephen O'Connell, the new president of the University of Florida. I'm looking forward to an escape from the rat race for a couple of days. Because I want to take my place in Florida higher education, I thought I would begin as a participant in the inaugural procession as a representative of our college. I shouldn't have any trouble finding my place in the inaugural procession; traditionally representatives of the oldest colleges lead the procession while the youngsters bring up the rear, and I doubt if there are many colleges younger than one week old.

I'd better close for now. Write when you have a chance.

Bill

October 8, 1968

Somehow this letter didn't get mailed, so I'll add a P.S. I just returned home from the joint meeting between the two boards, and I'm too frustrated to sleep. I had hoped by now our site problems would be solved but no decision was reached by either board.

The affair got off to a good beginning with a steak dinner for the school board, Ray Shelton and his administrators, our trustees and the administration, and members of the communications media. The presentation of certificates of appreciation to the school board was followed by the unveiling of a map showing all sites, free and otherwise, which have been offered to the college. After a comparision of McGuffey's recommendations and the merits of the Ybor City and Plant City sites, Hardcastle asked if we should proceed to evaluate all available sites or restrict our efforts to the Ybor City and other free sites. One of the school board members responded by saying as far as he was concerned under no circumstances would he change his vote; the offer was made in good faith because the whole board believed the junior

249

college should be located where the people who need it most could take advantage of it.

In the ensuing discussion a charge of misrepresentation was leveled at the state department of education. The school board claimed they had been told every junior college site in the state had been provided free. Said one of them: "If we had known when the junior college was proposed we'd be expected to spend money for a junior college site, we'd never have appointed the advisory committee." I can understand their hesitancy to give us money they so desperately need, but I wish I didn't feel like an unwanted child.

When discussing the Ybor City site, several references were made to the millions of dollars that would accrue to the college if it were a part of the Model Cities Demonstration Program. Personally, I'm enthusiastic about the program, but I hate to see a campus location chosen in anticipation of construction money which may or may not be forthcoming from the federal government. Finally, the conversation reached an impasse and Hardcastle agreed we would look further into the Model Cities application to be presented to Washington next month to see how much money could be channeled to the college. In the meantime we have both feet firmly implanted in mid-air.

Jeanny and I drove home from Gainesville this afternoon following the inauguration of Steve O'Connell. The ceremony, which was held in the large un-airconditioned gymnasium, featured dignitaries who presented honorary doctor's degrees and included the faculty in their long robes and colorful hoods. Am I glad I'm not responsible for initiating changes in educational methodology in this group. I got the impression the majority are older than I am and they simply reek with tradition. I much prefer our young faculty who will allow me a piece of the action.

Dr. O'Connell assumed the presidency after resigning as chief justice of the State Supreme Court. While he is the first alumnus of the university ever to serve as its president, he has had no previous experience in education, or in business or industry for that matter. He was a student body president and member of the boxing team at the university in the 1930's. It's interesting that a man

250

with this background heads one of the major educational institutions in the country. But on a campus with over 750 different buildings and almost 2,000 faculty members, his role as an educational leader is different from that of a junior college president.

The master of ceremonies was Chester Ferguson, Chairman of the Regents, and our landlord at the Hillsboro Hotel. He and many other influential and active supporters of the university system help to keep the legislature responsive to the needs of the university.

President O'Connell, in accepting his charge from Mr. Ferguson, voiced the feeling of commitment and dedication that most of us feel toward our responsibilities. I was so impressed by the clarity and forcefulness of his statement that I asked for a copy of his remarks so that when the going gets rough at Hillsborough Junior College during the next few years they can serve as an inspiration to me.

"I accept the presidency of the University of Florida with full knowledge of its many obligations, heavy responsibilities, and endless opportunities, and with deepest respect and gratitude for the high privilege of holding the office. To you, Mr. Chairman, to the Board of Regents and to the Board of Education, to the faculty, students, and staff of this institution, and to all the people of this State of Florida and their leaders, I say, with all the dedication that a human heart and mind can muster, that I humbly accept the charge you have laid upon me. I pledge to you that the cause of higher education at this institution, and in this state, shall be my cause. With the support, the assistance and the encouragement of you and guidance of Him who made us all, I am confident that this institution, and all who give it life, will satisfy to the fullest the highest expectation and the greatest demands that can be made on this University of Florida."

EPILOGUE

Editor's Note: The following statement was read to the trustees on September 15, 1970 when Dr. Graham submitted his resignation as president of Hillsborough Junior College.

THE BEGINNING   During the short period I have been its president, Hillsborough Junior College has been beset by a myriad of problems. From the time in March 1968 when we attempted to find appropriate temporary facilities for our classes to Mr. Oliva's report today on the completion of our relocatable campus, crisis has been superimposed upon crisis. In spite of these difficulties, however, HJC has blossomed into a college with a dynamic personality: one of which the state and community are already proud.

GROWTH   In retrospect, the growth of HJC has been truly phenomenal. Less than two years ago (and only three months after I reported for work), 17 full-time and 70 part-time instructors began classes with 1625 students at Hillsborough High School. A year later, courses were offered at six temporary locations to more than 3,000 students by 65 full-time and 86 part-time instructors. Finally, this fall for the first time, day as well as evening classes will be available in relocatable facilities on our own campus on Dale Mabry highway.

COMMUNITY COOPERATION   When I accepted the challenge to start with an idea and build a college, I was determined that HJC would become a truly comprehensive community college; that it would become a vital force in the community and in turn have the flexbility necessary to react positively to community needs. I have been gratified by the wholehearted support of community leaders and citizens groups. From the outset the Hillsborough County School Board provided our temporary classroom facilities and today, I received a letter from Dr. Shelton advising of the approval of our continued use of Hillsborough, Plant City and Plant High Schools and Mann Junior High for

252

evening classes this fall. This board also appropriated funds for a campus in Ybor City. The Urban Renewal staff continues to work diligently to secure title to the property for this campus. The Hillsborough County legislative delegation took the necessary steps to transfer the Gordon Keller School of Nursing facilities to HJC and the citizens of Plant City have provided 80 acres for a campus in East Hillsborough County.

The daily and weekly newspapers have given excellent coverage of our various activities and programs. Radio and television stations have been most generous in airing HJC public service announcements. The Greater Tampa, Greater East Hillsborough County, and Ybor City Chambers of Commerce, the Hillsborough County banks, and the City of Tampa's Data Processing center (with Mayor Greco's permission), all helped distribute information about the college.

Leaders in the community have responded enthusiastically and participate on the 12 advisory commitees to ensure that our occupational curricula will answer the employment needs of business and industry and support the career goals of the students.

PROGRAMS AND FACILITIES   Of necessity, our first year's offering consisted mostly of college transfer courses. This fall, however, we will have 19 two-year degree, career programs and 5 one-year certificate programs. Moreover, the college will offer more than 50 non-credit community services courses, many seminars, and a weekend-college.

Concurrently with improving and enlarging our instructional offerings, much time and effort has been devoted to planning the relocatable and permanent campuses on Dale Mabry highway and permanent campuses in Ybor City and Plant City.

CHALLENGES   Providing varied curricula and facilities are, of course, not only important but necessary. However, I have always felt it imperative that we devote as much time and energy as possible to solving the broad problems faced today by all institutions of higher learning. What can we do to lessen the attrition rate? What should we do to promote real and relevant learning? How can we cope with the needs of the masses yet not neglect the individual student? I believe we're on the right path to some of these answers through our experimental program. The 150 students participating this fall have been selected, tested and are ready to begin work. This program challenges the traditional role of the teacher and traditional methods of teaching. Throughout the coming year, no doubt, adjustments, and constant evaluation will be necessary. But I'm optimistic about the results.

HJC'S STATE AND NATIONAL INVOLVEMENT Even as HJC is becoming an integral part of Hillsborough County, it is also making a vital contribution both in Florida and in the nation. Many of our staff members have been recognized at state and regional conferences. Last week I received word that the college has been accepted in GT-70, a national consortium of innovative junior colleges.

PERSONNEL Faculty, administrators and other personnel have responded to our commitment with dedication and excellence of performance. Those of you who attended our charter graduation last June heard the spontaneous ovation given the faculty by the students. Working conditions have not been ideal — teaching at night, using borrowed facilities which meant lugging teaching aids to every classroom, crowded office space, moving records and other items not once but three times now. In spite of all this, morale has been high as evidenced by our productivity and low staff turnover. I am proud of my colleagues and consider it a privilege to have worked with them.

GOVERNANCE STRUCTURE To maintain a successful administration I believe communications within the college community must flow in many directions. Through our governance structure, faculty, students, administration and non-teaching staff members have a vehicle through which problems are identified. Thus, recommendations originating from many sources guide the president. Further, I am convinced that our climate of open, honest candor promotes an atmosphere which discourages the disruptive activities so prevalent in colleges and universities today.

PHILOSOPHICAL DIFFERENCES Yes, our progress has been great and with few exemptions the Trustees have approved and endorsed my recommendations. However, during the past year a schism has developed between three of the trustees and me. I had hoped that time would heal some of the old wounds created when the college was young and fighting to get underway. While I believe our conflict is more personal than professional, there appears to be a difference in philosophy as to the relative roles of the president's office and the board with regard to policy recommendations and operating procedures.

RESIGNATION Hillsborough Junior College has the potential to be the best junior college in Florida if not the United States. However, to achieve this potential, the president and the board must work together in harmony. The future of the college is more important than the achievement of any one individual. Therefore, after careful consideration I have concluded that HJC will best be served if I resign as President.

In closing, I should like to express my sincere gratitude to all HJC personnel for their hard work, cooperation and dedication to those in the community who have given, without remuneration, so freely of their time and expertise. I am confident because of them, this young college will continue on its road to greatness.